ALBERT SPEER

ALBERT SPEER
THE END OF A MYTH

Matthias Schmidt

Translated by Joachim Neugroschel

ST. MARTIN'S PRESS   NEW YORK

ALBERT SPEER: THE END OF A MYTH. Copyright © 1982 by
Matthias Schmidt. English translation copyright © 1984 by
St. Martin's Press, Inc. All rights reserved. Printed in the
United States of America. No part of this book may be used
or reproduced in any manner whatsoever without written
permission except in the case of brief quotations embodied in
critical articles or reviews. For information, address St.
Martin's Press, 175 Fifth Avenue, New York, N.Y. 10010.

Design by Kingsley Parker

Library of Congress Cataloging in Publication Data

Schmidt, Matthias.
    Albert Speer : the end of a myth.

    Translation of: Albert Speer : das Ende eines Mythos.
    1. Speer, Albert, 1905–   . 2. National socialists
—Biography. 3. Architects—Germany—Biography.
I. Title
DD247.S63S3513   1984   943.086′092′4 [b]
84–11784
ISBN 0–312–01709–X

Original title: *Albert Speer: Das Ende eines Mythos.* Published
by arrangement with Scherz Verlag, Bern and Munich.

First U.S. Edition
10 9 8 7 6 5 4 3 2 1

To Monika

CONTENTS

FOREWORD

This book is not about the personal life of Albert Speer. Rather, it deals with Speer the public figure, and with his autobiographical writings. In 1945, the Armaments Minister of the Third Reich was confronted with his own defeat. All his efforts had fallen short; the enormous armaments machinery, his work, had proven inadequate. Hitler's architect had been unable to bring into being the monuments of his architectural imagination. The end had come. But, unbroken by the judgment at Nuremberg and by twenty years in Spandau Prison, this academic among Hitler's paladins created another monument, in the form of autobiographical writings: *Inside the Third Reich, The Spandau Diaries,* and, more recently, *Infiltrations.* The great actor tried to undercut the defeat by once again assuming "responsibility." He took the guilt upon himself—the "legal guilt"—for the sake of the German people, whom his work was, and still is, meant to serve. He wanted to save the Germans from having to do forced labor for the victors. At least, that— according to his memoirs—had been the purpose of his conduct at the Nuremberg trials. The defeated minister also wished to clear himself and the Germans of any *moral* guilt. At the end of his memoirs, he warned of "depersonalization" due to the "technology" that he had served and admired; and he pointed out that "technology is depriving mankind more and more of self-responsibility."

The minister-cum-litterateur, taking the guilt upon himself, simultaneously produced a scapegoat by assuming the literary persona of a pessimist about civilization. Thus he permitted himself and the Germans to put on a portentous mien—and remain completely unbroken. Now, nothing was to prevent us from admiring not only the author of the autobiography but also the maker of the destroyed armaments machinery and the creator of architectural projects that never got beyond the planning stage. A great champion of mankind had presented himself, undaunted by the futility of human action. Scarcely anyone noticed the persistence of his old ruthlessness. A quotation from the theologian Karl Barth served as a motto for *Inside the Third Reich* and had to double as a decoration and protection for the monument. The litterateur Speer also had a knack for literary technique. But perhaps technique, like technology, exempts a man from "self-responsibility."

Historians have always scrutinized autobiographies; it is part of their job. Matthias Schmidt, in his examination of Albert Speer's autobiographical works, has done something that must always be done. His study of Speer is based on tireless research in archives and libraries, on arduous tracking of lost documents, on patient interviews with those witnesses who are still alive, and with the autobiographer himself, on meticulous checking of sources. In short, he has done all the detailed primary research that a trained historian must perform. Little by little, Matthias Schmidt uncovered the blueprint for the monument and the technique that was used to make it shine. He found that the monument resembles the man who erected it to himself—except that the resemblance discovered by Matthias Schmidt had not been intended by the author Speer. This revelation is what makes Schmidt's book so valuable.

Let me emphasize one more merit—at least, it strikes me as a merit. It is not Matthias Schmidt's intention to put Albert Speer on trial again or to turn historiography into a world tribunal. Such a grandiose pose would ill befit a historian. Schmidt is merely reporting—and certainly with the appropriate shrewdness and cunning—that Albert Speer was trying to pull the wool over our eyes, and that things were very different from what Speer tried to make us believe.

Professor Dr. Hans-Dietrich Loock
Free University, Berlin

1

BIRTH OF A MYTH

Two weeks after becoming Minister of Armaments, he proclaimed in a martial speech: "The war must be won."[1] Later, at a time when most Germans had already experienced firsthand the *Götterdämmerung* of the "Thousand-Year Reich," he offered a fighting slogan: "With the Führer, we will seize victory."[2]

On January 30, 1945, however, he bluntly told the Führer of the collapsing Greater German Reich that the war would be lost within a few short weeks.[3] A day or two earlier, he had assured the architect Hermann Giesler that Germany would only have to hold out for one more year: "By then, we will have won the war." Holding up a matchbox in front of Giesler, he made an oracular pronouncement: "An atomic explosive the size of this box is capable of wiping out New York."[4]

In February of 1945, he was planning to use poison gas to kill the dictator in the bunker of the Reich Chancellery.[5] A few weeks later, he assured Hitler unequivocally of his loyalty: "Mein Führer, I stand unreservedly behind you!"[6]

On May 1, 1945, when he put up a picture of Hitler in a room at Grand Admiral Dönitz's residence, he was unable to choke

1

back his tears. "That was the end of my relationship to Hitler. Only now was the spell broken, the magic extinguished."[7]

Six weeks later, a prisoner of the Americans, he wrote: "That period is still too close and his life ended too recently for me to be free of his personality."[8]

Albert Speer, the man capable of such contradictory words and actions, has become a legend. Twenty-three years after the destruction of Hitler's empire, Speer's memoirs (English title: *Inside the Third Reich*) saw the light of day, and readers were enthralled. They were fascinated by the honesty with which Hitler's friend and protégé described his past. They were amazed by Speer's apparent remorse about his involvement in the Third Reich. They were struck by his radical condemnation of the era in which he had played such a crucial role.[9]

As a young man, Speer had become Hitler's premier architect and then gone on to do an outstanding job of organizing the German armaments industry. Now, Speer became a myth. His credibility was debated at length in the halls of academe.[10] But what most people failed to notice was that he had become the ingenious architect and organizer of his own legend.

The Speer myth originated during the brief regime of Hitler's successor, Grand Admiral Karl Dönitz. At the end of the war, members of the United States Strategic Bombing Survey hunted for the man who had "worked visible miracles in the German war production."[11] They were hoping to obtain vital information that they could use in their aerial war against Japan, and they wanted to find out how the Germans had managed to keep increasing their armaments output up until the autumn of 1944, even though the accelerated pace of the Allied bombings had been wreaking ever greater havoc.

In their eager search, the Americans came upon "a member of the Nazi pantheon who may have been less well known than Göring, Goebbels, Himmler, Ribbentrop, Ley, or Streicher, but who was far more important."[12] This man was Albert Speer, and the Americans wanted to pump him for inside information on the effects of the bombings. Speer, who had meanwhile become Reich Minister of Economy and Production in the Dönitz administration, was residing at Glücksburg Castle near Flensburg.

Minister Speer turned out to be accessible and chock-full of information. For seven days, he answered the questions avidly put to him by his investigators. Next came countless interrogations at the "Dustbin" prison camp near Frankfurt.[13]

The interrogation team included George Ball (later Under Secretary of State during the Kennedy and Johnson administrations) and the economist John Kenneth Galbraith. In the course of the intense questioning, these two Americans realized that the prisoner was using a ploy: "He kept presenting himself as an outstanding technician and organizer. He could assume that his enemies would admire a good mind and a technological talent. . . ."[14]

The interrogation records, although declared top secret, passed through thousands of hands.[15] The many readers of these "classified" papers must have formed exactly the impression of Speer that he had tried to convey to his interrogators.

Then, at the Nuremberg war crimes trials, the Speer legend was made a matter of public record, so to speak. The man who had been Hitler's Minister of Armaments took the witness stand, and with his testimony he laid the cornerstone for the historical studies of his life that were undertaken during the next two decades.

At the very start of the questioning, Speer's attorney, Dr. Hans Flächsner, by prior agreement with his client,[16] read something that Speer had once written to Hitler. The quotation came from a memorandum of September 20, 1944: "The task that I am to perform is unpolitical. I have felt very good about my work so long as both I and my work were evaluated purely on the basis of my professional performance."[17] These words, read aloud in the courtroom, launched the postwar image of Speer. And twenty years later, this image was given what seemed its finishing touches in a brilliantly formulated study by the German journalist Joachim C. Fest.[18]

Speer was depicted as the prototype of the "man trapped in a narrow specialization."[19] Such a man does nothing but concentrate on his limited professional function, and he is obsessed with doing his job. His work is done in the service of technology, and neither his duties nor the performance of his work is subject to value judgments. The value of technology is technology itself. The sole frame of reference for the professional man is technology and its intrinsic problems; consequently, he lacks a political frame of reference. Such a man devises and produces, but never gives a thought to the human beings whom his work might help or harm. He ignores the fact that even strictly objective-oriented activity cannot be viewed apart from its social and political context.[20]

This attitude makes a man useful to any political system. And such useful specialists were highly welcome in the National Socialist system (which was not a system: its jungle-like lack of structure was both camouflaged and held together by Hitler's integrating personality).[21] It was these experts and technologists who, by doing their vital jobs without participating in daily political events, enabled the Nazi state to function even as it kept growing bigger and more unwieldy.

National Socialism, viewing itself as a monolithic Führer-state and suppressing or eliminating all opposition, encouraged such a mentality from its experts. If the specialists felt any hostility toward the regime, they were wise enough to voice no opposition. Instead, in their effort to maintain political order,[22] they struggled all the harder against Nazi bunglers. They encouraged utmost efficiency—which ultimately benefited the Reich. Indeed, these technical experts who had often failed to achieve professional success in the Weimar Republic (because of the poor labor market),[23] were greatly attracted to the National Socialist regime. It offered them a chance to do their technical work in "peace and order."

From 1942 to 1945, Albert Speer was the authoritarian director of Nazi Germany's armaments output, and thus the "Führer" of the technicians and engineers who had chosen the "voluntary isolation of the technological mind."[24] Speer is described by the English historian Hugh Trevor-Roper as the "real criminal of Nazi Germany."[25] Speer, he says, displayed more strongly than anyone else that necessary combination of deliberate political blindness and total willingness to serve the dictatorship.[26]

Historians regard Speer as the prime model for their detailed portrait of the politically ignorant specialist—an image that might have fitted men like Wernher von Braun, Otto Walther, or Walter Dornberger. These scientists were certainly "narrowed" by their specialization and blinded by their enthusiasm and inventiveness. Absorbed in their research, building their rockets, they never stopped to consider that they were helping a dictator to perfect his war machinery.

Speer, however, was anything but a man "trapped in narrow technology." As Minister of Armaments and War Production, he was certainly in charge of all those technicians and engineers, but it would be a fundamental mistake to view him as the prototypical "technocrat." His rapid climb to the top of the Nazi hierarchy, his abrupt moral about-face at the end of the war, and his self-portrayal as an apolitical National Socialist all point to the same thing. Speer had only one goal in mind: to make history. The positions he held during the "thousand" years of the Third Reich were purely means to an end. And Speer knew how to exploit them to the fullest.

Even at the Nuremberg Trial, Speer, ever mindful of his history, made sure that his life and work would be set down in detail according to his exact wishes: "I believe that someday [my work] will be valued."[27] Not knowing what the verdict of the court would be, Speer was uncertain whether he himself would be able to do this work. So he assigned this task to a man who had been one of "his closest [friends] since early youth."[28]

Dr. Rudolf Wolters played a very important part in Albert Speer's life. Their friendship began when they were students, and Wolters was Speer's closest colleague during the twelve years of the Third Reich. He then became a tireless helper during Speer's twenty years in prison. Wolters certainly knew Speer better than anyone else did. Yet, amazingly, historical studies of Speer mention Wolters only in footnotes, if at all.

Wolters was born in Coesfeld, Westphalia, in 1903 and attended the Humanistic Gymnasium in his home town. Then, like Speer, he studied architecture in Munich and Berlin.[29] It was in Munich that he became friendly with Speer, who was two years his junior. In Berlin, the two students attended the seminars of Heinrich Tessenow, whom Wolters called the "philosopher among the architects of his era."

In 1937, Wolters, a doctor of architecture, went to work for Speer, who had meanwhile become the Inspector General of Buildings for Berlin and also an intimate of Hitler's. Though burdened with a large number of duties,[30] Wolters kept a journal of Speer's successive offices and the later Ministry of Armaments from 1941 until the end of the war.[31] In 1943, he published a biography of his friend.[32]

There is another reason why Wolters is a good source of information about Speer. Since early childhood, Wolters kept a diary. This treasure-trove for historians contains not only general jottings but also excerpts from letters, reports, and other documents. Thus, anything that Wolters says can be verified by checking his diary.

In 1946, Speer evidently considered his friend and confidant Wolters the right man to take charge of recording his life story for future generations. From his Nuremberg cell, Speer asked Wolters "to describe my work for posterity and to set down a few things about my life."[33] Speer, who had not yet been sentenced by the court, had a very clear notion of the structure of his biography.

He wanted his life and work to be arranged in four parts.

Part I: The architectural work. Hitler's former premier architect suggested extant designs and photographs as the basis of this section. "This should be a straightforward job."[34]

Part II: His work as minister. "This should be a straightforward description of my organizational work and performance," Speer told his friend in Coesfeld.[35]

Part III: Aspects of the life of the former "second man" in Hitler's state.[36] "I believe," wrote Speer, "that I have the right to go down in history as different from all the repulsive 'bourgeois revolutionaries.' However, my positive relationship to Hitler should be depicted openly—in its idealistic form, which is the form it had."[37]

Finally, Part IV was to consist of memoirs, which Speer wanted to write in Nuremberg. "Later on, perhaps in several decades, this part should be published [separately] as a small book. It is to be open and honest."[38]

Speer used the recesses during the trial to set down Part IV of his historical legacy. He penned one hundred pages of *Scraps of Memories of the Twelve Years with Hitler.* [39]

However, Wolters did not get a chance to take charge of Speer's historiographic estate. Speer was sentenced to twenty years in prison. Since he was only forty-one years old, one could assume that Speer would serve his term and then go free to write his own chronicle.

During 1953–54,[40] Speer wrote detailed memoirs covering thousands of pages—pages of all kinds and sizes, even toilet paper. The material was smuggled out, little by little, from the Allied prison for war criminals in Spandau, Berlin. It wound up in Coesfeld, where Wolters had once again become a successful architect. One of his employees typed up the material, and the final typescript came to eleven hundred pages.[41] Nevertheless, as the prisoner Speer stated when this work was completed, it was "only a first draft."[42]

By 1964, when Hitler's former friend—now designated Prisoner Number 5—had already served eighteen years of his twenty-year sentence, his plans were made. After his release, he would embark on a writing career as eyewitness to the National Socialist era. True, he regarded his future literary activity as one of his great, albeit last, follies. "But," he philosophized, "perhaps it is my fate constantly to commit such 'last-minute'

Speer's letter to Rudolf Wolters, dated October 10, 1946, and sent from Nuremberg prison, requesting Wolters to present his life story to posterity.

nehmen. Wer von den alten Mitarbeitern
noch greifbar ist, kann sie am besten
feststellen. Einer von ihnen müßte die
Arbeit übernehmen. Das soll eine sachliche
Nrr. 1 Abhandlung über die Organisation u. ...
III. Beiträge zu meinem Leben. Ich
glaube, daß ich Anspruch darauf habe, als ein
anderer Mensch, wie all die vorderhand
„Bürgerrevolutionäre" der Nachwelt über-
liefert zu werden. Dabei soll das positive
Verhältnis zu Hitler offen geschildert werden, —
in einer idealistischen ..., wie es nun ein-
mal war. ... ... neben den ...
Bekannten wie Wittenberg'sche, von ..., Rohland
..., ... meine ..., ...,
Frank und viele alte Freunde, wie ...,
Kempf (Klavier!), Thorak, ..., ..., ... auch
Braunbach (der selbst ein Buch schreibt), ...,

follies." Prisoner Number 5 went on: "It would be best if I held my tongue, rather than ask the lighting technician on the stage of world history to focus the limelight on a dubious person like myself."[43]

Nevertheless, Speer's writing plans had widened in scope, for the material had grown in many ways. He finished the rough draft of his memoirs *(Inside the Third Reich)* in 1954. Then he went on to write an equal number of supplementary essays[44] and insertions. Next came a third batch, running to about the same length as the first two. It consisted of book reviews and scholarly discussions on *The Window* (a dissertation he had planned during the 1920s).[45]

Speer now outlined a six-part presentation of his past. The arrangement of this monumental opus had, accordingly, undergone a slight change. Parts I to III were to contain Speer's memoirs, a discussion of armaments ("which will be boring by its very nature"), and a discussion of his earlier architectural projects.[46]

Part IV was to include the Office Journal of the agencies run by Speer ("with the guaranteed concealment of the author's [i.e., Wolters'] name.") This part would also contain other documents, as well as Speer's commentary on all this material. Parts V and VI were to comprise his book reviews and his treatise on *The Window.*[47]

Although the former armaments organizer considered this literary enterprise a "folly," he nevertheless believed that he was one of the few people who could offer an unbiased account of the Nazi period. He also knew the exact point of view he would take. "In such matters, there is a hard-line position that goes beyond national interest."[48]

The prisoner was not without idealistic motives. He did not intend to "make money" with his memoirs, since it would be "dirty money."[49] After deducting his expenses, he would donate the profits to "charitable organizations."[50]

Meanwhile, in Coesfeld, Speer's friend Wolters had not been idle. After contacting the historian Walter Hubatsch and

Athenäum, a German publishing house, Wolters had met secretly with them to sound them out about the possibility of their working together on this project.[51] But Speer felt that Wolters was jumping the gun. He wanted to leave all avenues open. And so he admonished his overactive friend in Westphalia: "In my opinion, you've been moving too fast."[52]

Speer, it seems, had been flirting with the Propyläen-Verlag, another publishing house. One year earlier, Propyläen had gotten in touch with Speer through his daughter Hilde, who was living in Berlin. The publisher had offered Speer an option on his memoirs. But Speer had asked his family "to procrastinate politely."[53]

Meanwhile, something else was worrying him. Although historians dealing with Hitler and his retinue had certainly discussed Speer, there was still no comprehensive study of his achievements as Minister of Armaments. But just at that time, a young German historian named Gregor Janssen had obtained his *Staatsexamen* degree with an essay on the Speer ministry, and he was planning to expand his essay into a doctoral dissertation. Janssen's opus came into Wolters' hands by way of Professor Walter Hubatsch, who subsequently became doctoral adviser for the dissertation. Wolters promptly dispatched the essay to Spandau through the "secret mail service."[54] Speer, finding too many errors in the material, concluded: "On the whole, this study would do more harm than good. . . . [Janssen] is something of a conformist, like nearly all people in *all* times."[55] Adding some notes, the ex-minister sent the material back to Coesfeld, warning his friend Wolters not to let himself be misused as a source of information. Speer was relieved that there was no money available to finance Janssen's work. The prisoner also felt that "the author [sic], i.e., I, must express himself 'in a scholarly fashion' before the dissertations."[56]

Nevertheless, Janssen did write his dissertation on the Speer ministry. Published in 1968, one year before the German edition of Speer's *Inside the Third Reich,* Janssen's book enjoyed unusual commercial success for a scholarly work.[57]

After his release from prison in 1966, Speer finally signed up with the Propyläen publishing house. Wolf Jobst Siedler, head of Ullstein-Propyläen, hired Joachim C. Fest as historical adviser for Speer's book. Speer took back from Wolters the material that he, Speer, had busily produced during twenty years' imprisonment. Next, Speer went to the Federal Archives in Koblenz to study the files of the agencies he had headed.[58] He then retreated to his family home in Heidelberg in order to work on the project that he had outlined in Nuremberg. His goal was to set down his views of the Hitler state, "pulling no punches . . . so that the German people can understand once and for all the rotten corruption, hypocrisy, and madness on which the whole system was based."[59]

Yet Hitler's Armaments Minister and favorite architect seemed to have problems dealing with his own past. His view of bygone days had been altered by twenty years of incarceration, with a program of self-education that he had organized in an almost scholarly way.[60] "How strangely I find my viewpoints shifting," he noted after just three years in prison.[61] And later, while strolling with his publisher along the beach on Sylt, an island in the North Sea, Speer admitted: "Twenty years ago, I was a completely different person."[62] Siedler, intent on turning Speer's memoirs into a best-seller, sent his new author home more than once in order to rework portions of the manuscript, saying, "Herr Speer, you cannot write this in this way!"[63]

One can only speculate on the extent to which Siedler's and Fest's advice and "keen questions"[64] influenced the author. Nor can we tell whether their prodding led to any major changes in the content of the earlier versions. The first drafts done in 1946 and 1953–54 are not available for comparison. Nor did Speer intend to turn these manuscripts over to an archive.[65]

On the other hand, one may assume that Joachim Fest, a good stylist, must have semi-ghostwritten at least parts of the book. The almost literary-sounding prose of *Inside the Third Reich* is quite different from the language of a lesser work, *Technology and Power,*[66] that Speer wrote on his own. Its

12

clumsy diction recalls the language of Speer's speeches and letters during the Third Reich.

Speer's memoirs were published in Germany in September of 1969. The book soared to the top of the best-seller lists, and Hitler's former protégé achieved something that had eluded him during the Nazi dictatorship: He became popular.

Many factors may have contributed to the success of Speer's autobiography. The book was clearly of great interest to historians, who wanted to get informative primary sources for their research (and who were largely disappointed by the book). And, no doubt, a large section of the public, hungering for sensationalism, expected one of Hitler's most trusted confidants to supply juicy tidbits about their former Führer's "court." Speer not only chatted about the dictator's intimate fireside evenings at his Obersalzberg getaway, he also described the power struggles around the tyrant, the infighting that gave Hitler and his retinue a frightening and inexplicably demonic aura that explained nothing. All this information captivated a curious public.

However, a certain psychological factor may have played a part for hundreds of thousands of mainly older German readers. This autobiography of Hitler's onetime friend gave them an alibi in black and white. It relieved consciences, which, in varying degrees, had been heavily burdened by Allied "reeducation." They could all too easily identify with the man who had occupied a leading position in Hitler's state and yet—as he himself declared—had not been a National Socialist at heart.

For many amateur historians, Speer's memoirs were an eminently quotable document of contemporary history. Even the social psychologist Erich Fromm used Speer's text as a primary source for dissecting Hitler's psyche and analyzing his destructive nature.[67]

However, the success of Speer's memoirs is no proof that their author was telling the truth. Interestingly enough, many of Speer's friends and acquaintances from the Nazi era were skeptical and even rejected his present-day statements. A high-ranking officer who had been part of the former minister's circle said: "We are dealing here . . . with a Speer whom we did not know in those days."[68] And Rudolf Wolters, who had been the best-selling author's friend for over forty years and who had actively helped to nurture the memoirs along for twenty years, read the book and then wrote to his former boss: "I sit here . . . torn between old feelings of friendship and instinctive repulsion." He then waxed ironic: "No detective story could have been contrived more suspensefully."[69]

Nevertheless, Speer's memoirs, so appealing to his readership, consolidated the reputation he had established in 1945 as an apolitical mover and shaker of the Nazi state, who had then seen the light and felt sincere regret (Fromm).[70] Scholarly criticism by historians largely went unheeded and faded away. Thus, it came as no surprise that on the occasion of Speer's seventy-fifth birthday, the newspaper *Frankfurter Allgemeine Zeitung* published a laudation bristling with all the familiar platitudes about Hitler's protégé.[71]

However, if we investigate several important aspects of Albert Speer's life, if we consult files, documents, and eyewitness accounts, we cannot accept the cliché-ridden myth of Hitler's master builder and armaments organizer. Speer does not emerge as an architect with purely artistic ambitions. He was not an apolitical technocrat in a narrow specialization. Speer was Hitler's loyal paladin and minister, and he masterfully manipulated the instruments of power politics in the National Socialist state.

A few more things must be noted in regard to the documents on the Speer "case." A critical study of this material alone will impugn the credibility of the best-selling author.

Toward the end of the war, Speer reports, he sent for stacks of files during idle hours. Going through this material, he says, he found nothing that could incriminate him. "Consequently, I did not have any of the documents destroyed, except for the memorandum of an industrialist who had proposed the use of poison gas against the Soviet armies. On the contrary, I was reassured and ordered that my files be preserved in a safe place. A few weeks later, shortly before my capture, I had them handed over to the Americans as study material."[72]

However, the Armaments Minister's lack of qualms evidently had its limits. Several documents that might certainly have incriminated him are not to be found in the Bundesarchiv file on Speer's ministerial office, even though Speer, as Inspector General of Buildings and Minister of Armaments, invariably filed copies of all his letters and memos. Thus the archive of the personal staff of Heinrich Himmler, the SS-Reichsführer, contains documents reflecting the jurisdictional squabbles between Speer and Dr. Lippert, the mayor of Berlin, during the reconstruction of the Reich capital. These documents show that Speer the architect was involved in power politics.[73] The same file also contains a correspondence between the Armaments Minister and Heinrich Himmler about the Auschwitz concentration camp.[74]

There are further indications that Speer did not examine the documents as nonchalantly as he claims. ("Usually stretched out on my bed, I leafed through those documents at random.")[75] Take the manuscript of a speech that talks of "Jewish ringleaders and wire-pullers" [of the war—author's addition]. This speech had been given at Speer's orders. Yet when Speer came to this manuscript, he added a handwritten comment that he was not responsible for this speech and he noted: "Liebel's draft. [Speech] given by Liebel during [Speer's] illness."[76]

One Speer document from the Nazi period deserves special attention. It is the so-called *Speer Chronik* (cited here as "Journal"). As a daily office log of a government minister of the Third Reich, it is one of a kind. Its incredible background story is typical of many documents from the Nazi period. Furthermore, it demonstrates a specific instance of Speer's tampering with the historical record.

When Speer was Inspector General of Buildings, his friend

Wolters was his main division chief for Berlin and also his press and public relations officer. In late 1940, Wolters suggested to his superior that he, Wolters, keep a journal of all the important events in Speer's ever-widening area of jurisdiction.[77] Speer okayed the idea, and Wolters began his Journal on January 1, 1941. The Inspector General of Buildings issued a ukase to all department heads, ordering them to send regular reports to the chronicler.

Wolters selected facts and data that struck him as important for the Journal. He added his "own insights and knowledge from conversations and personal experiences." The Journal entries were then initialed by Speer, who never altered or revised them in any way.

Wolters kept up the Journal until September 1944. He then had to limit himself to a few diary entries because the general situation in Germany was getting worse by the day. At the end of the war, there were several copies of the Speer Journal,[78] but only one complete copy seems to have survived.

A complete copy of Speer's Office Journal, covering all the years, began an odyssey in March 1945. A woman on Wolters' staff brought this copy to the Höxter emergency depot, which had been set up at Speer's orders by Wolters and Heinrich Lübke (later President of West Germany). From there, the copy migrated to the castle library of Duke von Ratibor und Corvey. But not even this location seemed safe enough to Speer's chronicler. So, in early 1946, Wolters stored the material in soldered tin containers, which he buried in the garden of his family home in Coesfeld "in order to protect them from the occupation forces." During the early 1950s, Wolters then moved the material to his architectural office in Coesfeld.

In 1964, Wolters reread the Journal. He decided that "it was necessary to copy the entire text, and to correct grammatical and stylistic errors and remove several irrelevant and foolish things, especially a few passages that might incriminate Speer or one or two members of his staff, because the Ludwigsburg Central Agency for 'War Criminals' was still in operation."

Ultimately, the pagination was considerably altered.[79] There were two reasons for this change. First of all, Wolters had made substantial, sometimes *radical deletions*. Second, the original Journal had been typed not only on different typewriters, but also with different line spacings. The edited version, however, was typed on a single typewriter, and the spacing was consistent throughout.

After Speer's release from prison, Wolters gave him the "cleaned-up" version for his evaluation. (The Journal must have been useful to Speer when he wrote his memoirs.) Upon delivering the Journal to Speer, Wolters pointed out minor changes in the original copy. In 1969, after finishing his memoirs, Speer turned the sanitized manuscript over to the Bundesarchiv in Koblenz[80] without first notifying Wolters.

The Bundesarchiv then made a photocopy of this typescript and gave the copy to the Institute for Contemporary History in Munich. Both archive directors were aware that this was a retyped version of the Journal. But neither knew about the *deletions*.

The Journal, now available at these locations, was indispensable material for historians dealing with Speer or with the history of armaments and construction in the Third Reich. Scholars used the Journal as a primary source, never suspecting that it could, strictly speaking, be called a forgery because of the numerous deletions.

In 1969, the English historian David Irving, who is regarded as an *enfant terrible* by many of his colleagues, found a year's worth of entries of the original Journal at London's Imperial War Museum. He noticed that the text sometimes differed from the Koblenz and Munich versions.[81] Irving wrote to Speer, sending him a photocopy of the original text that he had found and asking him to comment on it. An astonishing correspondence then developed between the former Minister of Armaments and his chronicler Wolters.

"Now we're in for it," said Speer, when he told Wolters about

17

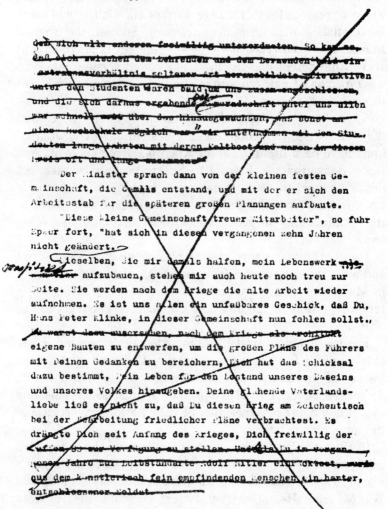

An example of an especially blatant deletion in the original
version of the Speer Office Journal.

- 35 -

gungsgegenstand: Allgemeine Fragen der OT, Generalin-
genieur, Berichte der Einsatzgruppenleiter über zurück-
liegende Arbeiten und zukünftiges Arbeitsprogramm. Auf
dieser Tagung wird am 16. März eine Dankadresse des Chefs
der OT an den Einsatzgruppenleiter Dr. F r ä n k und
die Einsatzleiter Direktor B o h r und Dr. W o l -
t e r s vom Leiter der OT-Zentrale verlesen.

Gegen 9 Uhr trifft der Minister mit seiner Begleitung
am 18. März in Liefering ein. Er wohnt im Kleeblattschlöß-
chen in Klessheim. Frau Speer kommt vom Obersalzberg aus.
Die Kinder kommen zu kurzem Besuch. Prof. M o r e l l
überzeugt sich von dem Befinden des Ministers. Herr von
B e l o w begrüßt Herrn Speer. Gegen 18 Uhr besucht der
F ü h r e r den Minister am Vorabend des Geburtstages, da
er nicht genau weiß, ob er am 19. wegen des großen Empfan-
ges der Feldmarschälle Zeit findet. Größte Sicherheitsvor-
schriften für den Aufenthalt in Meran werden befohlen. An-
schließend sind S a u r und von B e l o w beim Minister.

Der Geburtstag des Ministers am 19. März verläuft
ziemlich ruhig. Hausintendant K a n n e b e r g
gratuliert dem Minister mit einem Geburtstagskuchen.
Prof. M o r e l l und Herr von B e l o w kommen zur
Gratulation. Alle Mitarbeiter, Freunde und Bekannte mel-
den sich mit Glückwünschen oder schon auf die Reise mitge-
gebenen Blumengrüßen. Der F ü h r e r kommt doch noch
- mit Blumen. Am Nachmittag trifft der Reichsführer SS
H i m m l e r zum Besuch ein und zu gleichzeitiger Be-
sprechung allgemeiner Fragen. Der Tag klingt aus mit einem
gemeinsamen Glückwunschbesuch der Ärztin Frau Dr. H a r t
m a n n und der Heilgymnastin Fräulein D ü l t g e n .

In der vom Generalbauinspektor für die Reichshauptstadt
herausgegebenen Feldpostreihe "Vom künstlerischen Ringen
und Bekennen" erscheint als erstes Bändchen, das dem Architekten Albert Speer zugeeignet ist, "Vom Beruf des Baumei-
sters" von Wolters im Volk- und Reich-Verlag.

Mitte März finden auf dem Versuchsplatz des Luftfahrt-
ministeriums praktische Versuche über die Bewährung von Del-

An example of the revised 1964 version of the Speer Office
Journal (regarding the text, cf. Chapter 6, "Illness and Crisis").

19

the unpleasant matter. He was, at least, relieved that "fortunately, there are only slight differences, trivial for a historian."[82] Speer therefore suggested that his friend take the "first step" and replace the Journal copy in the Bundesarchiv with a photocopy of the original.[83]

In his reply, Wolters explained the background story "of this 'clean-up,' which I told you about when I delivered the manuscript [to you]."[84] As author of the Journal, Wolters felt entitled to make nonessential deletions, even after twenty years.[85] "Naturally," Wolters told his friend Speer, "I thought I should also delete a very tiny number of passages that, unfortunately, are not necessarily *unimportant* [author's italics] for contemporary history."[86]

In fact, these passages are of considerable historical importance. One of the things we learn from them is that, under Speer's aegis as the Inspector General of Buildings for Berlin, 23,765 Jewish homes were confiscated in the capital of the Reich and 75,000 people were resettled. "This is certainly an achievement!" Wolters commented ironically.[87]

Wolters offered to restore the deletions personally. If the Bundesarchiv did not agree, then Speer could inform its director that he, Wolters, would not turn over the original: "I will be delighted to give them my reasons." However, Wolters told Speer that "the original will be made accessible to the public only when no one can be harmed by it." He left the rest of the matter to his former boss. "And now you decide, great Armaments Master!"[88]

For best-selling author Speer, these revelations were understandably terrifying. Although his memoirs, which had appeared just a few months earlier, had stated that he could have known about the treatment of the Jews if he had wanted to know, he had had, according to his book, at most a vague idea of the terrible things that were happening in the concentration camps.

Although the deletions from the original Journal do not

expressly say that he knew about the extermination of the Jews, these passages do make it clear that, during his term of office as Inspector General of Buildings for Berlin, he was fully responsible for at least one aspect of the treatment of the Jews. The vague wording in *Inside the Third Reich* now seemed less believable than before. Speer was evidently worried about the credibility of his testimony. And he told his ex-chronicler that he, Wolters, had done the right thing in omitting these passages.[89]

Speer was nervous about his reputation. And so he made some astonishing suggestions to Wolters to prevent the original from surfacing. Speer used words that archivists do not like to hear. He also thought it would be better not to make the original copy of the Office Journal accessible to the public even in years to come.[90]

His friend Wolters helped once again. He wrote Speer a formal letter for the consumption of the Federal Archives in Koblenz, stating that he, Wolters, had been unable to locate the Journal among his papers.[91] But in a personal conversation with his former superior, Wolters said that after his, Wolters', death, the original typescript of the Journal would be turned over to an archive.[92]

Speer transmitted Wolters' letters to the Federal Archives in Koblenz. His own accompanying letter expressed his regret to Wolfgang Mommsen, the director of the Archive, that he, Speer, had not been more effective in this matter. "In any event, it is valuable for future historians to have available the extant documents located in the Bundesarchiv."[93]

Having done what he could to preserve his "integrity," Speer informed his friend in Coesfeld that Mommsen should have been "generally satisfied . . . since he also inherited a few films from me."[94]

Speer had thus tried "not to falsify the past."[95] But in so doing, he had—once again—given the past certain contours that fitted in with his own viewpoint.

This episode provides reason enough for a historian to investigate critically the literary monument that Hitler's friend set up to himself. We will see that a monument can easily develop cracks. Sometimes, it may even be in danger of being brought down from its pedestal by the historical truth.

2

THE ROAD TO HITLER

Albert Speer was born in Mannheim, Germany, on March 19, 1905. Sixty-four years later, in his autobiography, Speer gave the time and place of his birth an aura of fateful significance. It was twelve noon, he tells us, the bells of the nearby Christ Church were tolling, and there was thunder in the sky.[1] Speer the writer stylizes his birth as a historic event. Destiny apparently placed him among the great figures of the world.†

Speer then credits his mother with describing the circumstances of his birth. "As my mother often used to tell me . . ."[2] Thus, at the very start of his memoirs, the author shows that he is a writer of fiction rather than a historically accurate autobiographer. If he was born at twelve noon, there could scarcely have been any thunder, since on that day, storms were not observed over Mannheim until between 3 and 5 P.M.[3] And

---

†Speer is following an age-old literary tradition: Natural phenomena or other concomitant circumstances at conception or birth are presented as omens of the child's destiny. To cite just one example from ancient history: Before her wedding night and the conception of her child, Olympias, mother of Alexander the Great, dreamed that there was thunder in the heavens and that her body had been struck by lightning. Cf. Plutarch, *Parallel Lives.*

the bells of the Christ Church could not possibly have rung in the birth of little Albert, since the church was not built until six years after he saw the light of day.[4]

The Speers were typical of grand-bourgeois German families at the turn of the century. Grandfather Berthold Speer, an architect, had achieved prestige and prosperity in Dortmund. And his son, one of the busiest architects in Mannheim, had likewise "acquired a considerable fortune by the time he married the daughter of a prosperous Mainz businessman in 1900."[5] However, for Albert Speer's father, architecture was merely a means to a financial end, and he candidly admitted to a visitor in 1943: "It made no difference to me what I did. My main concern was to make money."[6]

Young Albert took all his privileges for granted: a fourteen-room apartment, servants, a chauffeur, a nanny.[7] However, the wealthy atmosphere of the Speer home took its toll on the boy, who received neither affection nor understanding from his parents. Their impersonal relationship to each other cast a shadow on the children. "Love," as Speer characterized their relationship in an interview many decades later, "was not provided for in the marriage contract."[8]

Little Albert felt lonely in the family of five. His brother Hermann, the firstborn, was his mother's favorite. His younger brother Ernst was his father's favorite. The adult Speer sees his childhood isolation within his family as the cause of his later communication difficulties and his inhibitions toward other people. "Warmth was shown to me only by Mademoiselle Blum, our French governess."[9]

Albert's education began in a private school. Then, in 1918, his parents moved to Heidelberg, and the boy had to attend a public high school there. Albert had a difficult time fitting in at the Helmholtz-Oberrealschule. However, a schoolmate named Quenzer helped young Speer to make a rapid adjustment to the dynamics of a public institution. The two friends vied to outdo one another in schoolboy nonsense,[10] and this rip-roaring fun gave Speer a chance to rebel against the totalitarianism of the teachers and the authority of his parents.

His heart swelled with pride whenever his name was entered in the classbook because of some mischief, and he thereby reveals his fondness for numbers and statistics: Every time his name was entered in the classbook, Speer punctiliously noted the event in his pocket calendar.[11] He further distressed his parents when Quenzer persuaded him to buy a soccer ball with his pocket money. "A plebeian impulse," writes autobiographer Speer, "which horrified my parents, all the more so since Quenzer came from a poor family."[12]

Speer rebelled once more against the bourgeois life-style of his parents when he made the acquaintance of Margarete Weber, the daughter of a Heidelberg cabinetmaker and town councillor. The parents of the seventeen-year-old schoolboy opposed his friendship with sixteen-year-old Margarete. Their sensibilities could not endure a relationship between their son and the daughter of a carpenter. But their opposition did not faze Albert. No sooner had he met Margarete than he began spending more time at her home than at his. In her family, he found all the warmth that he had vainly sought in the rigid atmosphere of his home.[13] Speer, Sr., was, of course, irked by his son's frequent visits to the Weber house. "He's down there again," the father snapped whenever Albert was at Margarete's.[14]

Eventually, the Webers became concerned about their daughter's close relationship with the boy from a better background. They packed Margarete, nicknamed Gretel, off to a girls' boarding school, and from then on the teenagers' romance had to be conducted by mail.

Albert's letters to his girlfriend were revealing of his character. Intellectual and long-winded, they lack the usual rapture of adolescent love. One year after becoming friends, Albert and Gretel had decided to marry as soon as he got his university degree.[15] Yet Speer was reluctant to show his feelings even to his future wife.[16] (Years later, after joining Hitler's cabinet, Speer was still a reserved, extremely withdrawn man. Even the members of his staff noted that their boss was often inhibited around them.)[17]

Albert had not yet made up his mind about his future profession. His favorite hobby was numbers. As the best mathematician in his school ("All my love focused on mathematics"),[18] he wanted to major in this subject at the university.[19] However, his father, who had gained money and prestige as an architect, had other plans for his son. He prophesized that if the boy became a mathematician, he would lead a life without money, without a position, and without a future. "In the end, you'll have to give private lessons to little numbskulls. Is this the kind of life you picture for yourself?"[20] As far as Speer, Sr., was concerned, there was only one possible profession for his son: architecture.

In 1923, when he was eighteen, Albert decided to take his father's advice and study architecture. He no doubt hoped to "buy" his father's love in this way. But the student of architecture still had to do without demonstrations of warmth from his father.[21] Ten years later, of course, young Albert's decision to study architecture was richly rewarded, and it gained him the unrestricted affection of the Führer and Chancellor of the German Reich.

For economic reasons, Speer had to begin his studies in Karlsruhe, near Heidelberg, since the Speers, like most Germans, were affected by the post–World War I inflation. Still, they managed to make ends meet during the financial chaos of those years; Speer, Sr., sold real estate for U.S. treasury notes. His student son profited from these transactions: Albert now received the cash equivalent of three hundred marks[22] (a month) and switched to the Institute of Technology in Munich. There Speer's fellow students regarded him as a Midas. While they had to make do with the meager food at the university cafeteria, Speer could afford better meals. His fare, as his biographer William Hamsher remarks, was richer "than in his [later] Spandau days."[23]

His free time was filled with hobbies that appealed to his romantic tendencies. He rowed, he was a passionate skier, he enjoyed hiking, and he loved to climb mountains.[24] Albert diligently wrote Margarete about his experiences, about the plays and concerts he attended. He assumed that his girlfriend was interested. "I was at the opera, . . . You want to know more about the play, . . . You would like to know my opinion, . . ." he wrote, in a strangely impersonal tone.[25]

In 1925, Speer transferred to the Institute of Technology in Berlin. In 1926, Professor Heinrich Tessenow began teaching there. This strong-willed man was a wonderful teacher "who was very different from all the other well-known architects."[26] Tessenow advocated a spare architectural style based on nature. "Simple is not always best," he lectured, "but the best is always simple."[27] Peter Koller, a pupil of Tessenow who later built Wolfsburg, the Volkswagen town, recalls: "You couldn't just study [with Tessenow]—only very few, colorless people managed to do that. You were either for him or against him."[28] Many of Tessenow's students emulated their mentor, and their opponents sneered: "They are Tessenowing."[29]

Speer too became an enthusiastic disciple and ardent follower of Tessenow. "My new professor is the most remarkable, most clear-headed man I have ever met," Speer enthused in a letter to Margarete.†[30] Powerfully motivated, Albert Speer set himself lofty goals. He wanted to be accepted at his teacher's master school and to become his assistant one year later.[31]

Nevertheless, his personal life-style was rather casual. Wolt-

---

†Speer's enthusiasm for his teacher was so intense that later on, upon becoming his assistant, Speer decorated his own apartment in Nikolasse, Berlin, in the "Tessenow style," according to a letter from Peter Koller, dated March 19, 1980, to the author.

ers, in his diary, offers a very detailed description of Speer the student, whom he met in Munich during the winter semester of 1925/26. "I remember him from the time of our early friendship as rumpled from head to foot: His shirt had an indefinable color, his tie—if he wore one—was knotted very loosely, his trousers dangled and had horizontal instead of vertical creases."[32] Speer's shabby attire inspired Wolters to draw a caricature of him in Tessenow's studio. Speer, revealing his sense of humor, kept the drawing.

Speer was casual not only in his appearance, but also in the way he worked. Wolters writes: "When I got to know Speer better, he struck me as brilliant but lazy. He would hire less fortunate but all the more diligent students to do his manual work for him—his drafting—and he paid them by the piece."[33] Speer could afford to farm out his work. He was the only member of his circle who did not have to wait impatiently for the monthly check from home. Speer had his own bank account. And when it came to helping others with his money, he was always ready and willing. If any of his fellow students had financial problems, Speer would gladly come to the rescue. His friend Wolters also was forced to avail himself of Speer's magnanimity. "For a long time, [I] would borrow from him on the twentieth of each month and then pay him back regularly on the first of the next month."[34]

When it came to the weekly competitions in class, however, Speer showed an intense desire to work.[35] A touch of the ambition that would catapult him to the top of the Third Reich was apparent quite early. Speer—so it seemed to his fellow students —achieved every goal with elegant ease. In 1927, he obtained his degree. Just six months later, he became Tessenow's assistant. Now, he could do what he had been planning for six years. He married his childhood sweetheart, Margarete Weber. The wedding took place on August 28, 1928, at Berlin's Gedächtniskirche (Memorial Church). Speer laconically informed his parents, who had never met their daughter-in-law:

MARRIED TODAY STOP
IN LOVE STOP
ALBERT AND GRETEL STOP.[36]

As Tessenow's assistant, Speer witnessed the political turmoil of the universities, where differences of political opinion often degenerated into free-for-alls. In 1928, Baldur von Schirach, who was majoring in German, became head of the National Socialist German Student Alliance.[37] In 1929, he called for the "storming of the universities"[38] in order to gain the support of young intellectuals for the National Socialist ideology. And Schirach's campaign was successful. Of course, the academic bastions could not be stormed with verbal arguments alone. "There is no room for cowards in the National Socialist German Student Alliance," said the organization's code of honor.[39] And so the political conflicts at the universities turned increasingly into slugfests. The NSGSA was proud of its brute force: "At least we are frank enough to admit we are ruthless," the organization announced bluntly.[40] In Berlin, there had been so much fistfighting between National Socialists and Communists since November 1930 that the university had to shut down temporarily in June of 1931.[41] Nevertheless, in the elections held by ASTA (Allgemeiner Studentenausschuss, or General Student Committee), the NSGSA made astronomical gains. It received its highest number of votes at the Institute of Technology in Berlin, where Speer was employed as Tessenow's assistant. Here the National Socialists won 38 percent of the votes in 1929–1930, and then 66 percent one year later.[42]

Although academic life in Berlin was constantly disrupted by student riots,[43] Speer the autobiographer can barely remember the heated political atmosphere he was working in. Indeed, he trivializes it: "Our Institute of Technology had in the meanwhile become a center of National Socialist endeavors."[44]

Nor did the National Socialist students overlook Speer the

assistant. Whenever he corrected their assignments, they used the opportunity to discuss politics with him.[45] Speer was practically defenseless against the trained propagandists of the NSGSA. He had been born and bred in an atmosphere in which current politics were not a topic of everyday discussion.†[46] He certainly did not turn a deaf ear to the arguments of the young Nazis. Peter Koller, a student assigned to Speer, had joined the National Socialist German Workers' Party in early 1930, because he saw it as the only German alternative to the "Red Front." Koller was on good terms with Tessenow's assistant, Albert Speer, and a frequent guest in Speer's home. "I can still remember," says Koller, "visiting him in his apartment and telling him about the class state, the political possibilities of reviving the economy, and the Nazi Party. Speer would listen, as calm and interested as ever, occasionally asking a brief question, never opening up, but thoughtfully weighing everything at length."[47]

Hitler put an end to Speer's thoughtful weighing. On December 4, 1930 (not in November, as Speer claims),[48] Hitler spoke to the students on the occasion of the student elections in Berlin.[49] "My students urged me to attend," writes Speer. "Not yet convinced, but already uncertain of my ground, I went along."[50] *Der Angriff,* the militant gazette put out by Berlin Gauleiter Goebbels, had announced Hitler's speech in its issues of December 2 and 3,[51] and thousands of students poured into the enormous auditorium of the Neue Welt, a beer hall in Neukölln's Hasenheide. More than five thousand waited for the Führer to appear. Hundreds had to be turned away after the police locked the auditorium because of overcrowding.[52]

---

†Speer depicts his childhood and adolescence in an unpolitical atmosphere, but we should take his account with the usual grain of salt. He might just as well be skillfully preparing the picture of an unpolitical architect and minister of state—a portrait that Speer subsequently draws of himself. Speer's teenage interests were anything but those of a political teetotaler. According to his autobiography, he "turned to what were then the advanced writers." *Inside the Third Reich,* p. 10.

A bloody piece of news was the curtain raiser for Hitler's speech. Von Bühnau, leader of the university Nazi groups, climbed to the pulpit and announced that "two SA-men had been killed by the murderous Red beast."[53] In light of these events, there was no way that Speer could have failed to notice the charged political atmosphere he was living in.

Hitler was greeted with a hurricane of applause. He offered his young listeners the following rhetorical fare: a Nazi philosophical discussion of nation, honor, and heroism, a lament on the mutual "massacring" of the Right and the Left, a call for political unification. He then wooed the young academics: "When nations abandon the old and traditional or, as they believe, old-fashioned ideas of honor, heroism . . . then the consequence is a gradual weakening of the nation. . . . A heroic idea rallies the heroic elements," Hitler explained to the students, "a cowardly idea rallies the cowards."

Nor did he conceal his feelings about the Weimar Republic and the politicians at its helm. "The war brought a continual extermination of the best and a preservation of the inferior—until finally, the latter became preponderant. And for twelve years now, we have been seeing the politics of these inferior creatures, a politics of sheer egotism." The mission of the National Socialists, said Hitler, was to turn the *Volk* into an organization of the most superior people and to unify the nation. When he presented the *Volk,* the Fatherland, and the German victory as ideals to strive for, the audience burst into tempestuous applause that lasted for several minutes. In conclusion, he appealed to the students: "Examine the times, examine the things that give life and impetus to these times. Then cast your votes and make up your minds. You must find the road that will make you a part of the life and future of the Nation."[54]

It was the right speech to warm the cockles of a young German heart. Shaken by misery, unemployment, and chaotic political conditions, these students were seeking ideals that were worth fighting for. The leader [Führer] "of that tremendous national movement that is now smashing its way across all the degeneration-products of a rotten and crumbling system"[55] knew precisely how to touch the keyboard of German national sensibilities.

Max Domarus, the foremost expert on Hitler's speeches, noticed as far back as the 1930s that Hitler's arguments made an impact chiefly on Germans: "Members of the Anglo-American powers, as well as Russians and Japanese, were unimpressed by Hitler's rhetorical displays, although these (non-Germans) sometimes appeared to agree out of tact or politeness."[56]

Thus the American journalist Louis P. Lochner could not understand the students who were repeatedly driven to frenzied applause by Hitler's oratorical skills. Lochner felt he had been confronted with a phenomenon that he could not explain. He wondered "how a man whose diction and way of speaking were by no means immaculate, who screamed, raged, and stamped his feet, could make such a deep impression on young intellectuals. In any case, I thought, they should have noticed the obvious gaps in his logic. . . ."[57] His summing-up: Hitler's young followers seemed hypnotized by their idol.[58]

The young intellectual Albert Speer was likewise carried away by Hitler's rhetoric, which, according to the American historian Rudolph Binion, always combined personal charisma and a national tiding.[59] Speer reacted emotionally, like everyone else in the audience. Of course, in his autobiography, he claims he behaved differently from those who "discussed that stirring evening over a glass of beer."[60] Speer needed to be alone. "Shaken, I drove off into the night in my small car, stopped in a pine forest near the Havel and went for a long walk."[61]

But ultimately, his reaction was the same as everyone else's. The others quaffed beer in order to cool emotions heated up by Hitler; Speer calmed his agitated soul in the nocturnal coolness of Berlin's forest air.

A few weeks later, Speer heard a rousing speech by Berlin Gauleiter Goebbels: "I felt repelled."[62] But his disgust did not break the spell of Hitler's speech. In January of 1931, the architect and teaching assistant Albert Speer applied for admission to the National Socialist Party. On March 1, 1931 (not January, as we are told in *Inside the Third Reich*),[63] he joined the Party; his membership number was 474,481.[64]

A crucial element in Speer's decision may have been the fact that his academic "foster-father," Heinrich Tessenow, although not a follower of National Socialism, was by no means hostile to its ideology. One day one of Tessenow's students discovered a copy of *Die Tat*[65] on the professor's desk. This was the "most interesting, most active, and most influential magazine in the 'struggle against Versailles and Weimar.' "[66] It steered very close to the National Socialist ideas but did not identify with them. For their part the Nazi ideologues—at least initially— put up with the philosopher-architect. A dance school he had designed in Hellerau was praised by National Socialist publications "as a model, an example of a good architectural spirit even during the 'degenerate period.' "[67]

"It was an utterly undramatic decision," Speer explained to a later German audience when he wrote about his joining the Nazi Party.[68] Nevertheless, in the English-language version of his memoirs, Speer tries to rationalize his action. He offers a more detailed apologia of his crucial step. If Hitler had announced before 1933 that he would involve Germany in a war, Speer writes, burn down the synagogues, and kill the Jews and his political opponents, he would have instantly lost Speer and most of the followers that he had attracted in 1930.[69] "How incalculable the consequences were," Speer naively tells his English and American readers. "And I thought that by paying my party dues of a few marks a month I had settled with my political obligations."[70]

In the speech attended by Speer, Hitler may not have referred expressly to war, imperialism, and annihilation of the Jews. Yet Speer could have hardly been unaware of the Nazi agitation during that period, when anti-Semitic slogans were anything but unusual. The Nazis were more than explicit about what

Hitler intended to do once he became Chancellor of the German Reich.

Ultimately, Speer's decision to join the Nazi Party was indeed politically motivated, however vaguely this may be defined. When he went on his nocturnal stroll through the Berlin forest after Hitler's speech, Speer saw the budding of new hope. "Here were new ideals, a new understanding, new tasks."[71] And, for the benefit of his British biographer William Hamsher, Speer explained his decision in a terse, but unambiguous sentence: "In a word, I joined the Nazi Party because I did not want Germany to go Communist."[72]

In any case, Hitler had found a new follower. Subsequently, he would treat Speer as a friend, maintaining a strange and total loyalty—what Germans call a *Nibelungen* loyalty—until the end of his life.

Speer's friend Wolters, who did not expect much of Hitler at that time, asked his fellow student why he had joined the Nazi Party. The reply was a rather loosely worded prophecy: "Don't worry, you'll see. That man is no fool. He's going to become someone someday."[73]

Speer's memoirs describe his joining the Nazi Party as an unpolitical act. However, ten years after that unpolitical act,[74] when Speer had become a leader in the Third Reich, he permitted himself to be hailed as an early struggler for the Nazi ideology. A 1943 biography informs us about his student days: "As an assistant at the Institute of Technology in Berlin, Speer was . . . one of those who fervently committed themselves to National Socialism. His staunch faith in the victory of the movement made him a true follower . . . of the Führer."[75]

The Armaments Minister did not care to recollect that before 1933 he had been politically uncommitted. He now presented himself to the German public as a "veteran" of the movement: "During the years of struggle, I often sat among you as an unknown Party member," Speer proclaimed at the Berlin Sports Palace in 1943. "I wanted to witness the Führer's unique demonstrations and to draw new courage for a new struggle from the passionate words of our Gauleiter, Dr. Goebbels."[76]

In 1943, Speer knew very well that he was not telling his Party comrades the truth. But it was convenient for the Armaments Minister to play the veteran National Socialist, who had been an early fighter for the victory of the Nazi revolution. Decades later, however, it was equally convenient for the writer Speer to don the literary guise of an "unpolitical National Socialist." Conveniences and opportunism may help a career, but they are useless for determining historical truth.

3

THE FÜHRER'S ARCHITECT

"At present, Berlin is an unsystematic collection or unsystematic series of residential and commercial buildings. The only monumental parts are Unter den Linden, the Castle, and their immediate surroundings." Reich Chancellor Hitler made this statement on September 19, 1933, to the mayor of Berlin and other high-ranking members of the municipal administration. The Führer, who had been Chancellor less than a year, was planning a complete overhaul: "As the Reich capital of a nation of sixty-five million, Berlin must be raised to such a high level of urban planning and culture that it may compete with all the other capital cities of the world."[1]

Hitler wanted to eliminate all the ugly aspects of Berlin. "The renewal of Berlin must be the very epitome of what can be accomplished with present-day means."[2] Hitler would allow no other city to rival this one. "Berlin is the capital of the Reich, and that is what it shall remain."[3] He could not afford to show any preference for other cities, and he excluded sentimentality from his urban planning. "What does 'heart' mean?" he once asked the people close to him. "One can't get things done with 'heart' alone. One needs an ice-cold mind!"[4]

However, at the time that Hitler was telling the Berlin city fathers about his plans for a thorough revamping of the Reich's capital, he had not yet found a suitable architect to make his dream come true.

So, for the time being, Hitler left the project with the municipal agencies, who were grateful for the Führer's interest. Dr. Heinrich Sahm, mayor of Berlin, was delighted. "Thanks to his sympathy and encouragement, the city of Berlin will be able to work actively toward a new and great era."[5] However, in trying to carry out Hitler's ideas, the Berlin officials had to struggle primarily with their own bureaucracy. First, the completely unresolved legal and financial problems had to be dealt with. These administrative obstacles were a thorn in Hitler's side, preventing the swift realization of his plans.[6] Nevertheless, Hitler left the Berlin administration to its own devices, and for three years, never interfering, he watched his project drag its way through the red tape. There was a good reason for his unusual patience: He still did not have a trustworthy architect to carry out his ideas. It was not until 1936 that Hitler was certain he had found a compliant man to implement his architectural notions; he had in fact "discovered" him three years earlier.

On July 28, 1932, Albert Speer was about to go on vacation. He was planning to paddle a folding canoe across the East Prussian lakes. His canoe and those of the other people in the party were already at the railroad station, and the train tickets had been purchased. But then a phone call cost the unemployed architect his holiday. Karl Hanke, head of organization in the Nazi Party in Berlin, had an assignment for him. Speer was to remodel the Party's district headquarters on Voss-Strasse.

This job launched a unique career. In just a few years, young Albert Speer became Adolf Hitler's favorite architect. Had Hanke called a few hours later, he would have been too late; Speer would have been on a train heading for East Prussia. Decades later, Speer even said that his career had been launched by a coincidence. And for years, "I regarded this coincidence as the luckiest turning point in my life."[7] Yet it was no coincidence that Speer was in Berlin at that time.

In early 1932, Reich Chancellor Brüning's budget cuts had led to a salary reduction for teaching assistants. Speer had therefore given up his position at the Institute of Technology in Berlin and moved to Mannheim, in order to manage his father's real estate holdings and also to try his luck as a freelance architect.[8] But projects were not forthcoming, and the unemployed architect had to make ends meet by continuing to run the family properties. This task, no doubt, neither kept him fully busy nor satisfied him, though it did spare him the financial plight of his jobless colleagues.

However, in the summer of 1932, politics brought him back to the capital. A national election was scheduled for July 31, 1932, and Speer went to Berlin "in order to feel a little of the exciting election atmosphere and—if possible—to help his Party commitment.[9] Thus, aside from the "coincidence" that Speer subsequently made much of on a literary level, his active interest in the political success of the Nazi Party was what really launched his career.

There was a reason why Hanke chose Speer to rebuild the new residence of the Berlin Party leaders. One year earlier, Hanke had entrusted Speer with a similar, though much smaller job. The Nazi Western District Leadership had a house in Grunewald, an elegant section of Berlin, and Speer had been asked to decorate the house in loud colors, with, says Speer, Communist [i.e., Bauhaus] wallpapers. Speer did the job for free.[10]

As a result, Speer was not unknown to the Party bigwigs in Berlin. Then two further assignments drew Hitler's attention to the hardworking and ambitious young architect. The First of May 1933 offered Speer a chance to demonstrate that he knew how to use architecture in order to turn mammoth events into high points of National Socialist manipulation. The Nazis, now in power, were planning a mass gathering for the night of May

1, at Berlin's Tempelhof Field. The Berlin city fathers had commissioned a design for this celebration, and the design landed on Karl Hanke's desk. Hanke's career had been advancing steadily. After the elections of March 5, 1933, the Nazi government had created the Reich Ministry for National Enlightenment and Propaganda, and Goebbels had been appointed head of the new ministry. Hanke, his brother-in-arms from the period of struggle, became the brand-new minister's secretary. And it was in Hanke's office that Speer saw the design for the city of Berlin. His reaction was unequivocal: "The design outraged both my revolutionary [!] and my architectural feelings."[11]

That very same night, says Speer,[12] he came up with his own design, one that was entirely consistent with the ideas of the National Socialists, who were using a mammoth celebration to pursue their goals. With the help of gigantic flags and searchlights, Speer created the setting in which the new power-wielders could display themselves effectively and make a lasting impact on the crowds.[13] The almost religious aura of the nocturnal celebration promoted a cunningly orchestrated feeling of national togetherness. The young man who staged the successful May First celebration concluded: "The *Volk* [people] has become the living bearer of the state. Its celebrations are therefore *Volk celebrations* in the deepest sense of the term."[14] Hitler, as Hanke could report to the happy architect, was thrilled.[15]

A man who could so accurately present the National Socialist ideology with the help of a gigantic panorama of flags and lights could also take charge of such national festivals in the future. Speer thus became Chief of Artistic Production of Mass Demonstrations in the Reich Propaganda Office.[16]

Speer had received an entirely different assignment at the same time, and he worked on it together with the May First celebration. This second project also aroused the Führer's interest. Propaganda leader Goebbels had commissioned Speer to remodel his ministerial residence and add a wing. The architect promised that both the remodeling and the new wing would be completed in two months. Goebbels told Hitler about the tight schedule, which the young Speer had recklessly set up for himself. Hitler regarded it as impossible. But Speer proved he could stick to the deadline that the Führer had called impossible. The house was finished on time.[17] Hitler was impressed. And he remembered Speer when he wished to have his own residence remodeled.

The problem was that since the start of his dictatorship, Hitler had been living in the state secretary's quarters, an apartment that was hardly suitable for the Chancellor of an "awakening" Germany. It was located on the top floor of the Reich Chancellor's own residence. Hitler was not outraged, he simply viewed the neglect as characteristic of the Weimar era. "Not only were large portions of the roof timbering rotted through, but the floors had completely decayed," he recalled indignantly years later. "During cloudbursts, the water came in not only from above, but also from below. On the Wilhelmstrasse side, a brook poured into the rooms on the main floor and was swelled by water flowing from all the openings, including the toilet."[18] As for the Reich Chancellor's office, Hitler compared it to a room "that . . . in its size and shape was more like the tasteless room of a salesman for cigarettes and tobacco wares in a middle-sized company."[19]

So Hitler decided to remodel the Reich Chancellor's residence from top to bottom. He assigned the job to his Munich architect, Paul Ludwig Troost,[20] and wanted it done as soon as possible. Troost did his designs in Munich and sent his building supervisor to Berlin to oversee the work. This supervisor, however, was unacquainted with the Berlin construction firms—an obstacle to the rapid completion of the project. Hitler now remembered the young architect who had remodeled his propaganda chief's house in such an incredibly short time. And thus Albert Speer was asked to step in, help them choose a construction firm, and lend a hand whenever necessary.[21]

Speer went to work. He wanted to get the official residence into move-in condition as soon as possible. Hitler, who was interested in architecture, could not be kept away. He showed up almost daily to check the progress of the work. His questions were "terse, but not unfriendly," reports Speer: Hitler asked which rooms had to be replastered, when the windows would be done, whether new drawings had arrived from his architect, Troost, in Munich, and so on.[22]

However, Hitler not only watched every step of the remodeling, he also observed the young architect, closely but inconspicuously. And Hitler evidently grew fonder and fonder of the tall, slender young man, whose answers were as terse and precise as the questions put to him, who spoke with a familiar South German accent and acted cool and distant, yet ingenuously friendly. The Chancellor must have enjoyed the fact that the young and unknown architect was not timid with him. Speer seemed unimpressed by Hitler's authoritarian personality and never tried to fawn on him. Such behavior must have offered a charming contrast to that of the officials around Hitler, toadies who were forever clicking their heels and whipping up their right arms with martial verve, or haunting his antechamber like Byzantine courtiers, trying to curry his favor. Nothing was more alien to Speer's unconventional mind than such posturing. And perhaps the fact that Speer—wittingly or not—was different made all the difference. His youthful, carefree ways appealed to most of the people he met. It is interesting to note that his teacher, Tessenow, was more and more surprised and displeased by his ex-student's development after 1933. Nevertheless, he remarked after the war: "In my opinion, Speer always remained a friendly and helpful person."[23]

Adolf Hitler also liked Speer. As Speer later recalls, the two men had already toured the remodeling site twenty or thirty times when Hitler invited him to lunch one day. Naturally, the young architect accepted. And naturally, says Speer, "This unexpected gesture made me happy—all the more so since I had never expected it, because of his impersonal manner."[24]

At lunch, Speer sat at Hitler's side. The conversation became personal—and the two men "fell in love at first sight," to use the words of the Hitler biographer Joachim Fest, who discerns "traces of an erotic element" in the Speer-Hitler relationship.[25]

The two men had a great deal in common. Hitler found it impossible to open up to anyone; a barrier that no one could pierce prevented him from feeling genuine friendship. Speer was equally aloof toward others; his light and casual manner actually disguised his inhibitions. At times, especially in a large group, he seemed awkward, almost embarrassed.[26] If he could not camouflage this timidity by acting youthful and carefree, he would cloak himself in reserve and coolness—a facade as impenetrable as the barrier that Hitler had set up around himself.

Their mutual enthusiasm for architecture overcame their inhibitions. The two men shared the same dream of going down in history by creating gigantic constructions that would far surpass anything ever done before. Hitler, actually a politician in spite of himself, and a passionate amateur architect, saw Speer as the personification of his life's dream. As the young architect's patron, Hitler now saw the possibility of emulating the patrons of earlier centuries and achieving immortality with the help of stone monuments. Speer, for his part, must have soon realized that the Führer and Reich Chancellor, a lover of architecture, could help Speer make *his* life's dream come true: He wanted to be immortalized as a second Karl Friedrich Schinkel.†[27]

However, architecture was not the only interest binding Adolf Hitler and Albert Speer. Even years later, when Speer became Minister of Armaments, little changed in the special quality of their relationship. Hitler still overwhelmed his protégé with demonstrations of trust and favor shown to no other paladin. Supposedly, he once even paid Speer the unique compliment of saying he loved him.[28] And Speer could take liberties that no one else in the leadership circle of the Third Reich

---

†Famous painter and master builder (1781–1841) in Berlin, with great influence in Prussia; he rebuilt Berlin and Potsdam.

would have been granted—not even Göring, Goebbels, Himmler, or Ribbentrop.

Admittedly, both Hitler and Speer poured such intense emotion into their strange relationship that it can certainly be called a friendship. But the peculiar thing about this friendship is that neither man ever managed to articulate his feelings in all the years that they knew one another. Still, the existence of such feelings became obvious during the final weeks of the war.

In fact it was inaccurate of Speer to state at Nuremberg that he would have been one of Hitler's close friends if Hitler had had any.[29] It would have been more correct to say that they *were* friends, but that neither had been capable of dealing with the other as a good friend.

After that lunch in 1933, twenty-eight-year-old Albert Speer could consider himself part of Hitler's retinue. And the Führer left no doubt that he had great plans for Speer. At first, of course, he gave Speer small assignments, "rush jobs."[30] Perhaps the Führer's promising "find" had to prove himself capable of carrying out the monumental projects that Hitler was dreaming of.

For Hitler was conspicuously holding back with his first large-scale construction, the development of the site for the Nuremberg Reich Party Rally. Indeed, even as late as 1933, Hitler may have been struggling with himself to decide whether to assign this task to his original architect, Troost, or to the much younger Speer. Still, despite the conjectures of certain historians,[31] Troost never worked[32] on any designs for the Reich Party Rally site, the "Nation's pilgrimage shrine."[33]

Before Hitler managed to make up his mind, destiny decided for him. On January 21, 1934, the architect Paul Ludwig Troost, whom Hitler venerated as a mentor, died after a brief illness.†[34] That same day, Walther Funk, Goebbels' state secre-

---

†Speer, contrary to his statements in *Inside the Third Reich,* had never met Troost. Frau Troost remembers distinctly that in early 1934, Hitler told her about a young architect he had met through Goebbels, and he asked whether

tary, spoke macabre words to Speer, probably verbalizing what many people close to Hitler were thinking: "Congratulations! Now you're the first!"[35]

And thus it was. In early 1934, Hitler commissioned Albert Speer to design a stone installation for the Zeppelin field in Nuremberg. In autumn of that same year, Speer became head architect of the entire Reich Party Rally project. He was thus awarded "the so-far largest artistic construction project of the new Reich."[36]

And Speer, now first architect to the Führer, was ready and willing to submit to his patron's architectural ideas: He designed and executed projects that became ever more enormous, ever more tremendous, ever more monumental. There is evidence of suggestions that Speer, driven by ambition, designed projects that actually surpassed Hitler's mammoth dreams. When Gerdy Troost attended a dinner at the Reich Chancellery after her husband's death, Goebbels asked her, in Hitler's presence, what she thought of Speer. She characterized the ambitious young architect with a comparison to her deceased husband: Had Hitler commissioned her husband to design a building one hundred meters long, Troost would have thought about it and then informed him the next day that because of structural and aesthetic factors the building could be only ninety-six meters long. The courageous woman then turned to Hitler: "But if you told Speer, 'I need a building one hundred meters long,' he would instantly say: 'Mein Führer, two hundred meters!' And you would say: 'You are my man.' "[37]

And indeed, Speer was entirely Hitler's man. He had moved farther and farther from the teachings of Tessenow, his once beloved teacher, and closer and closer to the notions of the dictator who loved architecture. Speer not only made these ideas his own, he virtually kowtowed to them. Whenever the Führer reached a decision after long discussions, it became

---

he could bring the young man to her deceased husband's studio (personal information from Frau Gerdy Troost to the author).

inviolable dogma for Speer. Criticism was inadmissible.[38] In 1936, in an essay entitled "The Führer's Buildings," Speer recorded the extent to which he had come to identify with Hitler's architectural ideas: "His large buildings, which are now beginning to rise in many places, are meant to be an intrinsic expression of the movement for millennia and thus a part of the movement per se. It was the Führer who created this movement, came to power through its strength, and is still shaping it in every last detail even today. . . . He has to build as a National Socialist."[39]

Decades later, in his autobiography, Speer claimed that he had seen himself merely as Hitler's architect and that he had never been concerned with politics.[40] Nevertheless, *as* Hitler's architect, he managed to offer political interpretations of his Führer's architectural ideas. "It will be a unique event in the history of the German people." Speer's essay prophesized, "that, at a decisive turning point, its leader is not only beginning the greatest philosophical and political restructuring in our history, but is also preparing, with his superior architectural knowledge, to create the stone constructions that will document the political will and cultural ability of our era for thousands of years."[41]

However, it was not just in architecture that Speer obediently followed his Führer. He became a willing underling of his master in other areas as well. The Protestant Speer left the Church and now described himself simply as "believing in God."[42] And he was Hitler's loyalist even in regard to church architecture: "Here too, I only advocate the Führer's conviction. The reconstruction of churches interests me only to the extent that they are architectural monuments with historical and artistic value."[43]

Such conduct was tantamount to surrendering his personal independence. But it was well rewarded. In 1933, Speer had already become head official of the Reich Propaganda Office.[44] In 1934, he was made a department chief on the staff of the Führer's deputy and head of the Beauty of Labor section[45] in the German Labor Front. In 1936, the title of professor was conferred upon him.[46] That was the year in which Hitler became certain that the thirty-one-year-old professor was the architect whom he could entrust with his greatest project. Just one year earlier, Hitler had voiced doubts "whether the architect Speer would be up to the task."[47] But then, in the summer of 1936, Hitler told Albert Speer to draft a complete urban-renewal program for Berlin. This assignment was to remain unofficial, however, and the plans were to be kept secret for the time being.[48]

On January 31, 1937, the *Völkischer Beobachter* announced: "The Führer has put an area of enormous responsibility in the hands of a man who, as both a National Socialist and artist, speaks for himself through his works. . . . A National Socialist and expert has received a great assignment."[49]

On the previous day—the fourth anniversary of the Nazi takeover—Hitler had officially appointed the architect Albert Speer chief planner for the reconstruction of Berlin. The Führer's edict made Speer Inspector General of Buildings for the Capital of the Reich,[50] a position that gave him wide-reaching powers. Subordinate to neither the Party nor any government agency, he was responsible to the Führer alone. His direct responsibility made him a virtual dictator in planning the Reich capital. He was empowered to take any necessary measures and issue any necessary orders to ensure that "all squares, streets, and buildings influencing the townscape are completed in a worthy manner and according to uniform standards"[51] The authorities and bureaucrats of the national government, the state of Prussia, and the city of Berlin had to knuckle under him. Any national or Party measures touching Speer's area of jurisdiction had to be submitted for his approval before they could be carried out.[52]

The Führer's architect had been an integral member of Hitler's private circle for years now and was, accordingly, respected by everyone who knew about his close relationship with the dictator. Speer could therefore be certain that Hitler would smooth the way for him in the implementation of his wishes and ideas.

If a man enjoyed the Führer's special favor, he could tackle problems with great self-assurance. This freedom was demonstrated by the newly appointed Inspector General of Buildings when he negotiated his salary. In March 1937, Speer, an intelligent tactician even in such matters, had suggested to Dr. Hans Lammers, head of the Reich Chancellery, "a monthly remuneration . . . to be set by the Führer."[53] But this was too vague for Lammers. He wanted to have some indication of how high a figure Speer would require, so that, said Lammers, "I can give the Führer and Reich Chancellor a guideline for establishing the amount."[54]

Encouraged to propose something himself, Speer expounded his salary ideas to the head of the Reich Chancellery, though not without a written bow to his employer: "First of all, I would like to state once again that I will be satisfied with *any* settlement insofar as it is made by the Führer."[55] Speer's suggestions were by no means to be viewed as conditions,[56] he said.

But then he got down to specifics. For the lower limit of his remuneration, they could look to the salaries of the city president and the mayor of the Reich capital. After all, "in its impact on Berlin, my work is not to be any less esteemed than the achievements of the city president." For his family's security, the pension requirements would have to be "similar to those of a top-level municipal leader," since, Speer argued, in this work in reconstructing Berlin, he could not be all too considerate of his health. He also wanted an expense account for representative purposes as well as an official car. And he felt he ought "to continue working as an architect" while holding his position as Inspector General of Buildings. However, he was willing to restrict himself to assignments from Hitler and not accept projects from anyone else.[57]

Lammers asked for the Führer's decision,[58] and Hitler gave his brand-new personal architect almost everything he desired. Speer would receive a salary of 1,700 Reich marks, which was somewhat higher than the salary of the mayor of Berlin (1,654 marks). He was also granted an expense account, though its limit is unknown since the figure was communicated orally to Speer. It was probably no lower than the mayor's expense account: 8,000 Reich marks per annum. Speer also had the right to continue working as a free-lance architect with the restriction that he himself had proposed: *i.e.,* to accept assignments only from Hitler.[59] But Speer had to forget about a pension, since, as a nit-picking bureaucrat in the Reich Chancellery had pointed out, "any guarantees regarding a pension for dependents [would] create a position similar to that of a government employee."[60] It seems that Speer, as Inspector General of Buildings, would have only a temporary position, "to be terminated by the Führer at a given time."[61] Hence, pension guarantees would be "more than a minor blemish."[62] The lawyers in the Reich Chancellery did not wish to break the civil service law, even though Speer's position had been created personally by Hitler. Besides, these public servants felt that Speer's income was high enough for him to provide for his family's security himself.[63]

Still and all, Speer could be more than satisfied. He would also be receiving 1,000 marks a month[64] for his construction work in Nuremberg, and he would be paid his standard fee for all assignments from Hitler. Writes Speer: "At the end of my career as an architect my fortune had increased to about one and a half million [marks], and the Reich owed me another million that I never collected."[65]

Within eighteen months, the office of the Inspector General of Buildings at 4 Pariser Platz mushroomed into a huge administrative apparatus. A salary list of September 1938 names eighty-seven employees—and this roster does not even include the free-lance architects and sculptors hired by the Inspector General of Buildings office, which even enjoyed the luxury of having an office physician.[66] As a planning agency for the reconstruction of the Reich capital, this office was less an artist's studio than an administrative apparatus, managed by the "employee" Albert Speer. It was officially given the status of a national agency *(Reichsbehörde).* [67]

And here, in his position as chief planner for the revamping of Berlin, Speer already revealed two traits of character that, according to the historian Karl-Heinz Ludwig, predestined him for political management: absolute subservience and authoritarianism. [68]

Speer was subservient when he had to keep the Führer company in Hitler's idle moments. As a "favored permanent guest and inhabitant of Obersalzberg" [Speer], [69] the architect evidently did not object to joining the retinue that formed the social framework of Hitler's musicales and movie evenings. Speer certainly must have realized the advantages of frequenting the Führer's round table. For the official political staffers, who were seldom permitted to enjoy Hitler's hospitality during those years, Speer was the Führer's friend and artistic colleague —a position that made him sacrosanct. For his own staff, Speer was Hitler's confidant and intimate, a reputation that he obviously cultivated with great care. Thus once, when he was dining with his staffer Wolters, Speer, in high spirits, told him, "Today, the Führer listed three great goals. Once he has reached them, he says, his political mission will be completed." When Wolters asked him what these three goals were, Speer replied, "Do you think he would have confided in me if he had thought I would tell you?" [70]

Speer secured his patron's favor by surprising him with architectural gifts. For Hitler's fiftieth birthday, Speer touched the Führer's heart by presenting him with an almost thirteen-foot-high model of an arch of triumph that Hitler had designed in 1925. [71] And it took Speer only nine months to put up the gigantic building of the New Reich Chancellery, [72] an achievement that moved Hitler to call his personal architect a "brilliant shaper and master builder." [73] Speer's earlier mentor Tessenow was less exuberant about the nine-month wonder: "I would rather you had devoted nine years to this project." [74]

However, such comments could not check Speer's soaring career. He became the most "influential architect" in Germany,[75] and he knew how to carry out his plans for power. For instance, the free-lance architects he commissioned to design his Berlin project were not permitted to accept outside jobs without his approval. Before designing anything for anyone else, these "free"-lancers had to obtain the consent of his office.[76]

Although these architects gave in to Speer unconditionally lest he terminate their contracts, other people stood up to him. Such a man was Julius Lippert, doctor of law, an old fellow fighter of Goebbels' from the Berlin combat period and mayor of Berlin since 1937.[77]

For a long time now, Speer had regarded Lippert as a nuisance, even though Lippert really had no objections to the overall reconstruction of Berlin. On the contrary, he had repeatedly stated that the city administration would unreservedly assist Speer in this project.[78] However, Lippert more and more stubbornly opposed Speer's high-handed omnipotence, since Speer more and more frequently went over the heads of the city fathers when carrying out his reconstruction plans. Jurisdictional squabbles erupted between the municipal authorities and Speer's agency, and a committee had to be formed to work out guidelines for facilitating cooperation between the two groups. However, "essential points" in the suggestions made by the committee did not chime with the ideas of the Inspector General of Buildings.[79]

Speer had entirely different views of his task. In his eyes, the revamping of the Reich capital would be "one of the Führer's most important personal concerns" after the war.[80] This, in Speer's opinion, determined the "status and administrative implementation" of the project.[81] "It would be inconceivable," sneered Speer the overhauler, "that the manifold individual measures necessary to [this project] should be regulated by 'arrangements' and compromises between myself and the official agencies that have previously been entrusted with similar urban planning projects. The unique nature of my project clearly demands that *one* agency bear [sole] responsibility for the entire work."[82] And Speer left no doubt which agency he meant. He told Lippert: "It is I."[83]

To avoid future arguments with the Berlin bureaucracy, Speer issued an edict to the mayor, hoping to settle all conflicts "according to instruction."[84] But Lippert, a veteran of the Nazi struggle, would not be intimidated. He refused to go along with Speer's demand that he agree to this edict. Lippert, a doctor of jurisprudence, argued that an edict that "bindingly regulated" his position in regard to the Inspector General of Buildings could be "issued only by the Führer personally."[85] Nevertheless, Lippert once again declared his willingness to cooperate with Speer. "My entire municipal administration is at your disposal for the Führer's gigantic work."[86]

However, such assurances of compromise did not suffice for Speer. He instantly put into force the edict "for greater cooperation between our offices," and he ordered Lippert to notify the proper administrative agencies.[87]

Despite these crude actions, Mayor Lippert stood his ground. He still believed he could reach a friendly understanding with Speer, but he did not hold back his opinion of the steps taken by the Inspector General of Buildings: "I must assume, to my regret . . . that your agency is intent on humiliating the administration of the Reich capital by refusing to reach a free compromise."[88] Lippert saw Speer's edict as a "unilateral diktat," and he refused to pass it on to his administrative offices.[89]

Speer's reaction was rude and gross. He sent the mayor a note with no salutation, demanding that Lippert acquiesce to his edict immediately.[90] However, Julius Lippert had no chance to give in to Speer's demand. On the same day that Speer sent his crass letter to the mayor of Berlin, the Inspector General of Buildings complained to Hitler about "Mayor Dr. Lippert's lack of understanding for my position, which is superior to his in regard to construction matters."[91]

Speer himself noted in a memorandum: "When I informed

the Führer ... that the mayor viewed my edict ... as humiliating for the city and had therefore ignored it, the Führer instantly stated that Dr. Lippert was to be 'immediately removed from office' as mayor and city president. Reich Leader Martin Bormann, who was present when the Führer gave this order, was told to have Reich Minister Lammers oust Dr. Lippert on the spot."[92]

Speer's *Inside the Third Reich* depicts the Lippert affair in very different colors: "Lippert could not work up any enthusiasm for Hitler's architectural ideas. At first, Hitler was merely annoyed, remarking that Lippert was petty, incapable of governing a metropolis, and even more incapable of understanding the historic importance he planned to give it. As time wore on, these remarks mounted in intensity. 'Lippert is an incompetent, an idiot, a failure, a zero.' ... After four years of this sort of thing, and right after a walk from the Berghof to the teahouse, during which he once more brooded over Lippert's stupidity, he telephoned Goebbels and categorically ordered him to replace his mayor."[93]

Speer himself made sure that the Lippert case left a bitter aftertaste: The entire correspondence about the conflict between the mayor of Berlin and Speer wound up in the office of Heinrich Himmler, the SS-Reichsführer and chief of the German Police. Three decades later, Speer still did not know how the Lippert files had come into Himmler's hands. The Führer's architect had forgotten that he himself had sent the documents to the SS-Reichsführer "for your confidential attention."[94]

This easy victory encouraged Speer to take further steps toward safeguarding his domain as Hitler's premier architect. Evidently, he feared competition from a certain colleague, "a personality in the Third Reich, who has so far been ignored," according to the historian Jochen Thies.[95]

Hermann Giesler, born in 1898, was an architect whom Hitler respected no less than he did Speer, though Giesler was not part of Hitler's private circle. Speer's trusted position as the

Führer's architect from 1933 to 1942 was not taken over by Giesler until the final year of the war, especially the last few months.

Giesler[96] had been busy with building the Sonthofen convent school since 1934. In 1936, Hitler personally assigned him the task of decorating Adolf-Hitler Square and the surrounding buildings in Weimar. Larger projects followed. In 1937, Giesler became a professor. In 1938, receiving the title of General Building Councillor, he was appointed chief planner for the reconstruction of Munich. Of course, Giesler had nothing like Speer's influence on the architecture of the Third Reich during the years that Speer spent at Hitler's side. Nevertheless, Giesler, an ardent National Socialist, was a more loyal liegeman of Hitler's than was Speer.

However, when Giesler was assigned the task of reconstructing Munich in 1938, his workload was as great as that of Berlin's Inspector General of Buildings—a fact that did not escape Speer's attention. In 1936, when Giesler had been assigned to do the buildings in Weimar, Speer had already been forced to watch jealously as the number of Giesler's assignments kept increasing. Speer had told one of his staffers: "We've got to keep an eye on Giesler."[97]

When Giesler was finally appointed General Building Councillor, Speer took him seriously as a rival. He cast about for a way of dealing with what he saw as an imminent danger. In late autumn of 1940, Speer hit on the idea of getting Hitler to issue an edict creating the position of "Führer's Commissioner in Charge of Architectural Art and City Planning for the National Socialist Party.[98] This commissioner's jurisdiction would go "beyond the tasks of the Party in matters of city planning."[99] There was no question that Speer was the only candidate to be considered for this job.[100] He would, in effect, become Germany's omnipotent national architect.

Naturally, the draft of the plan had to be approved by Martin Bormann, whose consent was by now indispensable for all such matters. Bormann, however, first asked Giesler for an opinion before requesting a decision from Hitler.[101] Upon reading the draft, General Building Councillor Giesler realized that if this plan was implemented, he would become fully subordinate to Speer. Giesler had already experienced the unpleasant aspects of being dependent on Speer, because, since 1939, Speer had been in charge of construction allocations for Munich as well as Berlin. Whatever his reasons, Speer had sometimes been slow in meeting the Giesler agency's requests for iron and steel, and he had sometimes ignored them altogether. For lack of material, Giesler, who still believed he had a genuine friend in Speer,[102] was sometimes forced to shut down construction sites in Munich.[103]

The new plan would assure Speer "total authority over all German construction projects on a downright megalomaniacal level," said Giesler.[104] The head of Munich's urban renewal imagined that if this plan was carried out, even worse things would be in store for him. In his report, he therefore completely rejected Speer's proposal. Reich Leader Bormann agreed with Giesler,[105] who also spoke to Reich Minister Dr. Fritz Todt, Plenipotentiary for Construction, and revealed his qualms to him.

Thus Speer's plan to achieve architectural omnipotence in Germany was doomed. Plainly, Speer knew all too well that he would lose this attempt to gain power and influence over Bormann and Hitler's number-two architect. So Speer retreated. He took back his proposal and dispensed with further discussion.[106] Indeed, he went even further. On January 17, 1941, in a fit of defiance, he went to Hitler and asked to be relieved of his numerous Party duties. Speer explained that he had developed "doubts about the expedience of a determination" of his "general duties." It would be better for him "to give up most of these duties." He intended to concentrate exclusively on his life's work: the constructions of Berlin and Nuremberg.[107]

The obvious defeat preyed heavily on the ambitious architect's mind. Two weeks after asking Hitler to release him from his many functions, Speer poured out his entire anger about

Giesler, who, with Bormann's help, had managed to show Hitler's minion his limits. Professor Speer, the Inspector General of Buildings, accused Professor Giesler, the General Building Councillor, of exerting a negative influence on Bormann and Dr. Todt with his opinion: Giesler should have first notified Speer. "An impossible action in a friendship," Speer fulminated in a letter to Giesler. "I will never be able to understand your behavior."[108] The result was a long period of bad blood between Hitler's two favorite architects.

For the Führer's sake, Bormann tried to bring about a reconciliation almost one year later. Bormann finally told Speer that it was time to end the feud; it was Bormann's "heartfelt wish" for the year 1942.[109] In 1942, one could not have simply ignored a "heartfelt wish" of Bormann's. And so, in his New Year's greeting to Bormann, Speer indicated that he was ready to make up. However, he felt that the relationship between him and Giesler would never again be as it had been. In any event, he said, he had never meant to cast any aspersions on Giesler's greatness as an architect. Speer also told Bormann: "Any other [*i.e.*, negative] opinion would be extremely foolish—although I strive to make my constructions such that their artistic quality will never and can never be surpassed, and I assume that this will never be the case."[110] Still, for all his hubris, Speer allowed his competitor to have the same peculiar view of the architect's profession.[111]

And in striking the heartiest of tones, Speer knew how to clear the air with Bormann. Decades later, Speer wrote in his autobiography that he had avoided Bormann: "From the beginning we could not abide each other."[112] Yet this letter has no trace of the antipathy that Speer subsequently reports. Instead, Speer penned ingratiating words to Bormann, who was intent on bringing the two feuding architects together:

"My best wishes go with you for the new year. All our wishes are only [sic] one in that we all have a chance to bring joy to the Führer and spare him any chagrin.

"Hence, my sole New Year's wish for you: May your highly

responsible work bring the Führer much joy and little disappointment in the year 1942." And Speer concluded his letter "in friendship and with heartiest greetings."[113]

The spring of 1942 actually brought a reconciliation—albeit shallow—between Speer and Giesler. Speer, as he informed the General Building Councillor, was delighted that he "could work [with him] again and enjoy their old confidence."[114]

In March 1942, of course, such friendly tones were easy for Albert Speer. He had long since reached a position that guaranteed him more power and influence than he might have ever attained as the Führer's personal architect.

4

THE MINISTER OF STATE

"I swear that I will be loyal and obedient to the Führer of the German Reich and nation, Adolf Hitler, that I will devote my strength to the good of the German people, obey the laws, perform my duties conscientiously, and carry out my responsibilities with impartiality toward all people, so help me God."[1]

Albert Speer was barely thirty-seven years old when he swore this oath to his Führer on February 15, 1942. (Two and a half years later, he was to break his word.) A few days before that February 15, Hitler had appointed him Reich Minister of Armaments and Munitions. Speer was replacing Dr. Fritz Todt, who had died in a plane crash.

Decades later, Speer mystically depicted death as having paved the way for his rise to power. "How often my career was affected by death. For I would never have become Hitler's architect but for the death of Troost, whose designs he so admired. And certainly he would never have appointed me Minister of Armaments if my predecessor, Todt, had not been killed in an airplane crash."[2]

Among the leaders of the Third Reich, Fritz Todt was an unusual person—something that Speer, as he subsequently presented himself, would have liked to be. Indeed, Todt and Speer were similar in many ways; but there was a vast difference between them.

Todt was a National Socialist out of profound conviction. ("For the man who lives in the era of Adolf Hitler, all wishes for personal comfort and convenience are as nothing compared with the sacred obligation to carry out the mission assigned by the Führer.")[3] Speer, on the other hand, had never made any effort to deal with the ideology of National Socialism beyond what was necessary for his career.

Todt, who had joined the Nazi Party back in 1922, had made a name for himself by building the Reich autobahns.[4] Even before Hitler's takeover, Todt had devoted much thought to the autobahn project, which he saw as a means of ending unemployment.[5] He was also attracted to the artistic aspects of the task. "The plan to build a network of connecting highways," he once said, "offered challenges which the master builders of many centuries had longed for in vain. . . . The autobahns must not be alien entities, they have to be integral parts of the landscape."[6]

On July 30, 1933, Hitler appointed Todt General Building Inspector of the German Road System.[7] On March 17, 1940, Todt became Reich Minister of Armaments and Munitions.[8] In July 1941, Hitler also made him General Inspector of Water and Energy.[9] Now, Todt was "virtually the minister of technology and the Führer's weapon-maker for the German Reich. . . ."[10]

This and other functions[11] had made Fritz Todt a central figure in the leadership of the Reich, yet he never got entangled in the omnipresent internal intrigues of the Party.[12] His personal modesty, his lack of the bragging and blustering typical of other Party functionaries gained him the respect of the general population, if only because he never touted his own virtues.[13] His technological expertise, his dislike of unnecessary bureaucracy ("I don't want a big office, otherwise I would suffocate in red tape"),[14] his lack of interest in Party infighting

Führerhauptquartier, den 15. Februar 1942.

66

Vor mir, dem Führer, erschien heute der Reichsminister für Bewaffnung und Munition, Diplom-Ingenieur
Professor Albert S p e e r und leistete mir im Bei-
sein des Reichsministers und Chef der Reichskanzlei
nachstehenden Eid:

" Ich schwöre: Ich werde dem Führer des

Deutschen Reichs und Volkes, Adolf Hitler,

treu und gehorsam sein, meine Kraft für das

Wohl des deutschen Vol..es einsetzen, die

Gesetze wahren, die mir obliegenden Pflichten

gewissenhaft erfüllen und meine Geschäfte

unparteiisch und gerecht gegen jedermann führen,

so wahr mir Gott helfe."

v.g.u.

. . .

g.w.o.

The record of Albert Speer's oath of office as Armaments
Minister, signed by Speer, Hitler, and Lammers.

brought him Hitler's "respect bordering on reverence."[15] This was entirely justified by Todt's accomplishments.

On February 7, 1942, both Todt and Speer were at Führer Headquarters in Rastenburg [now Kętrzyn, Poland]. Speer had been on a strenuous inspection tour of his construction staff in the Russian city of Dnyepropetrovsk. Flying back to Berlin, he had stopped off in Rastenburg.[16] After not seeing Hitler for several weeks, Speer hoped for "at least a brief greeting" from him, which he would have viewed as a special distinction.[17] Todt had likewise come for a conference with Hitler. It was to be his last meeting with the Führer. No one knows what they talked about, but statements by Todt's staffer Walter Rohland allow us to infer something of the content.

Todt, although a follower of Hitler since the years of Hitler's struggle for power, regarded the war with Russia as a national calamity.[18] True, when the autobahn to Vienna was under construction, Todt had voiced two ardent wishes: "One was the autobahn to Vienna, which is being built. My other wish is that someday an autobahn will run all the way to the Caucasus."[19] But Todt's desire to build a highway to Russia did not mean that he approved of Hitler's military goals. Despite his National Socialist conviction, Todt would not forgo the right to have his own opinion. He fully realized that Germany, especially after the United States entered the war, ultimately could not keep pace with the arms potential of the enemy.[20] "The crucial thing for him," according to his employee Rohland, "was the fact that Germany had to prepare for a *long* war, and that from month to month, the prospect of winning such a war grew dimmer and dimmer."[21] Todt made no bones about his attitude toward the war, whether talking to the Führer or to others.[22] After the war, Rohland stated that Todt had repeatedly urged Hitler to end the war politically. Rohland also presumed that a political solution to the war was the topic of conversation on the evening of February 7, 1942.[23] Todt had evidently failed to impress his views on the Führer. In any case, he seemed depressed when Speer saw him after Todt's meeting with Hitler.[24]

Todt wanted to fly back to Berlin the next morning. Since one seat in his airplane was still free, Todt could offer it to Speer, who had wanted to join him. But that was not to be. Speer was not received by the Führer until 1 A.M., and he remained with him until 3 A.M. This was not an unusual hour, given Hitler's eccentric schedule.[25] Speer, however, needed a full night's sleep; so he informed Todt that he would not be flying with him at 8 A.M. as planned.[26]

The weather was clear, and Todt left punctually on the morning of February 8.[27] The airplane took off without a hitch. But then, still within sight of the airport, the pilot abruptly turned the plane around and tried to land with the wind—an action indicating that there was some kind of emergency on board. "At that moment, a vertical flame, apparently caused by an explosion, darted up from the rear of the plane. The plane instantly plunged down from a height of some twenty meters, pivoting around its [right] wing and crashed on the ground almost perpendicularly, facing directly away from its flight direction."[28] There were no survivors.

The cause of the accident has never been cleared up. It has inspired speculation by countless more-or-less competent minds. Hitler's chief pilot, Baur, conjectures that Todt set off a so-called "airplane destroyer" with the boots of his fur flying suit, and that the pilot discovered it right after takeoff. Since Todt's own plane was being inspected at the time, he was using Field Marshal Sperrle's plane, a Heinkel 111, which, being a combat plane, was equipped with such a self-destruct mechanism.[29]

It is not out of the question, according to Speer, that the pilot inadvertently pulled the self-destruct lever himself. In Todt's plane, which had no such device, the identical switch had an entirely different function. But in Sperrle's combat plane, the pilot's mistake was fatal.[30] It took three minutes for the mechanism to work. The pilot did not have enough time to return to the airport and land before the kilogram of explosives blew up.

Postwar investigators who attempted to reconstruct the disaster by using an airplane carrying a time bomb only fed new rumors.[31] The SS and even Hitler himself were suspected of trying to assassinate Todt.

It is quite unlikely that Hitler was interested in killing his Minister of Armaments and Munitions. This talented man may have been an unpleasant Cassandra, whose opinion implied doubts about Hitler's invincibility, but the dictator greatly esteemed Todt's abilities and achievements. He had had good reason to entrust Todt with a wealth of offices vital to the war effort. His shock over Todt's death was genuine, though, in the next few days, he showed the stoic calm[32] with which he usually took unexpected strokes of fate—a seemingly unshakable leader.

Rumors about the SS responsibility for Todt's death persist even today. A top leader who felt it made no sense to prolong the war might have been too uncomfortable a prophet for the SS. Perhaps, in that black-uniformed elite, one might find the wire-pullers of a "deliberate" accident. Be that as it may, the death of Fritz Todt will probably always remain one of the unsolved enigmas of history.[33]

That very same day, the German public was informed: "On Sunday [February 8], in the fulfillment of his duties as a soldier, Reich Minister Dr. Todt died in an accident while carrying out his military assignments."[34] The nation was dumbfounded by the news of Todt's death.[35] Germans regarded him as one "of the few irreplaceable men"[36] at the top of the Reich, and they wondered about the cause of the disaster. The official announcement, described as "very terse," aroused criticism.[37] A flood of rumors resulted. Just a few months earlier, such idols as Werner Mölders and Air Force general Ernst Udet had died. Udet had shot himself, and his suicide had been officially hushed up;[38] Mölders had lost control and flown his plane into a factory chimney. Now, the wildest speculations were triggered by the lapidary data on Todt's death. It was generally conjectured that the accident had been caused by "sabotage or actions planned by enemy forces."[39]

And even Hitler voiced his suspicion "that foul play might be involved."[40]

The leaders of the Reich were also stunned by the news. "This loss is simply shattering," Goebbels noted in his diary. "Todt was one of the very great figures in the National Socialist regime. . . . Our loss will become obvious only in the next few months. . . ."[41] However, the fears of the Propaganda Minister turned out to be groundless. Todt's successor managed to fill his shoes more than adequately.

Speer's hour had come. Chance had saved Hitler's favorite architect from death. And in the aftermath, he never failed to tell his friends and staffers how easily he could have suffered the same fate as Todt. Field Marshal Erhard Milch could not conceal his cynicism: "Speer told me that he had actually wanted to fly back to Berlin in Todt's plane, but had changed [his mind] in the last moment. He always enjoyed flirting with danger!"[42]

When Hitler was informed of the plane crash around 9 A.M. that Sunday,[43] his Air Force adjutant, von Below, happened to be present. Hitler "reacted . . . almost imperceptibly. All he said, after a few minutes, was that Professor Speer was the only man who could replace Todt."[44]

Around noon, while soldiers and civilians in Führer Headquarters were excitedly discussing the problem of replacing Todt, Speer was summoned to Hitler.[45] Their conversation is documented solely by Speer's numerous accounts,[46] which, however, are generally consistent, aside from his statement at Nuremberg.

Hitler was standing when he received Speer. The now official atmosphere had nothing of the intimacy of the previous night's conversation. Speer, restrained and a bit shaken, expressed his condolences for Todt's death, Hitler "replied very briefly, then said without more ado, 'Herr Speer, I appoint you the successor to Minister Todt in all his capacities.' " Speer was floored. He thought he had misheard. Unsure of himself, he answered that he would make every effort to replace Todt in his construction projects. But Hitler insisted: "No, in all his capacities, including that of Minister of Armaments." Speer objected that he knew nothing about civil engineering or armaments; but Hitler assured Speer that he trusted him and that Speer could do it. Besides, added Hitler, he had no one else. Speer had enough presence of mind to cover himself. He asked for an official order from the Führer, "for I cannot vouch for my ability to master this assignment." Hitler issued the order in terse language, and Albert Speer wordlessly accepted this new honor.

Speer's appointment as Todt's successor has been widely discussed by scholars. The British historian Alan Milward sets February 18 as the date of the appointment;[47] and David Irving doubts that Speer was named successor in *all* of Todt's functions as early as February 8.[48] Finally, the question remains: Was Hitler's decision based on sudden inspiration or on his characteristic "dilettantism—he preferred to choose nonspecialists as his associates" (according to Speer)[49]—or had he made up his mind after long reflection?

At the International Tribunal in Nuremberg, Speer testified: "On February 8, 1942, my predecessor Dr. Todt crashed in his airplane. A few days later, Hitler made me his successor in his numerous capacities. . . ."[50]

Speer's testimony is consistent with the official process of his appointment, as described in the Speer Office Journal. "On February 9, the Führer appointed Herr Speer successor to Dr. Todt as Reich Minister of Armaments and Munitions, as Inspector General of the German Road System, and as Inspector General of Water and Energy. On February 10, the Reich Marshal appointed Reich Minister Speer Commissioner of Construction. Two days later, the Führer made the minister successor in all other functions that Dr. Todt had performed."[51]

Documents, if at all available, tally with the account in the Speer Journal. February 9, 1942, is the date appearing on the official documents of Speer's appointments to the positions of Reich Minister of Armaments and Munitions,[52] Inspector General of the German Road System,[53] and Inspector General of Water and Energy.[54]

Speer kept his statements at Nuremberg deliberately vague, omitting dates in order not to contradict the official data.[55] Nevertheless, his "unofficial" conversation with Hitler, described by Speer, must have taken place. Hitler's decision was spontaneous, and it was characteristic of him to act swiftly on his decisions. Even years later, when Speer was preparing for the Nuremberg Trial, he wrote his life story from memory, with no data at hand. Remembering that conversation, he noted: "February 8, 1942, several hours after Dr. Todt's death, transfer of all of Dr. Todt's offices."[56] The day after his arrival in Berlin, on February 10, 1942, he left no doubt among his closest staffers that Hitler had transferred to him all of Todt's capacities.[57]

David Irving may be highly suspicious of Speer's claim that he had been made Todt's successor in all his offices on that very same day. Nevertheless, in the account of a further event on February 8, Irving supplies evidence that Speer's statements are correct. For that afternoon, while Speer was conferring with Hitler, Göring came to see the Führer. Göring had been planning to visit Hitler the next day and had now hurried over "in order to get Hitler to transfer Todt's area of jurisdiction to his [Göring's] Four-Year-Plan Office. A dumbstruck Göring was told by Hitler that thirty-six-year-old Albert Speer would be succeeding Todt."[58]

The Reich Marshal was by no means naive enough to think that Hitler would hand him one of the three above-named offices, which were vital to the war effort. Göring could not complain of a lack of responsibilities. Furthermore, after the lost Battle of Britain, the Führer had far less confidence in the abilities of the head of the Luftwaffe. Nevertheless, Göring tried to get the office of "Inspector General for Special Assignments in the Four-Year Plan," which had been one of Todt's functions. Understandably, the Reich Marshal, vain and powerstruck as he was, nurtured ambitions about this office. If it were held by anyone else, there was bound to be trouble for Göring as head of the Four-Year Plan.[59] Indeed, Göring and Todt had

had certain conflicts, which the Reich Marshal wanted to avoid in the future by taking over that position.

Speer had kept abreast of the friction between Göring and Todt[60] and had been willing to take over Todt's offices only after Hitler assured him "that he would fully support Speer against all competitors."[61]

For Hitler, the matter was actually settled with the verbal assignment that Speer assume all of Todt's capacities. Next, it was the job of the bureaucrats to place the appointment on a legally sound foundation. Hitler held no brief for them: "Our administration often proceeds in an indescribably stupid manner."[62] Nor did the officials of the Reich Chancellery disprove Hitler's opinion to them. Speer's official appointment to the three most important offices was implemented with the most flagrant clumsiness of bureaucratic jurisprudence.

Hitler had not ordered Speer to take over Todt's duties until around noon of February 8; and since the plane crash had caused more than enough confusion, Dr. Lammers, head of the Reich Chancellery, did not have time to fill out the appointment documents until the next day. In a memorandum of February 9, 1942, Lammers wrote: "Today, the Führer personally handed the three relevant documents to Professor Speer in my presence. . . . The Führer approved the announcement that I drafted for the press and the radio."[63] Lammers relayed the "announcement" to Dr. Dietrich, Reich Press Chief, who then passed it on to the media.[64]

As the top man in the Reich Chancellery, Lammers concluded that the delivery of the three documents to Speer had made his appointment legally binding, so that there was "no need to inform the Supreme Reich Authorities and the agencies directly responsible to the Führer."[65] Nonetheless, Lammers insisted on sending a special letter to those agencies to notify them of Speer's nomination.[66]

In the best legal manner, Lammers also concluded that it would be advisable to run an announcement of the appointment in the *Reichsgesetzblatt* (legal newspaper), because Todt's appointments to those three offices had also been published there. To be sure, Todt's appointments had been made by way of "Führer edicts,"[67] and Lammers did not wish to bother Hitler "about issuing new edicts."[68] So "it was probably the correct thing for me to choose the form of an 'announcement' signed by myself for the *Reichsgesetzblatt.* "[69]

It took one of the officials of the Reich Chancellery five days to inform his superior that "if an announcement of Professor Speer's appointment to the three offices of deceased Reich Minister Dr. Todt is printed in the *Reichsgesetzblatt,* it will [have] only declaratory significance."[70] Thus the Herr Reich Minister need have no qualms about signing such a public announcement.[71] Next, on February 15, 1942, the business office of the *Reichsgesetzblatt* was asked by the Reich Chancellery to run the announcement as soon as possible.[72] The periodical acted quickly, publishing the news five days later.[73]

The bureaucrats of the Reich Chancellery were extremely meticulous when they drew up the document confirming Speer's appointment as Inspector General of the German Road System. Nevertheless, they made a "regrettable mistake," of which Reich Minister Lammers was then "obediently informed."[74] It seems that the document (both the original and the copy) described Speer as being appointed to the position of General *Building* Inspector of the German Road System, and neither Lammers nor Hitler had noticed the error when signing the document. Now the head of the Reich Chancellery did have to "bother" his Führer after all. Hitler had to sign a corrected document, and, on February 20, Lammers apologized to Speer for the "regrettable mistake."[75]

Twelve days after Speer's verbal appointment, the lawyers, whom Hitler called such names as "bacilli culture,"[76] were still busy with their punctilious implementation of the Führer's swift decision. But, of course, these problems did not concern the new minister.

Speer's appointment as Minister of Armaments put an end to his anonymity, which had been basically agreeable to him.

The Nazi bigwigs certainly knew of his close relationship to Hitler and showed him the cautious respect they showed to people enjoying the Führer's special favor. On the other hand, Speer was almost unknown to the general public. Germans had to learn who the man was who would be taking over Dr. Todt's many diverse tasks.

The *Völkischer Beobachter* promptly ran an announcement of Speer's appointment, a photograph of the new minister, and a two-column description of his background.[77] At the orders of the Propaganda Ministry, local newspapers followed suit.[78] "The development of the Party site in Nuremberg, the construction of the new Reich Chancellery, and the design for the total renewal of Berlin with its tremendous monumental constructions (a project interrupted only by the war) have demonstrated not only the artistic genius of the architect Albert Speer, but his organizational talent as well." These praises appeared in a Westphalian newspaper.[79] The *Völkischer Beobachter* placed the new Minister of Munitions on the same level as his recently deceased predecessor: "Party comrades Todt and Speer, distinguished by their professional knowledge and filled with an extraordinary wealth of creative ideas, belong to the loyal guard of the National Socialist German Workers' Party. By their actions, men of their stamp rebut the silly reproach of their political opponents that Adolf Hitler's movement lacks minds. . . ."[80]

The public was restrained and skeptical. Speer's replacement of Todt had come as a surprise. This reaction was heard by the inquisitive SD eavesdroppers from the lips of Germans. Still, the news had also had a "calming effect," since the "gap had been filled so quickly." The eavesdroppers also heard "statements to the effect that 'Professor Speer might be a capable architect,' but 'not a technical organizer and versatile genius on a par with Dr. Todt.' "[81]

On the whole, however, the Germans trusted the Führer, since he had made this important decision personally, and they considered "the swift choice of Dr. Todt's successor necessary and correct. . . ."[82]

Even propaganda chief Goebbels did not foresee such a somber future after his Führer's decision: "The Führer has appointed Speer as Todt's successor," Goebbels confided to his diary. "[He is] probably the only man capable of managing the dead man's great legacy in accordance with its purpose and its program."[83]

The new head of the Munitions Ministry was probably almost unmoved by the fact that the mass media had given him so much publicity. During the first few days after his appointment, he was completely involved in complex power struggles, because of the—already occupied—positions in Todt's agencies. Some of the lesser "Führers" were tempted to cut off a slice or two of the big power pie. But Speer, a newcomer to large-scale politics, immediately showed that he would not tolerate any encroachment on his new territory. Such attempts, as the Speer Journal laconically remarks, "were instantly recognized and nipped in the bud."[84]

Interestingly, these intrigues, which climaxed in the struggle around the man in charge of armaments production,[85] ultimately worked in Speer's favor. This was due to the complete support that Hitler had promised his new appointee and that he actually gave him. However, one problem remained for the architect who had just been promoted to minister. And solving it seemed a lot more difficult to him than his struggles to hold Dr. Todt's legacy together.

Speer's inhibitions in dealing with other people had not vanished even when he was Hitler's Number 1 master builder. He still made a shy and slightly awkward impression. Most of all, he was frightened by the thought "of speaking up easily at public meetings. . . ."[86] His only public speech as an architect had also been the shortest of his life, and it had left even Hitler rather nonplussed. On the eve of the dictator's fiftieth birthday, a stretch of Berlin's so-called "East-West Axis" was to be opened to traffic. As Inspector General of Buildings of Berlin, Speer could not avoid giving a speech. Looking forward to the occasion, Hitler hoped his architect would overcome his inhibitions. Speer's quick mind stood by him once again, and Hitler's great expectations were disappointed. Speer proclaimed in one breath: "Mein Führer, I herewith report the completion of the East-West Axis. May the work speak for itself!"[87]

Whenever Speer was asked to give a speech, he would tersely reply that "I do not make speeches myself" and he would send a member of his staff instead.[88] However, as minister, he could no longer afford this rhetorical restraint. On February 14, 1942, Speer officially greeted his new office staff with an address at the Reich Ministry of Armaments and Munitions. He was forced to give "the first speech of his life that was longer than two sentences."[89] Speer concealed his insecurity behind a mushy homage to the deceased Dr. Todt and to Hitler.

"At the zenith of his tremendous labors," Speer began bombastically, "our leader, Party Comrade Dr. Todt, was carried off. His work will remain indelibly imprinted for all time in the Book of History. . . . I am cognizant of the fact that I can never fully replace Dr. Todt's incomparable energy. . . ." And with somewhat embarrassing modesty, the minister struck a comradely tone: "I turn to you today and ask you to take me into your comradeship of veteran employees. . . . You may rest assured that I will be as concerned about your personal problems and plights as our late leader was." He linked an appeal to work with the admonition to recall the great loss that the Führer had suffered: "Great as our grief for the dead man may be, the Führer's grief is even greater. With our tireless work, we all will make it easier for him to get over this pain."[90] And with the customary threefold "Sieg Heil," Speer concluded what was actually his maiden speech.[91]

However, the young minister's rhetorical bow to his predecessor and to Hitler was apparently as ineffectual as his sentimental attempt to gain the confidence of his new subordinates. Xaver Dorsch, the senior member of the staff, gave his new superior a reserved answer: "Dr. Todt had our unlimited trust. Trust does not come by itself, it has to be earned."[92] (Two years later Dorsch was the ringleader of a conspiracy against Speer, when illness forced the minister to suspend all his activities.)

However, within ten days after his unsuccessful first speech, the new minister appeared to have overcome his insecurity when he spoke to the Gauleiters and Reichsleiters in Munich. During his first two weeks of office, the youngest minister of Great Germany had not been lazy. The first feuds in the area of jurisdictional disputes had been won. The system of "self-responsibility of industry," originally introduced by Dr. Todt to improve efficiency in armaments output, had now been expanded by Speer and approved by Hitler.[93] Speer had also made himself known in countless meetings with high-ranking industrialists and generals. And, last but not least, he had personally sat at the controls of a tank and a half-track motorcycle in order to have a close look at the products of the armaments machinery that he now commanded.[94]

All these activities may have given Speer a sense of security and ministerial authority. In any event, it was a warlike Speer who appeared before the Nazi bigwigs to speak on "New Methods of Increasing Efficiency in Armaments Production."

"First of all," said Speer, "in unison and with all our strength, we have to produce weapons and instruments that the Führer absolutely needs in order to win our victory in the coming years." The Gauleiters were told that any of their special wishes that did not contribute to the war effort would have to be put aside; in particular, the "peacetime constructions" were to be suspended. And draconic measures were called for to prevent "hoarding" of manpower and material in the factories: "The Führer, at my suggestion, has ordered that any factory directors and employees as well as governmental workers and [military] officers who try to secure material or manpower by means of false data are to be punished with death or long prison terms." Even the enemy in eastern Europe had to serve as a model: "The Bolshevists are ahead of us in one respect:

Their ruthless methods of applying drastic punishments for crimes that even slightly oppose the interests of the state. Here, in Germany, especially in the armaments industry, we must apply the severest penalties."[95]

The young minister had mastered the diction of the National Socialists in an astonishingly short time, and his vigorous words evidently drew applause from Hitler's "assistant Führers." His speech, according to the Speer Journal, "was, so we hear, well received by the sub-führers, who are a critical bunch."[96]

The staffers of what had been the Todt ministry soon noticed that their new superior had a different style of political management than their deceased boss. Dr. Walter Schieber, state secretary in the Munitions Ministry, explained the difference between the two men—a difference that lay chiefly in their mentalities: "[Speer] lacks Todt's human warmth. Even his heart is cool. All that counts for him is the object. He will squeeze everything out of us. . . ."[97]

The Goebbels press was full of praise for Speer's youthful dynamic energy in tackling the problems of German armaments production. "He has the traits of youth in the best sense of the word," an editor of the magazine *Das Reich* crowed, "he is endowed with clear, calm reason, a passion for creative action, and an optimism that neither knows nor tolerates any doubts about success."[98]

The "Speer Era" had begun.[99]

Later, Speer would call his appointment as Todt's successor a "recklessness" and "frivolity" on Hitler's part.[100] On the other hand, the British historian Hugh Trevor-Roper writes that Hitler made a more felicitous choice with Speer than with his other appointees.[101] Hitler's decision was prompted, no doubt, by the same intuition that had inspired him to put a bemedaled fighter pilot—Göring—in charge of the German economy or to make a champagne specialist—Ribbentrop—whose sole pretension to a cosmopolitan sophistication was a knowledge of languages, into his Foreign Minister.

Nevertheless, Hitler's decision to entrust Speer with the portfolio of Minister of Munitions had a sound basis. After a winter of heavy losses in the East, the dictator's top priority was to achieve maximum increase in armaments output. The solution to this problem required not so much a technologist as an organizer par excellence. Since Speer had completed the new Reich Chancellery in a record nine months, Hitler regarded him as a man with an "incredible organizational ability."[102] Furthermore, he could be fully certain of the loyalty of his thirty-six-year-old protégé. Hitler knew that he had an obedient human instrument in this ambitious young man, a tool that would willingly follow his orders.[103]

The question is: Did Speer actually aspire to a position so crucial to the war effort?[104] As Hitler's master builder, he had gotten his first taste of power and learned to appreciate its possibilities. A ministerial protfolio offered even more power to satisfy his ambitions. Nevertheless, he was well aware of the dangers attending his new position. As premier architect by the grace of Hitler, he had occupied a virtually unassailable position. The aura of artistic comradeship tying him to Hitler had protected him against the intrigues of other ambitious men. No one had dared to interfere with the obvious friendship of the architecture-loving dictator and his master builder.

Speer no doubt realized that, as a minister, he would be leaving his safe position of artistic outsider at Hitler's court; and Speer was smart enough to secure Hitler's backing from the very start. A calculating tactician, he had requested that Hitler order him to accept Dr. Todt's legacy. This obligated Hitler to support Speer completely. Besides, Hitler would thereby share responsibility for any professional mistakes that his new minister might make. Armed with these safeguards, Speer could not resist the temptation of joining the cabinet of the Greater German Reich.

His appointment astounded everyone around Hitler.[105] But even more astounding was the fact that, contrary to expectations, Speer proved to be a more successful weapons-maker than his predecessor.

5

THE SUCCESSOR
TO THE THRONE

Around 1943, as Field Marshal Milch recalled shortly after the war, Speer developed a new ambition: He wanted to be appointed Hitler's successor.[1] It was a propitious time for the Armaments Minister to nurture such plans. True, in a speech given on September 1, 1939, Hitler had named Göring as his successor or—in case anything happened to the latter—Rudolf Hess.[2] By 1943, however, Göring's star had waned, as far as Hitler was concerned. The head of the Luftwaffe had shown his incompetence by losing the Battle of Britain and by failing to keep up the supply lines to Germany's Sixth Army at Stalingrad.[3] Hitler, in deference to Göring's popularity with the German people, did not officially oust him as successor to the throne, but scarcely anyone in Hitler's retinue assumed that the head of the Luftwaffe would ever succeed the Führer. Hess, on the other hand, had burned all his bridges behind him in 1941 by flying to England on a naive peace mission.

By mid-1943, Speer had managed to attain a top position among the competing Nazi potentates. After taking office in February 1942 as Minister of Armaments and Munitions, he had more than doubled the German armaments output.[4] Speer had long since forgotten what he had described as the most important goal in the spring of 1942: "The war must be ended in the shortest possible time; if not, Germany will lose the war. We must win it by the end of October [1942] . . . or we have lost it once and for all."[5] Now, the Minister of Armaments kept driving his armies of workers to greater and greater achievements, and he declared that the war was a "fight until victory."[6]

On June 5, 1943, in a speech broadcast on all German networks, the Propaganda Minister did not fail to sing the praises of the successful leader of the Greater German weapon-maker:

> [I] believe I am speaking on behalf of the entire German nation when I thank our Party Comrade Albert Speer with all my heart and congratulate him for a crucial achievement that will enter his name forever in the book of this war. He has thereby earned the gratitude and boundless appreciation of the German people.[7]

The dynamic armaments organizer could be certain of his Führer's esteem in any case. Just six months after Speer took office, Hitler stated in regard to his Armaments Minister's successes: "For the first time, we have come at least so far that . . . no more eggs are taken on strolls through the Reich. Earlier, every egg had to be transported by railroad a thousand kilometers and more, until it arrived more or less where the hen had laid it. . . . That [waste] is over and done with."[8] The Armaments Minister climbed from one production increase to the next, and in mid-1943, he was as high in Hitler's esteem as ever. "Speer is still tops with the Führer," noted Goebbels in his diary on June 23, 1943. "He is truly a genius at organization. . . ."[9]

Meanwhile, the armaments chief, who had zoomed to the peak of the Nazi hierarchy, had been dealing with highly political issues that went far beyond the duties of an "unpolitical professional minister."

Before the war, when Speer had still been Inspector General

of Buildings for the Reich capital, he had suggested to Goebbels that the architect Rudolf Wolters be made exhibition commissioner for the exhibition "New German Architecture." In this capacity, Wolters visited all the major European cities until 1943—Copenhagen, Madrid, Belgrade, Athens, even Ankara.[10] He also met personalities like Franco, Salazar, the Bulgarian king and queen, and the Yugoslav prince regent and his wife. In this way, Wolters gathered "informative political insights,"[11] which he always transmitted to his boss. Around that time, February 1943, when, according to Speer, Goebbels was trying to take Ribbentrop's place as Foreign Minister,[12] Wolters returned from his last "exhibition trip." He had just been in Ankara, where he had met ex-Reich Chancellor Von Papen, whom Hitler had shelved by putting him in the German embassy in Turkey. Von Papen had asked Exhibition Commissioner Wolters to transmit to Speer the—for caution's sake "Turkish"—opinion of the political situation. German peace negotiations with Russia at any price. "This will be our last chance to achieve an admittedly very harsh peace; but it will avert a catastrophe.[13] [Moreover] a constructive foreign policy demands that Ribbentrop be replaced by someone with imagination, for instance, Speer."[14]

The Armaments Minister passed the "Turkish" opinion on German foreign policy on to Hitler after crossing out Papen's suggestion that Speer become the new Foreign Minister.[15] Speer had good reason to omit this remark. He had recently witnessed the Propaganda Minister's futile attempt to get Hitler to remove the vain and simpleminded Ribbentrop and replace him with Goebbels.[16]

Such failures curbed the ambitions of several of Speer's fellow ministers. But they did not discourage the Armaments Minister (who was "only doing his job") from staying involved in high-level politics and revealing his crown-prince aspirations. The thing that prompted Speer to set himself such lofty goals was what Propaganda Chief Goebbels called simply the "Führer Crisis."

Since the start of the war, Hitler had withdrawn more and more from the actual business of politics. He now saw his main field of endeavor in his role as supreme commander of the Wehrmacht. For this reason, he found little time to concern himself with political problems. This was quite all right with three men who, despite their extremely diverse natures, had one thing in common: ambition. The three were Martin Bormann, head of the Party Chancellery since Hess's flight into English captivity[17] and a loyal servant of his master; Dr. Hans Lammers, head of the Reich Chancellery and a bureaucrat in the best sense of the word; and Wilhelm Keitel, head of the Supreme Command of the Wehrmacht, whose fawning on Hitler had inspired his military colleagues to nickname him "Lakei-tel" (a portmanteau word fusing *Lakai,* lackey, and *eitel,* vain). The ambition of these three men was to manage Hitler,[18] and they had the advantage of daily access to the dictator. The other ministers had to go through Bormann if they wanted to see the Führer.[19] The only exception was Armaments Minister Speer, whose appointments with Hitler were set by the dictator's military aides, since Speer's area was of a military nature.[20] In this way, the Führer was isolated from his ministers, while the influence of the three-man committee increased, much to the annoyance of the Propaganda Minister. "[It] is undeniable," Goebbels suspected, "that these three intend to establish a kind of cabinet government and erect a wall between the Führer and the ministers! This cannot be tolerated under any circumstances."[21]

The little doctor instantly began to organize a campaign against those three "Führer managers" in order to undermine their ambitious project. He wanted Walter Funk, Robert Ley, and Speer to support his campaign. "The choice was typical of Goebbels," autobiographer Speer remarks, "for we were all men of academic background, university graduates."[22]

One day, according to Speer, Goebbels was with these ministers. After a critical analysis of the political situation following Stalingrad, Goebbels said something that one would scarcely have expected from the Führer's ardent admirer. Nevertheless, these words did come from Goebbels' cool, intellectually trained mind: "We are not having a 'leadership crisis,' but, strictly speaking, a 'Leader crisis.' "[23]

At once the quartet of academics decided to turn to Reich Marshal Göring, who was paying far more attention to his diverse hobbies than to his countless duties. The ministers wanted to reactivate his function as chairman of the Ministerial Council for the Defense of the Reich.[24] Their goal was to form a countercabinet headed by Göring in opposition to Bormann, Lammers, and Keitel. Their overall plan was to destroy the power of the three-man committee that was isolating the Führer.

However, they first had to deal with a certain problem. The relationship between the Reich Marshal and the Propaganda Minister was more than cool. After his famous Sportpalast speech of February 18, 1943, Goebbels had shut down the Horcher, a fancy Berlin restaurant that was a favorite eatery of Göring's and many other high Party functionaries. The propaganda chief had wanted to show the general public that the leaders were willing to accept restrictions as part of the all-out war effort. However, the closing of the restaurant had infuriated Göring. The resulting "state of war" between Goebbels and Göring now had to be terminated if they wanted the Reich Marshal to join their projected campaign.

The group of academic ministers saw Speer as the right man to make amends with Göring; indeed, it must have been Goebbels who suggested the Armaments Minister for this mediator role. After all, Goebbels regarded Speer as one of his most reliable allies in his efforts to bring about a total war. A short time earlier, Goebbels had described Speer as being, as always, entirely committed: "I can rely on him blindly."[25] And Speer, the "outsider," showed that he was an equal among equals with the intriguing politicians. Without a moment's hesitation, Speer set out for Obersalzberg on February 28, 1943, to arrange a reconciliation talk between the Reich Marshal and Goebbels at

Göring's country house. Speer had to meet with Göring twice before the latter agreed to receive the propaganda chief.[26]

Goebbels arrived in Obersalzberg the next day[27] and was welcomed by Göring in a baroque attire.[28] They exchanged a few civilities and then, after a political *tour d'horizon,* the two men came to the real problem: the lack of leadership in foreign and domestic politics.[29] Needless to say, they talked about the "three magi," Bormann, Lammers, and Keitel, who were also a thorn in the Reich Marshal's side. The Propaganda Minister had now come to his real topic. He suggested to Göring that they resurrect the Ministerial Council for the Defense of the Reich. They would "surround themselves with courageous, upright, and loyal men," then "slowly deprive the three-man committee of its influence and shift its powers to the Ministerial Council."[30]

Göring was by no means ill-disposed toward the idea, and he spoke of getting SS-Reichsführer Himmler to join them. Goebbels had already won over Funk, Ley, and the Armaments Minister (Goebbels: "Speer is entirely my man").[31] "We have a group," the Propaganda Minister commented, not without pride, "that is not at all bad. In any case, we've got men who enjoy the greatest prestige and the greatest authority in political life today."[32] On the whole, he was delighted by his talk with Göring. Any ill feeling between them was gone. Goebbels: "The petty tensions that had crept between our offices in the course of time were not even mentioned."[33] The propaganda chief had attained his goal: The Reich Marshal's support had been won for the alliance against the "three magi."

Minister Speer did his bit to mobilize Göring, and he did it cunningly. During a walk across the grounds of Obersalzberg, he told the Reich Marshal about the path that Bormann was following. Autobiographer Speer writes: "I explained quite openly to Göring that Bormann was aiming at nothing less than becoming Hitler's successor, and that he would stop at nothing to outmaneuver him [Göring] and, actually, all of us in regard to Hitler. I took the occasion to tell Göring how Bormann seized every opportunity to undermine the Reich Marshal's prestige."[34] Göring was still the officially designated successor to the Führer, and Speer had skillfully struck the Reich Marshal in his most sensitive spot—his vanity. Göring's reaction: "Göring listened with mounting feeling."[35] Speer the politician was a master of his trade.

The Armaments Minister then did more preliminary work for the next step in Goebbels' plan. First, Göring, who was chairman of the Defense Council, had to be made acceptable to his Führer again. No easy enterprise this, for, says Speer, "the massed Allied air raids, which had been going on for weeks, and meeting almost no opposition, had further weakened Göring's already imperiled position."[36] So, on March 5, Speer flew to Führer Headquarters in Winniza[37] and got Hitler to summon Goebbels. Speer hoped that he and the eloquent Propaganda Minister could at least drop hints to the dictator about their "plans for activating the Council of Ministers for the Defense of the Reich."[38] Three days later, the Propaganda Minister arrived in Winniza, and Speer instantly informed him about his efforts to sound Hitler out. Goebbels praised his fellow minister: "As usual, his preliminary work was intelligent and skillful."[39]

However, Speer had to point out to Goebbels, who was raring to go, that "the Führer [is] rather inaccessible . . . to Göring at the moment."[40] Göring's prestige with Hitler had suffered tremendously because of the Luftwaffe's total fiasco. Goebbels already envisioned his carefully hatched plan dissolving in air, since the whole undertaking was dependent on the prestige Göring enjoyed with Hitler. But then, since the Propaganda Minister was seeing the Führer anyhow, he decided to go ahead with his plan.[41] During a nocturnal conversation, in Speer's presence, Goebbels pulled out all the stops of his rhetoric in order to create the right atmosphere for discussing the delicate topic of the Reich Defense Council with Hitler.[42] However, the news of a nighttime air raid on Nuremberg destroyed all of the Propaganda Minister's efforts.[43] The result, according to Goebbels, was an all-out battle. Together with Speer, they had their hands full "getting the matter under control."[44] The Reich Defense Council and Göring were no longer suitable topics of discussion that evening.

Goebbels refused to give up. On March 17, the five confederates met to discuss further ways of putting their plan into action. Their goal was still to destroy the power of the "three magi" at Führer headquarters. Göring made no bones about his dislike of the three shadows around Hitler: "In regard to their power domain, they rank [in downard order]: Bormann, Lammers, Keitel; and Keitel is an absolute nonentity. . . . He's like a locomotive without fire, running along and then suddenly grinding to a halt."[45] To get anywhere with the Führer, said Göring, offering a psychological explanation that was oddly original, "you have to handle him properly and approach him at the right time with the right arguments."[46] He pointed out that Bormann, Lammers, and Keitel had proceeded a lot more skillfully. "That has to be changed."[47]

But nothing was changed, and the Propaganda Minister's campaign remained a dream. Göring sank back into his apathy, while a resolute Bormann climbed a further rung up the ladder of his career. On April 12, 1943, he was "named secretary to the Führer."[48] Goebbels, clever tactician that he was, instantly recognized the change in the power dynamics and switched over to the side of the enemy whom he had just been fighting. And Bormann, no doubt informed about the thwarted plot against him, made sure not to attack Speer openly. After all, he knew what a high opinion the Führer had of his Armaments Minister.

Speer's sally into high-level politics had not cost him his lofty position in the Nazi hierarchy. This was reason enough for him to pursue his political ambitions on his own. The Armaments Minister knew that Hitler had no intention of remaining dictator of the Greater German Reich for the rest of his life. Hitler had once said in Speer's presence: "One cannot be Führer all one's life, there has to be a limit."[49] Hitler had also confided to his Armaments Minister "that he was planning great things for him and had placed him after Göring on the list of successors for the position of Führer."[50] (An honor that, Speer claimed shortly after the war, he had not aspired to by any means.)[51] However, even when the dictator was in a large group, he was not chary with praise of his weapon-maker.[52] For example, writes Speer, Himmler had to put up with Hitler's greeting his loyal Heinrich and Speer with the words "You two peers."[53]

Thus heartened by the "First Man" in the Reich, the Armaments Minister began to test the possibilities of becoming the "Second Man."

During October 1943, Speer had a series of meetings with his office chiefs. The Armaments Minister was planning to have industrial representatives work with his most important office chiefs, so that if any of the latter were to leave, his job could be taken over by the appropriate industrial representative.[54] President Hans Kehrl, as intelligent as he was self-assured, was unpopular because "he [could] get sarcastic, pedantic, and offensive in negotiations whenever he sensed hollow claptrap and incompetence."[55] Kehrl was one of the office chiefs with whom Speer conferred about his plan. The main problem was dealt with quickly: They postponed it. Kehrl had more important things at this time to worry about than finding a replacement in case of the Big Emergency.[56]

However, the office chief and the minister had a lengthy talk, and Speer steered the conversation to a different topic.[57] He was interested in hearing Kehrl's opinion of the most important figures in the Third Reich. According to Kehrl, "We finally came to the question of which of them could possibly succeed Hitler." Speer felt that the Führer would make the choice himself, and his authority would guarantee the man's acceptance by both the Party and the German people. Speer and Kehrl also agreed that the Reich Marshal would not be picked to succeed Hitler. "His physical and mental instability," said Kehrl, "his lack of thoroughness and his inconsistent behavior as well as the obvious decline of his energy made him completely unsuitable [for the job]."[58] On the other hand, the Armaments Minister and his office chief were uncertain whether the dictator had already unofficially revoked the choice he had made at the beginning of the war: his designation of Göring as his successor.

Finally, Speer and Kehrl reviewed all the possible candidates for the office: They mentioned Himmler, Goebbels, and Bormann. Speer asked Kehrl what he thought of these three men. The office chief had once met the SS-Reichsführer,[59] and his opinion of Himmler was quite clear. Hitler—Kehrl was convinced—realized "what a hidebound and irresolute if not cowardly man Himmler was. Speer fully agreed with his office chief. Goebbels, said Kehrl to his superior, was not in the running, if only because of his appearance. Furthermore, there was a widespread distate in the Party for the methods of Goebbels' public work. Speer, for his part, could tell his staffer that Goebbels now saw Hitler relatively seldom and did not seek his advice frequently, as he had once done. The idea of Bormann as a possible successor to Hitler, said Kehrl, was a "bad joke."[60]

After these three candidates were crossed out, the Armaments Minister got down to cases. He threw his hat into the ring, as it were. Did Kehrl "consider it possible that Hitler was thinking of [Speer] as his successor?" The office chief did think so, and he listed good reasons for his assumption. Speer, he said, was the only possible candidate "who was on the same wavelength [as Hitler] because of their mutual artistic interest." Furthermore, Kehrl knew of no one else who had such a close personal relationship to Hitler. Finally, the office chief added, Hitler had the best possible impression of the Armaments Minister's capabilities. "Speer nodded in satisfaction," says Kehrl.[61]

Minister Speer made no secret of his aspiration when speaking to others.[62] He evidently felt so secure about his position in the Nazi hierarchy that he dared to voice these both ambitious and dangerous thoughts. Thus, Bormann was correct when he maintained that Speer was "ambitious to become Hitler's successor."[63]

Speer's openness about his goal was not without its consequences. Göring, Bormann, and Himmler were merely waiting for the right opportunity to get rid of their incautious rival. And opportunity knocked several months later, when Speer fell ill. The bed-ridden minister was far away from Hitler, the center of all power. As Field Marshal Milch describes it, Speer "had the whole pack at his throat."[64]

In his memoirs, however, Speer devotes only a few scant pages to his plans to succeed Hitler. "I recall," he writes, "having had several conversations with Milch about the matter."[65] Speer's literary taciturnity is understandable. Such ambitions can only have a political motive, which does not fit in with Speer's self-portrait as an "unpolitical specialist."[66] Just two years after his illness, he would once again be seized with ambition to become his country's top leader. At that point, however, the German Reich would be under the treads of Allied tanks, and there would be nothing left for anyone to lead.

6

ILLNESS AND CRISIS

In his memoirs, Speer devotes a whole chapter to the illness he suffered when he was Minister of Armaments. His account clearly demonstrates the extent to which the writer distorts his own past. Something that was good yesterday is bad today, and the physicians he once trusted completely are now excoriated as quacks.[1]

Even as a child, Speer had health problems, which were probably psychosomatic in origin. Young Albert was plagued by circulatory disorders and frequent blackouts.[2] And when the adult Speer, barely thirty, could consider himself part of Hitler's entourage, the tremendous construction tasks assigned by the dictator would sometimes cause Speer to have claustrophobic fits, especially in closed rooms. His heart would race wildly, he felt a tingling in his hands and feet, and he was overcome with anxiety. He would lie down to keep from collapsing. Doctors could find no organic causes for his condition.[3]

In 1936, a new face turned up in Hitler's circle. Dr. Theo Morell had been introduced to Hitler by Heinrich Hoffmann, the court photographer. The Führer soon trusted the corpulent physician and made him his personal doctor.[4] Following Hitler's example, the Nazi elite quickly beat a path to Morell's office, and his patients now included Göring and Goebbels, Dietrich and Ribbentrop.

In 1936, when Speer was not only bothered again by circulatory problems, but also tormented by gastric disorders, Hitler advised him[5] to consult Morell at his office at 216 Kurfürstendamm, Berlin.[6] Speer recalls: "The sign at the entrance read: DR. THEO MORELL. SKIN AND VENEREAL DISEASES."[7] However, this specialization, also indicated in other sources, is quite improbable, for Morell was a general practitioner and a specialist in diseases of the urinary tract, and that was how he was described in the Berlin telephone book.[8] Morell, according to Speer's memoirs, examined him superficially and then prescribed intestinal bacteria, dextrose, vitamin pills, and hormone tablets.[9] Speer wanted a second opinion, and the Berlin University professor who then examined him could find no organic illness. He blamed Speer's problems on overwork. Writes Speer: "I slowed down my pace as best I could and the symptoms abated."[10] However, the architect did not wish to annoy his patron Hitler; so he told everyone that he was following Morell's directions to the letter.[11]

Yet Hitler's hardworking master builder could not have been dissatisfied with Dr. Morell's treatment. In mid-1941, when he was afflicted with new gastric and intestinal disorders, he again sought advice from Hitler's personal physician. However, Morell was not in Berlin at that time, so Speer consulted a radiologist, Professor Henri Chaoul at the Landhaus Clinic.[12] Chaoul, examining the Inspector General of Buildings, only X-rayed the patient's gastrointestinal tract and then sent his written diagnosis to Morell. Chaoul did not recommend any therapy.[13]

Morell instantly wrote Speer a long letter, informing him of the findings and making detailed suggestions for treatment. According to this letter, Professor Chaoul had found both an inflammation of the duodenal mucous membrane and chronic appendicitis.[14] Morell knew perfectly well that Speer's problems were mental in origin. This time, he did not prescribe intestinal bacteria, dextrose, vitamin pills, or hormone tablets, as he had in 1936 (according to Speer).[15] Instead, he suggested a diet.[16] He also felt it would be rash to remove Speer's appendix. He merely told his patient to take piperazine.[17] Speer, a gourmet, who frequented the epicurean Horcher Restaurant in Berlin, did not care for the diet. In fact, his dietetic lunches sometimes triggered "ugly outbursts against his staffers."[18] Nevertheless, he seemed quite satisfied with Morell's therapy. Otherwise, he would scarcely have asked Hitler's personal physician to treat Hilde, his daughter, two years later.[19]

In early 1944, Speer fell seriously ill. During his trip to Lapland at Christmas 1943, he had felt pains in his left knee joint. Now, in the first half of January 1944, these pains were growing more and more violent, and they were accompanied by a crippling swelling.[20] At first, Speer consulted his friend Dr. Karl Brandt, Hitler's other personal physician and commissioner of public health. Brandt talked Speer into going to the Hohenlychen Clinic, which was run by Dr. Karl Gebhardt, the top physician of the SS and an intimate friend of Himmler's.[21] On January 18, 1944, the Armaments Minister entered Ward I, a private ward in the SS-hospital. Germany's weapons manufacturers had to get along without their master for a while.

This was hardly an escape into illness because Speer felt he had reached "the end of a lifelong lie."[22] For the minister was neither resigned nor inactive. On the contrary: As dynamic as ever, he tried to rule his armaments empire from his sickbed. His secretaries moved into several rooms at the hospital, and a direct telephone line was established between Speer and his ministry.[23] Speer had no intention of letting any intrigues encroach upon his realm of power during his illness.

Day after day, he received members of his staff and met with visitors often until after midnight—much to the annoyance of Gebhardt, who had to step in more than once to remove "visitors interfering with his therapeutic activities."[24] And since Speer did not care to neglect his close tie to Hitler, the all-decisive focus of power, he sent four letters to the dictator as early as January 26.[25] They were symptomatic of his fear that a lack of personal contact with his Führer might result in a loss of power for Speer. At the moment, he had no cause for concern: The Führer was openly worried about his favorite minister and ordered that all reports on Speer's state of health should be submitted to him, Hitler, personally.[26]

Speer's passion for working in his sickbed was not without its consequences. When he entered the Hohenlychen Clinic, his problem was diagnosed as only a "purulent rheumatoid infection of the left knee joint in connection with an old injury of the ligament."[27] But then, on February 10, the patient suddenly got worse,[28] showing symptoms of great exhaustion. He explicitly asked that Dr. Morell come the next day. However, Hitler could not get along without his personal physician, and so Speer agreed to let Professor Friedrich Koch, an internist at the Berlin Charité, take over his treatment. It was not Speer's wife or Dr. Brandt (according to Speer) who called in Koch,[29] but, as the lengthy medical reports show, SS-physician Dr. Gebhardt and Dr. Morell.[30] At Hitler's request, Gebhardt had been giving Morell constant written and oral reports on Speer's condition. Now, Morell was also kept abreast by Koch.

Professor Koch, arriving at Hohenlychen on the night of February 10, took over all the clinical examinations and decisions.[31] He had come just in time. During the night of February 11, Speer's illness took an ominous turn. He had trouble breathing, he developed cyanosis, he was spitting up blood, and his pulse, at 120, was unusually high. Koch diagnosed Speer's disorder as pulmonary embolism.[32]

Upon receiving detailed information about the patient's condition, Morell issued some comprehensive directions for his therapy. He not only recommended injections of vitamin K[33] (as Speer reproachfully writes), a not uncommon treatment for a patient who was spitting up blood,[34] Morell also prescribed thrombovit and ultraseptyl, along with other medicaments.[35] Twenty-five years later, Speer claimed[36] that Koch had ordered Hitler's influential physician not to interfere with his, Koch's, treatment of the Armaments Minister. However, the pertinent documents do not reveal whether this was the case or whether Koch did, in fact, follow Morell's recommendations. All that can be maintained with certainty is that an intensive series of phone calls took place between the Charité professor and Morell, who was at Führer Headquarters.

According to Speer's memoirs, mysterious things occurred during his medical crisis. The surgeon Gebhardt supposedly asked the internist Koch to operate. But Koch refused, because such an operation would have threatened the patient's life.[37] The specter of a "medical assassination" by the SS-physician Gebhardt haunts Speer's description of the episode. However, toward the end of the war, Koch could tell his ex-patient only that he, Koch, had had an angry dispute with Gebhardt about how to treat Speer's illness.[38] Even in 1947, when Koch could have testified openly against the head SS-physician, all he remembered was that there had been "in the course of treatment differences between Gebhardt and me." Koch did not mention any life-threatening operation suggested by Gebhardt.[39]

On February 13, Koch informed Führer Headquarters that Speer's condition had improved.[40] The Armaments Minister was recovering visibly.[41] However, Professor Koch, feeling that the damp climate of Hohenlychen was not conducive to his patient's convalescence, recommended that Speer be moved to Merano, Italy. So Speer told Gauleiter Hofer to "prepare a large house with about sixteen to twenty rooms."[42] Gebhardt immediately informed his friend and boss Himmler of Speer's intention: "Reich Minister Speer has expressly asked me to transmit this request to the supreme SS and Police Chief, so that SS-Obergruppenführer Wolff may support it." Furthermore, Gebhardt told Himmler, the Reich minister had requested that he [Gebhardt] accompany [Speer] to his destination, and he had also invited his family to come along. "I am to watch over him by way of transition until he has completely adjusted to the climatic conditions there. I agreed to this plan for the time being and I would like to request a decision from the Reichsführer. . . ."[43]

However, Himmler, as it turned out, had a good reason for not yet allowing the Armaments Minister to leave his "supervision." Hence, Gebhardt, citing Himmler,[44] opposed Koch's suggestion. In the end, Koch was forced to call the SS-Reichsführer himself in order to obtain permission to move Speer to Merano.[45] Meanwhile, in Italy, SS-Obergruppenführer Wolff received orders to "investigate the convalescence site scrupulously and determine whether it would ensure total security for the patient, according to the standards of the State Police, especially in regard to aerial attacks."[46] Himmler made his friend Gebhardt responsible for the minister's safety. "Within the framework of this responsibility," the Reichsführer instructed the SS-physician, "only your orders are valid and binding."[47]

Decades later, Speer dramatized the fight that was fought over him. But at the time, it did not strike him as particularly important—to the extent that he even noticed it. He took leave of this "oppressive place"[48] with a concert for the staff of Hohenlychen; the concert featured the pianist Wilhelm Kempff. On March 17, Speer headed south.[49]

At Merano, the convalescent and Dr. Gebhardt appeared to get along famously. After his stay there, Speer thanked his doctor by sending him a photograph with a personal dedication. And the "devoted" Gebhardt reciprocated with a note: "Upon returning to my clinic from Italy, I was instantly reminded of your illness and the lovely time afterward. . . . Please permit me," the physician waxed a bit sentimental, "to thank you once again with this note, not only for all your demonstrations of personal sympathy and your comradeship, but above all for everything you have done for my family."[50] Without doubt, Speer must have been convinced of the medical capabilities of Gebhardt and Morell. When Hitler gave his personal physician the Knight's Cross to the War Merit Cross in February 1944, the minister promptly offered Morell his heartiest congratulations from his sickbed. "May you continue to work this success-fully for many more years and, above all, remain at the Führer's side and help him." Speer then added a request: "If you have any time left over from your important tasks to tend to my needs every now and then, I would be extremely grateful to you."[51] Several months later, Speer voiced similar praises when Himmler's intimate friend Gebhardt was awarded the same distinction as Morell. "After all, I was able to experience your great skill personally," Speer wrote in his congratulatory letter, "and I am therefore all the more delighted at the distinction that you have received."[52]

However, his "comradely gratitude" to his former gods in white did not prevent Speer from describing them twenty-five years later in his autobiography as sinister and dubious repre-sentatives of their profession. He even claimed that he had already doubted their qualifications in the old days. To docu-ment Gebhardt's lack of medical ability, Speer blamed him (albeit indirectly) for the death of Bichelonne, the French Min-ister of Production, with whom Speer had "a distinctly personal relationship."[53] "Toward the end of the war," writes Speer, "French Minister Bichelonne had Gebhardt operate on his knee at Hohenlychen. He died a few weeks later of a pulmonary embolism."[54] A quarter of a century later, Speer forgot that in October 1944, he himself had advised his French colleague to be treated by Gebhardt as Speer's guest.[55] Speer had been de-lighted to hear that the operation had been a success.[56]

Speer's illness was viewed by some of his jealous rivals and competitors as a stroke of luck for them. Intrigues were not long in coming. Göring, Bormann, and Himmler had not for-gotten Speer's ambition to become Hitler's successor. The trio of conspirators quickly got together to launch an attack on the helplessly bedridden Minister of Armaments. They just as quickly hit on a plan for knocking Speer off his high horse.

Xaver Dorsch, Speer's deputy as head of the Todt Organiza-tion, was the right man for the job. When Speer had become

Minister of Armaments and Munition, Dorsch had initially been reserved, but had then shown at least an outer loyalty. Now, during Speer's absence, he knew how to play up the old rivalries between the Todt Organization and the Construction Section of the Ministry of Armaments.

Dorsch reported to the Führer, and the indefatigable Bormann was also present. Hitler then asked Dorsch if he had any problems. Dorsch held back, and Bormann eagerly leaped in, saying that Dorsch did have problems at the ministry.[57] The ambitious Dorsch did not fail to proudly tell his staff that the Führer had inquired sympathetically about the problems of the Todt Organization.

This brought the head of the Todt Organization a rebuke from his bedridden boss: Dorsch, said Speer, had personally exploited a meeting with the Führer, a meeting that Speer had arranged, and Dorsch had then promptly gone to his staff and repeated Hitler's remark. "He probably told them that this was a powerful boost for the Todt Organization." According to Speer, conflicts between the central office of the Todt Organization and the Construction Section had led to personal struggles. "People are deliberately circulating rumors that poison the atmosphere even more." The Armaments Minister wanted to take drastic measures. In the future, if the "maliciousness" of rumor-mongers was demonstrated, they would be sent to a concentration camp.[58] Immediate declarations of loyalty by Dorsch, said Speer, were the sole condition for their further work together, and the Armaments Minister made his feelings ominously clear to his subordinate: "I do not regard you as indispensable to the central office of the Todt Organization."[59]

But then the patient at Hohenlychen received an even worse shock. He learned that Dorsch and other veteran staffers of the Todt Organization had been thwarting Speer's personnel politics—with Bormann's help.

Furious, Speer appealed to Hitler. On January 29, 1944, he informed his Führer that he had been deceived as a Reich minister. A certain small group of former Todt employees had irrefutably demonstrated their disloyalty to him. "I must absolutely apply the severest penalties if I am to maintain my authority in my ministry." He told Hitler that he intended to remove Dorsch as head of the central office of the Todt Organization.[60]

However, Göring, chief of the Luftwaffe, sided with Dorsch and enlisted his help in launching a campaign against the hospitalized Speer. Göring felt it was time to polish up Hitler's tarnished image of Göring and work against the Armaments Minister. The Reich Marshal accused Speer of failing to obey an order issued several months earlier by the Führer: to set up gigantic bomb-proof concrete factories.[61] Göring was thinking mainly of converting caves and tunnels for this purpose. Speer, however, had favored Dorsch's idea of building so-called "mushrooms": concrete ceilings twenty feet thick were to be poured over artificial hills, and the resulting "mushrooms" were then to be hollowed out. In October 1943, the Armaments Minister had approved construction of one or two of these factories to produce fighter planes, even though he basically opposed such mammoth projects. He felt they were too expensive, and they also held up production for many months.[62]

On April 14, 1944, when Speer was convalescing in Merano, Hitler met with Göring and Dorsch at Obersalzberg. The dictator was indignant about the slow progress of the factory construction. The Reich Marshal blamed it on the lack of cement deliveries. Dorsch hastily assured his Führer that the "Luftwaffe had received its full quotas of cement . . . from the Todt Organization."[63] Speer's subordinate had thereby skillfully passed the buck to the absent Armaments Minister, who was responsible for supplying all construction material in both the Reich and the occupied territories.

Hitler then asked for an explanation of how the "mushrooms" were to be built. Dorsch had just told him that this "construction method was so reliable that they could be certain of its successful implementation."[64] The dictator promptly decreed that the "mushrooms" could be "built only by the Todt

Organization," which he called the largest construction concern of all time. "He said he would see to it that the Todt Organization took over all future large-scale constructions in the Reich."[65]

Courted in this way by Hitler, Dorsch indulged in a gesture of seeming generosity toward the convalescing Speer. Dorsch said he would first have to consult the Armaments Minister, since Speer wanted the Todt Organization to operate only in the occupied territories, and he, Dorsch, did not want to have any internal conflicts. Hitler promised to clear the matter up with Speer.[66] However, Hitler did not clear up anything with his absent Minister of Armaments. Instead, two days later, in Göring's presence, he ordered Dorsch to begin construction on ten "mushrooms" without further delay. Ignoring Dorsch's request to clear up the administrative problems with Speer, Hitler said: "Göring, I am no longer needed in this matter. Discuss any further problems with Herr Dorsch."[67] Speer was more than irritated that the Führer had made such a decision over the head of his Armaments Minister. Ultimately, this decision would reduce the latter's sphere of power, since Hitler was, in effect, handing the entire construction apparatus of the Luftwaffe over to the Todt Organization—and thereby to Dorsch.

Earlier, in Hohenlychen, a depressed Speer had been forced to realize that the Führer had not reacted to his letters. Furthermore, the Führer's demonstrations of favor had come more and more seldom: "A bowl of flowers with a standard typewritten note," one or two brief telephone calls, which Speer still remembers.[68] The Armaments Minister was deeply disappointed by his lord and master's obvious cooling of affection. And Speer reacted emotionally when Hitler visited him on March 18, 1944, at Klessheim Palace, where Speer was spending five days en route to Merano. In his autobiography, Speer uses the language of a rejected lover: "Seeing him again after . . . ten weeks, I was for the first time in all the years I had known him struck by his overly broad nose and sallow color. I realized that his whole face was repulsive."[69]

In Merano, the minister was also annoyed that Hitler had allowed his paladins Himmler and Bormann to go after three of Speer's office chiefs. Responding to Hitler's decision, Speer sent him an angry and disappointed letter on April 19: "Mein Führer, it worries me that I have to sit passively on the sidelines while you make decisions on new and important construction matters. . . . This is the first time that you have been dissatisfied with things done in my area of responsibility."[70] Without naming names, he again complained about the disloyal Dorsch. He said he wanted to make some personnel adjustments in the Todt Organization. Dorsch was to continue construction work in the occupied territories, while another veteran Todt staffer was to take over the projects inside the Reich. Speer wanted to place the overall supervision in the hands of Walter Brugmann, who was devoted to him.[71] Speer skillfully tried to get Hitler to accept his suggestions by reminding him of his old passion as an architect: "You will understand, mein Führer, that as your architect, I am passionately devoted to architecture, and at a later time, it will be very difficult for me to have to realize that, at a critical moment, I did not perform as I should have in this area."[72]

Speer used any weapon he could to cling to his position of power. If Hitler did not go along with his wishes, then the Armaments Minister was planning to resign from every office he held.[73] Speer may have reached this decision when his ego was wounded by Hitler's disdainful behavior; however, his defiance was short-lived. For the day after he sent Hitler his letter, Speer received a visit from his staffer Walter Rohland, head of the Tank Committee. Rohland, nicknamed Panzer-Rohland by the press, had a serious talk with Speer: Given the way the war was expected to end, said Rohland, panicky measures by the Supreme Command were quite possible, and Speer was the right man to prevent the worst.[74] Panzer-Rohland managed to talk the offended minister out of resigning, but he had the impression that Speer "did not fully understand my reasons."[75]

On April 20, 1944, Hitler's fifty-fifth birthday, someone

joined forces with Speer and confronted the conspirators who were trying to oust the convalescent Minister of Armaments. Ever since Speer had taken office as minister, Field Marshal Milch had been his devoted friend—something that the people around Milch did not quite understand.[76] A man of great organizational talent, Milch had employed "a mixture of brutality and humanity" (David Irving) to increase production of fighter planes fifteen-fold from November 1941 to July 1944.[77] The high-spirited field marshal was both popular and unpopular, partly because he always offered his frank opinion, whether or not the other person wanted to hear it. At times, he did not hesitate to bellow out his views like a drill sergeant. (He said one could make an impression on Göring only by yelling back at him.)[78] Milch enjoyed great prestige with Hitler, who respected his undeniable achievements and perhaps even his straightforwardness.

The dictator was angry about Speer's ultimatum-like letter of April 19, but on his birthday he nevertheless showed that he was open to reconciliation. Milch recalls: "Hitler, who knew about my friendship with Speer, summoned me to Obersalzberg on 4/20/44 and asked me to go to Speer in order to clear the matter up on his [Hitler's] terms. I noticed that a break with Speer would have been difficult for Hitler at this time."[79] Milch used the opportunity to act as Speer's advocate. He pointed out to Hitler that since Speer was ill, he was more sensitive than usual; Hitler would lose his best man, who was irreplaceable. And then Milch commented, not without a sideswipe at Göring, Bormann, and Dorsch: "And only because of intrigues by rivals of dubious value."[80] After a long pause, Hitler replied that he esteemed Speer more highly than any of his other people, but that Speer would have to be reasonable and not overstrain himself. If Dorsch took over the construction work, this would not lower Speer in Hitler's eyes.[81]

In his role as Speer's advocate, Milch then suggested a compromise: Speer would remain in charge of construction, and Dorsch would be given more independence. "Above all, the minister would no longer have to be consulted about construction matters."[82] The field marshal was focusing on the objective problems. Such a compromise would eliminate the old rivalries between the Todt Organization and the Construction Section of the Armaments Ministry. Hitler accepted this suggestion. However, Milch the mediator wanted even more. He asked the Führer "for a message for Speer . . . to restore the relationship of personal trust." But here, the obstinate Milch came up against Hitler's armor of personal reserve, and he had to keep urging the dictator. At last, Hitler gave in: "Tell Speer I love him!"[83]

That same night, around 1 A.M., Milch arrived in Merano with two members of Speer's staff, and a histrionic scene unrolled during the next few hours. Although the Armaments Minister had yielded to Rohland's persuasion and dropped his plan to resign, he nevertheless put up an adamant front. The field marshal had to talk away at his stubborn friend for several hours. When Milch transmitted the Führer's declaration of love, Speer even became insulting. "The Führer can kiss my ass!" But the field marshal put the Armaments Minister in his place: "You're much to small to act like that toward the Führer!"[84] It was not until five in the morning that Speer finally came round.[85]

Speer recalls: "After hours of argument I yielded, on the condition that Dorsch would be placed under me again."[86] But this can scarcely have been the main issue of that four-hour conversation, since, on the previous day, Milch had gotten Hitler to agree to keep Dorsch under Speer. And this must have been the first thing the field marshal told his combative friend. Ultimately, the whole business was nothing but a four-hour dispute over the minister's wounded ego.

That night, Speer drafted a letter ordering Dorsch, head of the Todt Organization, to construct six "mushrooms." Hitler signed the letter the following day.[87] Naturally, the pragmatic Speer realized he would encounter problems on two fronts if Dorsch was restricted to those huge constructions. The necessary quotas of manpower and material would have to be taken from other construction projects being implemented by the Building Section of Speer's ministry. If he favored the Todt Organization with these supplies, then he could reckon with complaints from other Reich agencies. But if he supported the projects planned by these agencies, then he could be certain of renewed friction with Dorsch.

A skillfull tactician, Speer left the foreseeable problems to the ambitious Dorsch. On April 25, 1944, Hitler had refused to allow the removal of the entire construction industry from the jurisdiction of the Armaments Ministry. So Speer made Dorsch his deputy as head of the Construction Section in his ministry.[88] The Armaments Minister was not compromising himself in any way, and Dorsch thus remained his subordinate.

A falling-out between Hitler and his favorite minister was prevented, and on the evening of April 25, Speer once again joined the intimate group around Hitler.[89] According to Milch, "Speer spent a lot of time with Hitler in May and June, and their relationship was as good as it had been earlier."[90] Göring, Bormann, and Himmler had lost their cunning campaign against a basically defenseless foe, and Speer "felt cheerful"[91] about the outcome. Nor do his memoirs conceal how greatly he valued his influential position: ". . . I had been bribed and intoxicated by the desire to wield pure power, to assign people to this and to say the final word on important questions, to deal with expenditures in the billions."[92]

On May 10, 1944, when the Armaments Minister was about to resume his leadership of the Greater German weapon-makers, he viewed his position as so solid that he could venture to mention the infighting of the past few months when he "officially returned." "I would like to speak openly about various matters," he told his section chiefs, "that have come up during my illness." He said they had the right to be informed of things "that ultimately spelled a crisis in my work as minister."[93]

However, Speer's openness was quite limited. He concealed the hard struggle he had waged to maintain control of the construction industry, his passionate appeal to Hitler to let him keep this control, and his threat to resign. He truthfully reported that he himself had suggested to the Führer that the building industry be separated from the armaments industry. But then Speer grotesquely distorted his stand on this issue, claiming he had told Hitler "that I would not personally be annoyed or angered by such a separation, that I was above such a reaction, and that I would not feel bad about it, even though my background is in architecture." He had assured Hitler, said Speer, that it was right to do these things, "with no consideration of my person." Such were the fabrications that Speer offered his section chiefs.[94]

How ever Speer may have presented his own behavior, he drew certain inferences from the in-house intrigues. Two years earlier, when taking office, he had offered his staff comradeship as a basis for efficient cooperation. But now, he felt this attitude was no longer suitable. So he made it clear to his section chiefs "that from now on, 'the minister' would be emphasized more strongly than before. . . . It is necessary that the leader, who must be embodied in the minister, must in any event stand out as the authority."[95]

Still, the minister's new emphasis on this authority and the strenuous work of increasing the output of Germany's armaments machinery did not protect him against a new crisis. This new crisis, however, involved all the leaders of the Third Reich.

7

THE TWENTIETH
OF JULY 1944

Little has been written about Speer's part in the attempted assassination of Hitler on July 20, 1944,[1] the only detailed description of his role having been written by Speer himself.[2] This gap is not surprising; for the scholar dealing with the whole story of this resistance movement, Speer was merely a supernumerary.[3]

But for Speer personally, the near assassination was extremely important. The "Rebellion of the Conscience" evidently undermined his unshakable ignorance and forced him to confront an ethics that he had long since given up in his struggle for power. It is characteristic of Speer's ambivalent nature that, in the aftermath of those events, he managed to maintain the shield of his protective ignorance while making more than one gesture toward ethics.

Speer's account of the Twentieth of July in his memoirs and his other published statements on this topic are certainly a masterful component of his postwar rehabilitation. As an autobiographer, he leaves no doubt that he rejected the abortive putsch at the time. Yet, in the way he depicts his own conduct in regard to those events, he presents himself as a neutral observer of the uprising.

"I myself," he writes in *Inside the Third Reich*, "in spite of my spontaneous repudiation of the uprising, had a curious feeling of merely being there as a nonparticipant, as if all this . . . did not concern me."[4] His subsequent dichotomy is something he now describes as "loyalty not only to Hitler but also to the conspirators."[5] Hitler's favorite minister goes even further; he now tries to identify with those rebels. Looking back, as Speer admitted in an interview shortly after his release from Spandau, he would have liked to join the putsch.[6]

These may be phrases of self-stylization. Nevertheless, they obfuscate Speer's clear-cut and vehement behavior after the abortive putsch, when he insisted on his allegiance to his Führer and the National Socialist state.

Speer was at the Propaganda Ministry with Goebbels and Funk when a telephone call from Führer Headquarters informed them of the uprising and its defeat.[7] (A bit earlier, the Armaments Minister had delivered a lecture at Goebbels' ministry to members of the Reich government.)[8] During this telephone call, mention was made of Hitler's suspicion that the would-be assassin was a Todt Organization employee working in Rastenburg. As head of this organization, Speer was responsible for all the employees working on the fortification of the bunker installations at Führer Headquarters. The Armaments Minister therefore felt implicated, especially since he could not tell Goebbels what kind of security screening the workers had undergone when they were being selected.[9] Throughout the day, Goebbels seemed very distrustful of his fellow minister.[10] Consequently, he was lying when he claimed, in his speech of July 26, 1944, that he had instantly known that none of the construction workers at Führer Headquarters could have committed the crime.[11]

Meanwhile, Hitler had gotten information about the conspirators, and he gave up his suspicion about the workmen on the very same day. Mussolini visited him in Rastenburg as scheduled on July 20, and when Hitler was taking him back to the railroad station, he stopped to talk to the construction workers, who had been arrested. He told them they were free now. "I knew from the very first that you weren't the culprits."[12]

The Armaments Minister spent most of the day at Goebbels' ministry. In his memoirs, Speer describes the Propaganda Minister as the "most competent antagonist of the conspirators."[13] However, Speer was scarcely the neutral observer here. On the contrary, he spent hours in the office of Wilfred von Oven, Goebbels' press and PR officer. Here, Speer gave "well-meaning advice for quelling the revolt of the generals"[14] and offered active help.[15]

During the evening, both Goebbels and Speer were astonished to receive a bit of news that arrived in the palace of the Propaganda Minister: Investigators had found a list of the men who were to make up the cabinet in the government planned by the conspirators. Speer had been appointed Minister of Armaments. Speer's and Goebbels' reaction was unequivocal. "Both [men] laughed," reports Von Oven, "indeed Speer laughed so heartily that only a highly experienced actor could have managed to put on that good a show if he had really been involved in the conspiracy."[16]

The Armaments Minister could afford to laugh, since his name was followed by a question mark and the words: "To be asked only after the revolt."[17] This restrictive note could not be misinterpreted. It exonerated Speer of any possible complicity in the putsch.

However, the fact that Speer was to keep his position after the putsch showed that the conspirators sympathized with him. This "sympathy" was not unanimous, however, and it would be an exaggeration to claim that they were willing to view Speer "as one of them."[18] Such a thesis would presume that Speer and the conspirators had the same ideology; but this was not the case. Everyone knew how devoted Speer was to the Führer.

This was probably the reason why the conspirators did not wish to approach him until after the revolt.

We can be certain that Speer enjoyed "sympathy" from the army, which was best able to judge his organizational achievements as Minister of Armaments. On the other hand, Carl Goerdeler, a civilian, has nothing positive to say about Speer. He may have been a good architect, Goerdeler wrote in 1943, but he lacked any professional knowledge for his present office [as Armaments Minister].[19] Nevertheless, a long time before the assassination attempt, Geordeler had tried to contact Speer through a high-level member of the latter's staff in order to present his idea on the war situation to the Minister of Armaments.[20] Geordeler's attempt failed, however. Indeed, considering his low opinion of Speer's abilities, it is a mystery why he wanted to get to him in the first place.

A large number of the leaders of the Reich had been summoned to Führer Headquarters on July 21 to offer their congratulations. Speer, too, flew to Rastenburg to pay his appropriate homage to Hitler for being "saved by Providence."[21] Here, Speer sensed that his Führer was unusually reserved when greeting him. Hitler moved past him with a "careless handshake," according to *Inside the Third Reich.*[22] However, SS-Adjutant Otto Günsche, who remained near the Führer as he reviewed the phalanx of high-level Nazi well-wishers, cannot remember that Hitler was blatantly restrained in his behavior toward the Armaments Minister.[23]

Hitler's vengeful anger focused primarily on those army officers who had repeatedly asked for a unified Wehrmacht leadership and who had now been found in the ranks of the putsch.[24] Understandably, Speer took Hitler's reactions as a personal affront, since, for organizational reasons, he shared their conviction. In a memorandum dated (with fateful irony) July 20, 1944, Speer had vehemently advocated a Wehrmacht unification as a prerequisite for a German victory. "We can win the war," said Speer, "only if total commitment at home is accompanied by organizational unification of the branches of the Wehrmacht and the organizations attached to it."[25]

Hitler had not yet seen this memorandum. However, it was generally known among the leaders that in regard to the organization and leadership of the Wehrmacht and ultimately the Reich, Speer had the same opinions as prominent representatives of the army, who had now been degraded to a "clique of traitors." Even at the Armaments Ministry there were people who did not hesitate to verbalize their critical thoughts.[26] And at Hitler's Obersalzberg retreat, Speer and certain army representatives had even had open conversations analyzing the harsh reality.[27] Thus, it comes as no surprise that the Armaments Minister was regarded as an "alienated Party man," especially by Hitler's secretary, Bormann, and his Propaganda Minister Goebbels.[28] These two masters of the game of power and influence had probably expressed their opinion to their Führer.

Before July 20, 1944, all this may have been of little interest to Hitler, since intrigues among his subordinates fitted in with his principle of divide and conquer. But after the assassination attempt, Speer's well-known opinion must have aroused Hitler's distrust, particularly since Speer's agreement with some of the conspirators had led to good personal relationships—an equally well-known fact that was bound to increase Hitler's suspicion. This was probably the reason for Hitler's aloofness toward his favorite minister on July 21. But it did not mean that he was planning to dismiss the organizer of his war machinery; for, according to Speer's memoirs, "the next day, Hitler was more friendly to me again. . . ."[29]

Nevertheless, the Armaments Minister seems to have felt uneasy. Ultimately, he must have been extremely nervous about the inclusion of his name in the cabinet list drawn up by the conspirators. Also, his good relations with some of the putsch leaders must have been disagreeable to him now, since they offered his rivals a target for new attacks. Thus, Speer felt threatened in his position by the events of July 20. He feared intrigues—and rightly so—although he probably overestimated any personal danger he was in, even making too much of it decades later.

It was all the more important for the Armaments Minister to be certain of Hitler's favor if he hoped to forestall new schemes by his adversaries. At the loyalty demonstration that he staged at his ministry on July 24 after returning from Führer Headquarters,[30] Speer was simply rapturous in pledging his allegiance to Hitler. His speech, given before two hundred section chiefs,[31] is described in his autobiography as his feeblest and most insecure. Indeed, he devotes only one sentence to summing up the contents.[32]

However, informative in many respects, this speech is worth quoting in detail. Speer's office chiefs sat at a long table on either side of their boss, like the disciples flanking Jesus in Leonardo Da Vinci's *Last Supper* (according to the Speer Journal).[33] Minister Speer, in a solemn atmosphere, spoke to his staffers:

> After the events of the past few days, I felt a need to speak to you, and I feel this need especially now that I have had the opportunity to spend the past three days with the Führer. Because of this visit, our faith in our victory can be greater than ever for all of us. After witnessing the forcefulness with which the Führer is tackling the problems of these days and the unswerving confidence with which he is looking forward to the events of the next few months, I know we have an obligation to emulate him. . . .
>
> I am firmly convinced that Thursday [July 20] was a turning point in our fateful struggle, a sign that victory will be ours.

This time, the total war was not merely a "basis of discussion," said Speer, but a fact; and he demanded that his people actively help as "servants of the Wehrmacht." He then ended

105

his speech bombastically: "In conclusion, we hail the Führer: *Sieg Heil!*"[34]

Nothing could be more unequivocal than these vociferous indications of where the Armaments Minister stood. His enthusiastic declaration of loyalty was prompted by his sense of logistics as well as his intrinsic opportunism. After all, he knew very well how dependent his power was on Hitler. In 1946, Speer claimed he had stuck to the "monster Hitler" after July 20, 1944, because it was simpler. But this oversimplifying statement misses the mark.[35]

There is no doubt that his "Magnificat" to the Führer was sincere—a sign of Speer's unbroken bond with Hitler. But something else is far more revealing. In a postwar interrogation, the incarcerated Armaments Minister alleged that by February/March 1943 he had realized that the war was lost. When the systematic bombings of the hydrogenation plants began on May 12, 1944, he had concluded there was no way that Germany could win a military victory.[36] This testimony does not seem credible. The Armaments Minister's speech of July 24 demonstrated his utter confidence that Germany would win the war; and the term "final victory" *(Endsieg)* was part of his standard vocabulary in nearly all the speeches he gave during the next few months.

A further aspect of his speech of July 24, 1944, should not be neglected, since it distinctly reveals Speer's ambivalent character. This is clearly shown by a comparison between this speech and the ones given on the same topic by Göring,[37] Goebbels,[38] and even Dönitz.[39] For one thing, Speer does not explicitly mention the assassination attempt. Along with their statements of loyalty to the Führer, those unshakable liegemen poured out their wrath on the "miserable clique" of officers. Speer, however, did not indulge in such vituperation.

Nevertheless, his basically negative attitude toward the conspiracy was unequivocal. Nor did he leave any room for doubt when he gathered his section chiefs around him on July 24, after the bigwigs' demonstration of loyalty. Speer wanted to give his employees details of the putsch, the quelling of which he had witnessed from a very close vantage. He expressed his great appreciation, nay, admiration for the Propaganda Minister, the successful adversary of the putschists. "He articulated his undisguised respect for Goebbels, who had had the 'sangfroid of a general in battle.' He doubted," said Speer's section chief Kehrl, "whether he [himself] could have dealt with such a difficult situation as effectively as Goebbels."[40] Before July 20, one of the conspirators, Claus Schenk Count von Stauffenberg (chief of staff to General Friedrich Fromm, the supreme commander of the reserve army) had repeatedly invited Speer to meet with him at Bendlerstrasse, the center of the putsch. Speer, however, had been unable to attend because of his scheduled speech at the Propaganda Ministry. After July 20, the Armaments Minister described those invitations as a coincidence. Kehrl, who seldom blue-penciled his own opinions, commented: "Only a minister of state could be that naive."[41]

Speer's rhetorically mobilized rejection of the conspiracy had repercussions among his staffers. The Speer Office Journal says: "A positive consequence of the assassination attempt is a new wave of dynamic decisions. The blame for the bad weeks and months has been placed on the hidden ulcer. The flame is again blazing bright in the active men."[42]

Speer demonstrated to the architect Hermann Giesler that he was worried about Hitler's overall condition. Just a few days after the abortive coup, Speer asked Giesler to stand by for a flight to Führer Headquarters in order to divert Hitler with construction plans for Linz, his favorite city.[43]

If Speer had ever been truly worried that he had lost favor in his Führer's eyes, his fear turned out to be groundless. The inclusion of his name on the cabinet list of the conspirators did not implicate him in any way, since the restrictive note proved he had known nothing about their plans. His relations with the putsch leaders were due simply to the professional and organizational cooperation between his ministry and the army. Not even the fact that (as mentioned in Speer's memoirs) the putschists had occasionally used his term "nodding donkeys" for the yes-men around Hitler[44] could be a problem for him, since he could hardly be identified as having coined this epithet.[45]

Hitler's continued affection for his minion was made clear by a special gesture. The Party and its power-wielders were more than willing to get rid of Speer. So in order to facilitate continued cooperation between his ministry and the Party, Hitler gave Speer his moral support and expressed his esteem of Speer's achievements to an inner circle of the Gauleiters on August 4, 1944.[46] This was a clear signal to his governors that Hitler still regarded the Armaments Minister as a man above suspicion.

Goebbels, too, insisted on holding up the banner of his fellow minister before the public. In his report on July 20, 1944, the Propaganda Minister praised Speer's achievements, lauded his "tireless work," his use of a "brilliant process of simplification" to increase German armament production to an astonishing level.[47] In regard to its effect on the public, this "rehabilitation" —if we are to view it as such—was far more important than Hitler's talk to the Gauleiters, since Goebbels's speech was broadcast over all the radio networks of Greater Germany.[48]

Nevertheless, these efforts by Hitler and Goebbels did not discourage the rumors about the Armaments Minister and the Twentieth of July. The fact that Speer's name had been on the conspirators' list leaked out at least in Berlin, circulating there as a rumor.[49] The source of the leak was probably the Armaments Ministry itself, since Speer had revealed this fact to his section chiefs in his meeting with them.[50] The rumors got more and more involved. In Münster, for example, people were whispering that "Reich Minister Speer has been shot because of his ties with the clique of traitors."[51] In order to halt the rampant speculations about Speer, the Report of the Offices of the Reich Propaganda Ministry (October 16, 1944) recommended that Speer "make a public appearance in the near future."[52] One month later, the Armaments Minister himself felt it was necessary to speak to his staff about the underground whisperings.

Rumors were frequently false, he explained, "for otherwise I would be under arrest somewhere instead of sitting here."[53] He advised that they take all the chitchat about the Armaments Ministry with a necessary sense of humor.[54]

These rumors, which are also mentioned in *Inside the Third Reich* to emphasize Speer's shaky position,[55] should not be overestimated. They should not be seen as indicating the supposed seriousness of his involvement in the events of the Twentieth of July. For Speer was by no means the only Third Reich bigwig about whom rumors were spreading. The lack of information, especially during the first few days after the assassination attempt, helped to ignite rumors.[56] Thus, Germans conjectured that Field Marshals Von Rundstedt and Von Manstein were also part of the conspiracy.[57] Nor did Reich Marshal Göring, who was still rather popular at that time, remain untouched by the events that followed the putsch. His nephew was arrested and held for several days,[58] and it was said that Göring himself had participated in the coup and was under house arrest and guarded by SS-men at Karinhall, his country estate.[59]

Speer knew very well that he was not the only Reich leader victimized by popular speculation.[60] Nevertheless, decades later he insisted, in an almost embarrassing way, on exaggerating the alleged danger he had been in after the Twentieth of July. In a *Playboy* interview, he put an entirely different meaning on the July 20 invitation to Bendlerstrasse, which, in 1944, he had waved off as sheer coincidence. Now, he claimed that "Fromm wanted to have me under supervision on that day in order to ensure my participation in the new military government. . . . Turning down [the invitation] saved my position in the government [of the Third Reich] and presumably my life."[61] Yet at the time of the interview, the best-selling author, who was working on his postwar rehabilitation, must have known that he was retrospectively exaggerating any personal danger he had been in. After all, Hitler himself had not done anything to Speer even when the latter had sabotaged the Führer's Scorched Earth policy toward the end of the war.

However, Speer went further in the *Playboy* interview. He
stated that he had been at Führer Headquarters the very day
that Hitler had indulged in a special pleasure. "That night, in
the screening room, they ran a color film of the execution of
some twenty conspirators for Hitler and his guests. Each man
had been hung on a meat hook and slowly strangled to death
with piano wire. The pressure was periodically decreased to
intensify his agony. Hitler loved the film and would screen it
over and over again. It became one of his favorite entertain-
ments. . . . I myself could have easily been among the victims."[62]

We can only wonder where Speer got his detailed knowledge
of the executions, since not even the historian Peter Hoffmann
could offer such particulars in his standard work on the resistance.[63] In *Inside the Third Reich,* Speer claims he had never
seen the film: "I could not and I would not see it."[64]

Survivors of the group around Hitler at that time flatly deny
that such a movie was ever shown at Führer Headquarters.[65]
For instance, the architect Hermann Giesler, who spent all of
August at Führer Headquarters, was once looking at photos of
the executed conspirators. Hitler, waving him off, exclaimed:
"Leave that alone, Giesler! I don't want to see those men."[66]

Nevertheless, during the months following the assassination
attempt, Speer showed that his mind was not entirely closed to
the moral and idealistic stand taken by the conspirators. The
ruthless government measures against their accomplices as well
as innocent people led to countless executions and to the arrests
of thousands of Germans who were merely related to suspects.
This drastic situation may have triggered Speer's first moral
reaction. Still shielded by Hitler's favor, he used his position to
intervene on behalf of the countless unfortunates who had been
arrested.[67] And he did this even though he ran the risk of
arousing new suspicions. Nor was he bothered by the fact that
Kaltenbrunner, who, in December 1944, was still ubiquitously
feared, had not yet fully cleared him of suspicion.[68]

To be sure, Speer's interventions had little success.[69] Furthermore, the people working closest to him must have been ir-

ritated by his dichotomous behavior in regard to the Twentieth of July Affair. He kept wavering between loud rejections of the failed putsch and repeated efforts to intervene on behalf of arrestees. Such annoyance among his staffers can be the only explanation for a mysterious unsigned memorandum of August 23, 1944, to Wolters, who was keeping the Speer Journal. Plainly ironic in its intent, this memorandum read: "Our minister has been so active in clearing up the confusion caused by the Twentieth of July that his helpfulness should be recorded in the Office Journal. What do you think? (Also, his 'passive' contribution!!)"[70]

The events of the Twentieth of July had no fundamental influence on Speer's attitude. He still pinned all his hopes on Hitler and the ultimate German victory, and he helped to encourage a large part of the population to believe that Germany could still win the war.

8

STICK-IT-OUT SPEECHES
AND THE
ASSASSINATION ATTEMPT

At Nuremberg, Hans Frank, the Nazi governor of Poland, was complaining about Albert Speer to Gustave Gilbert, a prison psychologist. "Don't forget," said Frank, "that Speer himself helped to spread faith in the [German] victory—with bombastic speeches about how he would deploy his new airplanes and sweep the heavens clean of all enemy aircraft. What else do you think kept us alive in Cracow? Faith in the victory of the German Army!"[1]

Goebbels and Hitler were certainly not the only Nazi leaders who tirelessly proclaimed the superiority of German weapons and prophesized the German victory. Speer's speeches also constantly fueled popular faith that Germany would win the war. Granted, the impact of his addresses was not due to a thrilling voice or polished eloquence. Speer was never an orator who could enthrall his audience with his rhetoric. Instead, when he promised his audience weapons that would decide the outcome of the war and when he announced technological innovations that would stun the enemy, he lent credence to his words by seasoning them with figures. Displaying a cool, intellectual air, he would enthuse about rising armaments capacities, increased production, greater output. His braggadocio had the authority of a man who must have known what he was talking about; he was, after all, in charge of all those factories in which the miracle weapons were supposedly being manufactured.

By September 1942, Hitler and Speer had agreed to pull all the propaganda stops "so that the German people and especially German armaments workers might know the value of [German] weapons—compared with foreign weapons."[2] For Speer, such "enlightenment" was not unimportant for his own plans: He hoped that his advertising campaign would heighten the motivation of his workers, thus ensuring higher output. This was crucial for the Minister of Armaments, whom even his friend Field Marshal Milch described as "ambitious, indeed greedy, for power."[3] Speer must have realized that his power was contingent on the amount of matériel produced by his weapons factories.

By 1943, the wider German public sensed that Germany could not hold out against the mass of the Allied arms potential. Now, none of Speer's talks lacked some variation of the statement that "the sheer quantity of Allied weapons could be not only balanced but outdone by higher *quality.* "[4] That year, according to the judgment of the historian Karl-Heinz Ludwig, the slogan "qualitative superiority" introduced "a new phase of lying to the German people—a phase that culminated in the myth of miracle weapons."[5]

In September 1943, Speer addressed a gathering of Reich orators and Gau propaganda leaders at Berlin's Kroll Opera house. "In this war of technology, it is absolutely necessary to place the quality of weapons over the quantity of weapons. Given the enemy's present and future superiority in the number of his weapons and the size of his manpower, we are forced to outdo the foe by producing weapons that are increasingly better than his in all areas. That is the great chance we have in this war."[6]

Two weeks later, Speer promised the Gauleiters that astonishing improvements in quality were just around the corner. "I can emphatically assure you that the aerial weapons that we will soon be mass-producing are superior to those of the enemy." Nor did Speer neglect to offer the Gauleiters a vague hint of something that had become the fondest of German hopes: the miracle weapons. "We have a national secret that the whole German nation already knows. Of course, the details are still not sufficiently known." The Armaments Minister did not care to reveal these details, since, as he explained, the secret weapon was now being converted from single to assembly-line production, and a few problems might be encountered in the process.[7] Speer proclaimed that 1944 would be a "year of technological surprises in all areas."[8] At the beginning of the year, he announced optimistically: "We armaments people are starting the year 1944 with great hopes. We know that it will bring us great successes."[9] One of the things on which Speer was pinning his hopes of success was the retaliatory weapon that he had been pushing forward with all his energy since July 1943. That month, the Führer had decided that this weapon, "which can be produced with relatively low resources, will decide the outcome of the war and relieve the homeland of its burden."[10]

One man who yearned for the completion of this weapon was Goebbels, since "retaliation" was a cornerstone of his propaganda campaign to make the population forget its devastated cities. Goebbels was completely dependent on Speer's armaments machinery and he fully trusted the Minister of Armaments. At the start of 1944, when Goebbels and Hitler were standing in front of a huge map of London, the Propaganda Minister indicated the "most rewarding targets" for the V-1 flying bombs. When he spoke to Wilfred von Oven, his press and PR officer, Goebbels made no bones about his feelings; he was delighted that this year, the "Armada of Revenge," which he had been promising the Germans for such a long time, would finally overwhelm the English. "The offensive weapons that we are deploying are new and unique. There are no defenses against them and no warnings. No flak will help and no siren.

They will smash right into the unsuspecting metropolis. Bang! I can't paint too horrible a picture of the effect such attacks will have on [British] morale. . . . If only our industry keeps pace now. We can rely no more on the Air Ministry than on the Four-Year Plan. Luckily, we've also got Speer. He'll do it."[11]

However, the V-1 did not fulfill expectations.[12] Still, the Armaments Minister was unfazed, since his engineers were already feverishly working to make the V-2 rocket operational. To keep up the Propaganda Minister's mood, Speer screened a film for him in July 1944; the film had startling shots of a V-2 takeoff repeated a dozen times. The screening was so secret that only Goebbels, Milch, and Speer were present. The Propaganda Minister, who had had no precise notion of this rocket, was thrilled. "I do not want to spread any unfounded optimism," he stated afterward, "but, after mature deliberation, I believe that this weapon will force England to her knees. If we could show this film in all German movie theaters, I would not have to give any more speeches or write any more articles. Even the most hard-boiled pessimist could no longer doubt our victory."[13]

The Armament Minister's subtle and "secret" movie propaganda had a smashing effect, as was revealed a bare three weeks later. In late July, Goebbels, evidently spellbound by the shots of the soaring V-2, wrote an editorial for the weekly *Das Reich*. The Propaganda Minister prophesized to his readers that the Führer would "soon bring the war to an end . . . by launching terrible weapons."[14] Yet the V-2 was not deployed and the war was not ended. The morale of the population was correspondingly low. The Allied invasion, the advances of enemy troops toward the borders of the Reich, and the unhindered raids by bomber fleets were undermining the Germans' faith in their victory.[15] The growing pessimism, which also spread through the armaments industry, angered Minister Speer, who wanted "to wipe out this depression and replace it with our optimism."[16] Once again, he had encouraging words at hand. The enemy, he declared in a speech, would get a resounding shock one day. If he pulled another daytime raid on Germany, two or three hundred of his aircraft would be shot down from the sky. Or else two or three hundred thousand tons [of enemy ships] would be destroyed at one blow in a convoy battle. For Speer, in late August 1944, it was merely a matter of sticking it out until the utopia of new German weapons hove into view. "We have to hold out . . . through this period, until these new weapons come, the weapons you all know, the jet fighters, the jet bombers, the U-boats, the small U-boats, the new retaliatory weapons, which will soon do the talking [for us]." That was Speer's suggestion to his armaments leaders.[17]

In 1944, Speer's attitude toward his office was unusual for a minister. Armaments factories had to be rebuilt constantly after bombings, and their reconstruction was usually improvisational. Speer saw all this from the viewpoint of a sportsman. In fact, he told his fellow minister Schwerin von Krosigk "that the race between destruction and reconstruction was the most exciting contest in the history of the world."[18] So it was not surprising that Speer demanded "a certain athletic [i.e., competitive] behavior at all times "from his people.[19]

It may have been such a youthful athletic spirit and a certain taste for adventure that inspired the forty-year-old minister during the final months of the war, when he kept visiting the front lines as well as endangered cities and burning factories. Speer felt that his visits would have a profound psychological effect on munitions workers, especially when he exhibited his faith and confidence within earshot of artillery fire. And he also expected his staffers to follow his example.[20]

But by late 1944, not even the Armaments Minister could fail to realize that the V-2 would not turn the tide of battle, as had been hoped. So, in November, he informed his colleague Goebbels that he felt it was useless to keep up the hopes of the population if those hopes could not be fulfilled in the foreseeable future.[21] At a rally held in January 1945, Speer was asked when they could count on the introduction of the new secret weapon. He replied: "For my part, I can say only that I will fight these rumors with all my strength. After all, I did not launch this propaganda. You cannot have heard such things from my lips."[22] (!)

Nevertheless, his specific denial of the miracle weapon did not prevent the minister from giving further stick-it-out speeches to maintain faith in a German victory and to make oracular announcements of new weapons.[23] He told his staffers to behave optimistically[24] and to work with "fanatical faith" toward "victorious peace."[25] Sometimes, he even resorted to allegories in order to keep up the spirits of his subordinates. In November 1944, Speer told them: "Before every ascent there is always a deep valley, and, in terms of our production, we can be certain that in these months we are getting past the nadir and are about to advance toward new successes."[26]

Apparently, Speer's buzzwords—"success," "stick it out," "victory"—exerted a hypnotic effect on him, operating as verbal mechanisms that he needed to block reality. Indeed, he went even further in his stick-it-out speeches. After Germany lost the Battle of the Bulge in December 1944, Speer turned up in Aachen-Düren to visit the division headed by Hitler's former army adjutant, Major Gerhard Engel. The minister confronted the senior officers, junior officers, and troops, and, without being asked, he harangued them to hold out. "The form [of his speeches] was simply embarrassing," said Engel.[27]

Even when most of the Reich territory was already occupied by enemy troops, Speer still wanted to inveigle his compatriots into believing that Germany would win. But he did not get a chance to do so.

(Of course, shortly after the war, Albert Speer no longer recalled his unflinching and vociferous faith in the German victory. In June 1945, he claimed he had been of "the opinion by February/March 1943 that the war was lost."[28] In his memoirs, a forgetful Speer depicts Hitler and Goebbels as the chief engineers of the stick-it-out and wonder-weapon propaganda, which he—needless to say—sharply opposed.)[29]

Eventually, the repeated promises of new and decisive weapons that would bring victory closer for the Germans and the seemingly unshakable optimism flaunted by the leaders lost their impact. The longer the war dragged on, the more harshly reality mocked the propaganda.

Indicative of this development was the number of factory employees who called in sick. By the end of 1942, their absenteeism became a serious problem for the leaders of industry. To be sure, the mass of workers kept building, producing, and repairing dutifully until the bitter end. But still, no small number were tardy, sick, or absent without an excuse and frequently had to be replaced by others. At a meeting in October 1942, Labor Commissioner Fritz Sauckel[30] complained about the "tremendous [employee] fluctuation" in the factories; he called it an "abnormal" situation that had to be eliminated.[31]

Speer could increase output only if he pushed down the high absenteeism in the factories. Mere promises of speedy victory did not suffice to guarantee a high work morale among all armaments employees. So their supreme chief did not hesitate to fight the problem with the weapons available to him in the Nazi state. Speer said that one could not be finicky in this matter, for "Ley has established that whenever a factory has a house physician who examines the employees, the number of sick workers drops down to one-fourth or one-fifth. The SS and the police could take harsh measures, by all means; they could arrest the malingerers and put them in concentration camps. There is no other possibility. It only has to happen a few times. Word will get around."[32]

Nevertheless, one year later, the problem of absenteeism had still not been solved to Speer's satisfaction. He evidently saw workers as machines, whose efficiency could be increased by the proper measures. At least, such inhumane thinking is apparent in the words he spoke to the Gauleiter in October 1943. He told them he shared the opinion of the German Labor Front "that generally a German worker has a 10-percent performance reserve, which could be raised even further."[33]

The reason why this 10-percent potential had not been ex-

S p e e r /K.   Berlin W.8, den 31.Okt.1944   18

Herrn C l a h e s :   abgesandt am 7/11 44
—————————————————   KL

   Ich bitte Sie, ein Schreiben etwa folgenden
Inhalts an den Wehrmachtführungsstab aufzusetzen
und mir zur Unterschrift vorzulegen:

   "Ich habe ein Interesse daran, dass mir alle
Verfehlungen, die innerhalb meines Aufgabenbereichs
(einschl. OT und Transporteinheiten) zur Kenntnis
kommen und auf das schärfste geahndet werden.

   Ich bitte Sie daher, die Heeresgruppen anzu-
weisen, dass sie derartige Fälle mir unmittelbar
über meine Hauptabteilung ....
im Zentralamt zur Kenntnis bringt, damit ich mich
unmittelbar wegen der Strafverschärfenden Massnah-
men mit den zuständigen Kriegsgerichten in Verbin-
dung setzen kann.

                                        ~~4361~~

Vermerk des Ministers:
"Diese Mitteilung soll selbstverständlich keine aufschie-
  bende Wirkung bei der Durchführung evtl. Verfahren haben".

                    gez. S p e e r

Speer's order for more drastic punitive measures in cooperation
with court martials, 1944.

ploited, said Speer, was that the "so-called goldbricks . . . are corrupting the spirit of the ready and willing workers in the factories."[34] The efficiency-minded Minister of Armaments fully concurred with the method that the German Labor Front wanted to use to cope with this terrible situation. "I am thankful that, at the behest of the Labor Front, several thousand goldbricks have been arrested in the factories and taken to concentration camps. I am of the opinion that these goldbricks, who are certainly known in the factories, have gotten their just desserts."[35]

On the other hand, the man in charge of the concentration camps was anything but edified by such methods of intimidation. Earlier, in May 1942, SS-Reichsführer Heinrich Himmler had angrily pointed out that the Party and the state all too frequently threatened to send delinquents to concentration camps in order to "place a supposedly greater emphasis" on directives.[36] Himmler therefore told all the supreme Reich agencies, including Speer's ministry, and all the Gauleiters "to give up such habits." Otherwise, the SS-chief planned to announce publicly that if such cases came up, he would not turn the culprits over to his police or send them to a concentration camp.[37] His rationale was that "even the most serious penalties no longer inspire dread if they are threatened on every occasion. . . . A concentration camp, with separation from one's family, isolation from the outside world, and the hard labor that must be done there, is a harsh punishment."[38] Himmler felt that even without such coercive methods, most people would follow orders voluntarily and with understanding, for "on the whole, Germans are extremely decent."[39]

In 1942 and 1943, Speer may have simply been flexing his rhetorical muscles by threatening to send culprits to concentration camps. But in 1944, he showed that he meant business. Several days after taking office as minister, he had asked Hitler for the legal instrument for such drastic measures, and Hitler had given it to him in the form of an edict.[40] Now prison and, in more serious cases, the death penalty loomed for anyone—clients, factory directors, plant managers, civil servants, or construction and armaments employees—who supplied false data on the need for, or available amount of, manpower and material.[41]

In 1944—the year of the stick-it-out and retaliation propaganda, the year that Speer had proclaimed the year of technological surprises in all areas—the Minister of Armaments made use of Hitler's edict. That February, he asked Otto Thierack, Reich Minister of Justice, to institute preliminary proceedings against August Pagels, manager of the Linden Iron and Steel Works. "According to the documents in my possession," said Speer, "there seems to be an especially flagrant case of sabotage of our war effort."[42] In March of that same year, Speer asked the Minister of Justice to bring criminal action against Walter Kamaryt, a Viennese, who, according to Speer, had supplied false figures on the need for, and available supplies of, material crucial to the armaments industry.[43]

An interesting case is that of Rudolf Egger, general manager of Büssing. This time, the Gestapo anticipated the Minister of Armaments and took Egger into preventive custody, stating that he had removed for his own use material allocated to his factory.[44] Minister Speer instantly notified the "dear and honored Party Comrade, Dr. Kaltenbrunner," that he had reached an agreement with Himmler: "All criminal proceedings occurring in my work domain should be carried out together with your representatives—in order to increase rather than mitigate the punishment."[45] The Egger case, according to Speer, should have been handled jointly by the Gestapo and his ministry. The Minister of Armaments felt that the manager of Büssing had received too light a sentence: "If the charges against General Manager Egger have been proved beyond the shadow of a doubt, then three days' preventive custody is, in my opinion, inadequate. He would deserve at least three months. I am picking out this case because I expect only good things to come from a severe penalty, especially the effect it has on other plant directors."[46]

Looking back thirty-five years later, Speer offers an entirely different account of the Egger case in his last book *Infiltration (Der Sklavenstaat).* [47] He uses it as an object lesson to depict his jurisdictional squabbles with the SS. He also tries to prove that the SS kept attacking him and his industrial managers for political reasons. Speer reprints the first part of a letter that indicates his annoyance at not being informed of Egger's arrest; Speer then doesn't forget to quote the last sentence: "I must protest against linking such proceedings with interventions by political offices based on political grounds."[48] In his book, however, Speer conscientiously hides the fact that he wrote this letter in order to make three requests for a harsher punishment. Indeed, his distortion of the facts goes even further when he concludes his description of the case: "Egger was instantly released from custody. The accusations against him had proved to be unfounded."[49] What reader would not conclude that Büssing's general manager had been set free only because of Speer's speedy intervention!

Speer was using all means at his disposal to continue producing armaments as the war situation kept making his task more and more difficult. Even though he was making this all-out effort to enable his Führer to keep fighting the war, Speer was dismayed to note that Hitler himself—following his Scorched Earth Policy—wanted to destroy the industrial installations that would fall into the hands of the advancing enemy. This was a frightening thought for Speer, since the manufacturing plants were the foundation of his power.

In September 1944, a distraught Speer asked Hitler whether they could reckon with a speedy German reoccupation of the lost territories. Hitler said they could.[50] The Armaments Minister concluded that if the lost areas were indeed reconquered, then the demolished industrial installations would be worthless to him since it would take months to get them running again. He therefore ordered only "crippling" of the factories: Important machine units were to be removed in case the enemy drew near, so that he could not utilize the factories for his own armaments production.

These actions were carried out according to Speer's policy of "crippling instead of destruction." There is no telling whether his chief motives were highly moral, whether he was moved primarily by ethical impulses—by the obligation to preserve these places of work for his workers. One thing is certain, however: He had a very strong personal interest in preventing the destruction of these bastions of his power. And it is equally certain that although Speer gave the necessary orders, the factories could be crippled only with the assistance of most of his staffers.

Nevertheless, the collapse of Nazi Germany was inevitable; and during the final weeks of the war, Speer, wavering between unrealistic hope and sober perception of the situation, was probably seeking a way out of the looming disaster. It may have occurred to him at that time that everything must come to an end—a thought that surely crossed the minds of many Germans who could survey the overall situation. But for Speer, as he stated at the Nuremberg Tribunal, such reflections became an "intention,"[51] even a "plan";[52] and decades later, Speer the autobiographer spoke of a "decision."[53]

At his trial, Speer went into detail about his reflections.[54] He said that by early February 1945, he had seen no other way out than to kill Hitler: "It was clear that if Germany lost the war, [Hitler] would confuse his own fate with that of the German people and that he would view his own end as the end of the German people." But Speer, according to his testimony, was already convinced that the war was lost and that "unconditional surrender would have to be accepted." It was then, he claims, that he developed his plan to kill Hitler, Bormann, Goebbels, and Ley, who often gathered together at night in the bunker of the Reich Chancellery. Speer meticulously explains how he planned to carry out these assassinations. He wanted to introduce poison gas into the ventilation system of the bunker and thereby into all the underground rooms. But, he says, he encountered problems. It was not so easy to get hold of the right gas; furthermore, he had to talk the maintenance man of the Reich Chancellery into turning off the gas filters of the fresh-air system. It took weeks, says Speer, to deal with these problems —and by then it was too late.

There seems to be no doubt that the Armaments Minister did toy with such ideas. He spoke to Dietrich Stahl, head of the Main Committee for Munitions, about his deliberations: Stahl was to get hold of the poison gas. In 1946, Stahl testified that Speer had had such ideas in 1945.[55]

However, Speer was not the last "frustrated assassin" of the Third Reich. One cannot call his reflections an "assassination attempt," and even the word "plan" would lend too much importance to his idea. He did not think it through, he did not consider the overall consequences.

The picture of Speer as an assassin on the prowl seems bizarre and grotesque. Imagine the head of the German armaments industry in the dead of night, shrouded in a dark overcoat, holding a briefcase containing several vials of poison gas, stealing through the garden of the Reich Chancellery, peering in all directions, wondering whether he has been sighted by any of the sentries, then attempting to introduce the lethal gas into the air shafts, and finally sneaking away from the scene of the crime! Even against the overall tragic background, this portrait is not devoid of comic features. Some historians evidently did not have enough imagination to conjure up such a fantasy. Otherwise, they would have recognized the surrealistic absurdity of Speer's reflections and they would not have been so ready to accept the thesis of "Speer the Assassin." Shortly after his release from Spandau, Speer himself, in a moment of honest self-knowledge (though without casting doubt on his "assassination plan") admitted that if an assassination attempt does not succeed, it can have "a strong touch of the ridiculous."[56]

Further imponderables, not thought out by Speer, supposedly made the enterprise even more questionable. Hitler lived in the Reich Chancellery until mid-March 1945,[57] retreating underground only during bombings. So the Armaments Minister would have had to wait until Hitler withdrew to the bunker with Bormann, Ley, and Goebbels. At the same time, he would have had to make sure that the gas filters were switched off. This was a matter of chance, since he could hardly ask the maintenance man to turn off the gas filters in the midst of an air raid. Hence, it is rather doubtful whether his attempt would have succeeded the first or second time. By the third or fourth "genuine try" at the very latest, the minister was bound to arouse suspicion with his gas-filled briefcase.

And perhaps it might have occurred to him shortly before his deed that Hitler and his liegemen were not the only people in the bunker; there could have been others—secretaries, adjutants, domestics, who were only doing their duty. All of them would have perished. The successful assassination would have brought Speer not the fame of a classical tyrannicide, but the infamy of a mass murderer. For he could not muster up the courage to face his Führer with a pistol—virtually as a twentieth-century Brutus.[58] He certainly had enough opportunities to do so. He still had unobstructed access to Hitler, only a casual glance was cast into his briefcase, and he was never searched for weapons even at the very end.[59]

And what would have happened after the assassination? Would it have brought a swifter end to the German catastrophe? Reich Marshal Göring was still Hitler's officially designated successor, and there is no telling whether he would have agreed to unconditional surrender. Speer did not think about these things; he had no concrete ideas, no overall design.[60]

The Führer's fears terminated Speer's vague reflections. Hitler suspected that the Russians might fire gas grenades at the Reich Chancellery. The gas would have spread out on the floor and penetrated into the ventilation shaft, which was on the ground floor. And if the dictator did not fear death, then his greatest anxiety was that his corpse might fall intact into enemy hands. So, in order to forestall a Russian gas attack, he had a thirteen-foot chimney built on the intake shaft of the fresh-air mechanism. That was the reason, Speer testified at Nuremberg in 1946, why he had been unable to carry out his plan.[61]

In early April 1945, Rudolf Wolters met once more with his friend Speer in Berlin. The minister asked him about the general mood of the Germans. Wolters said that it was very bad in Höxter, where he had come from. "I told him that people couldn't understand why the men around Hitler didn't hold him back or put an end to his activities. Speer then asked why they couldn't kill him. When I replied that no one could do that more easily than Speer himself, he pulled a gun out of his pocket and placed it on the table without a word."[62] Albert Speer's assassination fantasies never got beyond this silent gesture of resignation.

Most of the people who knew the Armaments Minister during the Third Reich were more than surprised when they heard him claim that he had wanted to kill his patron with poison gas. Having known him as a faithful disciple of Hitler, they were taken aback by his words, which they simply could not believe. Speer's friend Wolters skeptically shook his head when he heard these statements by his former boss.[63] Dr. Theo Hupfauer, who was in close contact with Speer during the final months of the Third Reich,[64] even living next door to him for a while, expresses doubts about Speer's statements on this topic. Speer, he says, must have realized that it was, in general, technically impossible to carry out such a plan.[65] And Hermann Giesler, Speer's adversary then and now, can only poke mordant fun at the "assassination plan" supposedly hatched by Hitler's one-time minion: "The second most powerful man in the state lacked a ladder."[66]

John Kenneth Galbraith criticizes the former Armaments Minister with charming irony and sees his poison-gas notions from the viewpoint of a man who interrogated Speer shortly after the end of the war and read his memoirs decades later. Galbraith says the following about Speer's assassination intention: "In 1945, it was more of a fantasy."[67] And he adds that Speer's thoughts along these lines have "obviously gained importance in the course of time."[68]

Whatever may have gone through Albert Speer's mind in February 1945, it was not in vain. It helped him in his defense at the Nuremberg Tribunal and it served his postwar rehabilitation before an international audience. Had he not had those assassination thoughts, then the Speer legend might have been less fascinating.

During the final weeks of the Third Reich, the ambivalence in Speer's character became more and more obvious, so that his fellow minister Schwerin von Krosigk, who had close contact with him during that period, voiced the following opinion after the war: "His intelligence and his heart went their separate ways in the moody soul of this excitable and changeable man."[69]

One moment, the Armaments Minister was forced by his intellect to realize how hopeless the situation was; but a moment later, he nurtured the strangely sentimental hope that fate would eventually bring a change for the better. On the one hand, his intelligence led him to undermine Hitler's orders for destruction; but on the other hand, his emotions kept drawing him to this magical figure that had been the center of Speer's life for twelve years.

On March 19, 1945, his fortieth birthday, Speer handed Hitler a memorandum that contained a warning: "Every backward step [taken by the soldiers] will bring defeat that much closer." But, in the next sentence, he fueled an unrealistic hope: "A sudden persistence on the present front lines for several weeks can gain respect from the enemy and perhaps spell a favorable end to the war."[70] At the same time, he pointed out to his Führer that any differences of opinion between them did not encroach upon their personal relationship. The birthday present he requested from Hitler was a picture of the Führer with a personal dedication. For twelve years, he had been the only person close to Hitler who had not asked him for such a distinction. Now, at the end of their relationship, he wanted to show his patron that "I still revered him and valued the distinction of a personally dedicated photograph."[71]

For his part, Hitler too had a strange emotional dichotomy toward his protégé. He was annoyed at the memorandums in which Speer used defeatist words—a Cassandra among his colleagues. At the same time, Hitler was so worried about Speer's life that he lent him his personal chauffeur, Erich Kempka, when the Armaments Minister wanted to drive to the Western Front. Hitler would not entrust Speer's life to anyone else. He told Kempka that "the reliability of Speer's own chauffeur was no guarantee for [Hitler]."[72]

But no sooner had the Armaments Minister driven off than the dictator signed the infamous order known as "Scorched Earth." All military installations for transportation, communication, industry, and supplies that were located within the territory of the Reich and that could possibly be used by the enemy to continue the war were to be destroyed, with no consideration for the population. The agencies that Hitler put in charge of implementing this order were the military-command authorities, the Reich defense commissars, and the Gauleiters.[73] Thus, Hitler had virtually deprived Speer of all his power and possibility of ordering "crippling" instead of "destruction."

Hitler's attack on his Armaments Minister did not lessen the artist/politician's personal feelings for his minion. When Speer returned to Berlin on March 21, Hitler went over to his driver after the conference on the situation and shook both his hands. "He thanked me over and over again for bringing back his minister . . . safe and sound."[74]

A few days later, Hitler pleaded with Speer, even begged him to state that he at least still hoped that the war was not lost; otherwise, Hitler told him, he would have to send him on sick leave. Speer refused to comply. But twenty-four hours later, he demonstrated his loyalty to Hitler. With the words, "Mein

Führer, I stand unreservedly behind you," he announced his submission.[75] Hitler rewarded this declaration of allegiance: He signed a decree that put Speer in charge of implementing Hitler's destruction edict. With the Führer's signature, his Minister of Armaments regained his power and could once again "cripple" instead of "destroy."[76]

On April 11, Speer wanted to give a speech in order (he says in his memoirs) "to call upon the public in general to avoid senseless destruction."[77] However, these appeals constituted the smallest part of the address. Generally, the speech appears to have been written by a man who still—or once again—failed to realize that the motor of his armaments machinery would spin only a few more times and then come to a halt.

An astonished Speer stated in the draft to his speech that some sort of armaments production could still be kept going. A few months earlier, he had been preaching the slogan "Quality instead of Quantity." But now, he wanted to proclaim the necessity of "primitive weapons" to enable Germany to keep fighting. He celebrated the hand-carried *Panzerfaust* tank-destroyer as a symbol of the improvisational skill of his armaments industry and, at the same time, he appealed to the soldiers to hold out and keep fighting. "These primitive weapons are useful," the speech draft says, "only if we fight hard and are ready to give our all. [These weapons] demand every last bit of commitment from the soldier as a lone warrior."[78] And, a man obsessed with figures, Speer insisted on announcing that over three million of these tank-destroyers had been produced during the first quarter of 1945. As for the future, he did not see it in dark colors—at least according to his projected speech. "The fact that . . . a high number of heavy devices are still being manufactured shows that our supplies are not yet exhausted, so that we can still keep delivering [these products] for a long time."[79] And, on that April 11, 1945, Speer intended to broadcast an amazing justification over all German radio networks; he wanted to explain why the factories of the German worker should be spared: "We are all profoundly convinced of the ultimate victory of our German nation." After that, the un-demolished industrial installations could resume operations.[80]

In his memoirs, Speer reports that his speech was edited by Hitler and then never given: "In the cut version the speech had lost all point."[81] However, Hitler's revisions were not so sweeping as to adulterate the gist of the text. Most likely, the Armaments Minister himself realized that the speech as a whole was patently absurd. For just a short time later, he shook off the unrealistic attitude that had permeated the draft of his speech; now, he once again seemed to have a clear sense that defeat was inevitable. Still, he knew how to embellish his realization with the heroic bombast of the finest Nazi rhetoric.

On April 14, 1945, Speer sent a letter of farewell to his friend Karl Hanke, who had helped him early in his career. Hanke, Gauleiter of Lower Silesia, was in charge of defending Breslau. Speer's letter to Hanke demonstrates that, during the last days of the Third Reich, the Minister of Armaments was still indulging in the same heroic romanticism that Propaganda Minister Goebbells kept proclaiming over and over again. "With your achievements as the Defender of Breslau, you have given so much to Germany," Speer praised his friend Hanke. "Your example, which has not yet been fully recognized in all its grandeur, will someday have the inestimably high value for the nation that few heroes in German history have attained. . . . You are not to be pitied. You are advancing toward a worthy and beautiful close of your life."[82]

Speer had miscalculated. After fanatically defending Breslau, Karl Hanke flew out of the city shortly before its surrender. Decades later, Speer was evaluating his former friend along with other bigwigs of the Third Reich whom he described as gangsters with animal drives. However, he called Hanke a man who had had at least a few human instincts.[83]

On April 23, 1945, the Armaments Minister, who had been traveling through the as yet unoccupied territories almost all month long, flew once again to the beleaguered capital. In his autobiography, Speer lists several reasons for his return. He says he wanted to obtain the release of his friend Dr. Karl Brandt, who was imprisoned in a suburban villa. He also wanted to talk another friend into going west in order to flee the Russians. "But the far more powerful magnet behind these reasons was Hitler. I wanted to see him one last time, to say good-bye."[84]

There may have been an even more compelling reason, however. On April 22, Martin Bormann, who still had direct Tele-type contact with the Gauleiters, sent a telex from the underground rooms of the Führer's bunker. Along with directives and information for the Gauleiters, the telex asked: "Where is Speer?"[85]

Speer was staying with Karl Kaufmann, Gauleiter of Hamburg. Here, he must have read Bormann's call for him. Perhaps Speer feared that Hitler or Bormann had told SS-killers to liquidate the Minister of Armaments for sabotaging the Scorched Earth orders. So on April 23, 1945, Speer took the bull by the horns. In his usual casual way, he entered the bunker vault and greeted the stunned secretaries: "I guess you didn't expect to see me again."[86]

According to Speer's memoirs, when he then faced Hitler, he confessed that he had failed to carry out his destruction orders.[87] For Hitler, this must have been tantamount to admitting treason—but there were no consequences. The Führer would later repudiate Göring and Himmler for treason; but he forgave his friend and protégé for his breach of loyalty. The object of Hitler's "unrequited love"[88] could leave the bunker unhindered.

On April 24, 1945, at 4 A.M., Speer took off in a Fieseler Storch from Berlin's East-West Axis, leaving the burning capital behind him. He could look forward to the future, having already provided for his family's security. In early April, he had given his friend, the sculptor Arno Breker, a tin can to safeguard for his, Speer's family. The can contained 80,000 Reich marks.[89] Speer's head was filled with adventurous plans, which he had revealed only to his friend Milch several days earlier, and for which he had already made the necessary preparations.

9

SPEER AND THE DÖNITZ GOVERNMENT

"An operetta government!" That was what Speer called the twenty-three-day administration headed by Grand Admiral Karl Dönitz as Hitler's successor.[1] However, the Armaments Minister, who now had nothing to produce armaments for, was anything but a supernumerary on this ruin-covered "stage." Karl Dönitz unexpectedly played the leading role, attempting to settle Hitler's estate to the best of his knowledge and belief.[2] The interesting thing about Speer's part was that during the brief span of twenty-three days, he kept demonstrating, more effectively than ever, his extraordinary capacity for adjustment —like a "quick-change artist."

After his farewell visit to Hitler's bunker, Speer had gone to northern Germany. There, on April 25, 1945, he moved into makeshift quarters near Lake Eutin in Schleswig-Holstein.[3] In Berlin, the final act of the Greater German drama was coming to its horrible finale under many feet of concrete. Meanwhile, the unemployed architect and Armaments Minister was thinking about how he could carry out his plans, which he had revealed to Field Marshal Milch two days before his last flight to Berlin. The code name for Speer's fantastic project was—of all things—Winnetou.[4] This was the name of a character in the Wild West novels of Germany's most popular writer, Karl May, a producer of pulp superheroes. Hitler enjoyed reading Karl May, who was condemned decades later by Speer for being Germany's greatest dilettante.[5]

Speer's plan was to join forces with Colonel Werner Baumbach, a fighter pilot, and several other friends. The group would then fly a seaplane to Greenland, where they would wait for the end of the war and the occupation of Germany. Speer assumed he would return home two months after the capitulation "in order to take over the German government."[6] In his memoirs, Speer tells about his escape plans ("Ever since seeing the Udet film *SOS Iceberg* I had dreamed of a lengthy vacation in Greenland"[7]) but he conceals his political goals. He claims that he and his friends intended to fly to England in the autumn of 1945 and surrender there.[8]

His both fantastic and ambitious plans thrived in the right atmosphere. On April 25, fighter pilot Baumbach and Armaments Minister Speer met "in the forest camp at nightfall."[9] Four days later, the preparations for the Karl May flight were evidently well under way. "Winnetou plans rising high," Speer noted.[10]

While Speer was at his lakeside idyll, indulging in romantic thoughts of icy wastes, Grand Admiral Dönitz, commander in chief of the German Navy, was in the nearby town of Plön. On April 20, Hitler had named him commander in chief of the northern zone, authorizing him to issue directives for "all national, Party, and Wehrmacht agencies in that area."[11]

Dönitz regarded Speer as a friend,[12] and the Armaments Minister, for his part, felt more than just official friendship for the admiral. Although their relationship was not marked by the buddy-buddy tone of Speer's friendship with Milch, their feelings were nevertheless rooted in mutual liking and respect as well as faith in the Führer and the Reich. When Dönitz's sons were lost at sea during the war,[13] Minister Speer expressed "profound and heartfelt sympathy" for their heroic deaths;

when Dönitz's son Klaus failed to return from a mission in May 1944, Speer told the Grand Admiral that "our mutual comradely work will assure that he and his . . . brother Peter, who sacrificed themselves for the Führer and our Greater German Reich in their enthusiastic and unconditional willingness to give their all, shall not have fallen in vain."[14] In October 1944, Speer and Dönitz exchanged pictures, demonstrating their "comradely friendship."[15] Such gestures would have been all but impossible between Speer and Goebbels or Göring.

Speer's relationship with Dönitz, then, was more than "quite friendly in the line of our official duties,"[16] as author Speer characterized it years later when he more or less strongly dissociated himself from former colleagues in the course of his literary maneuvers. On April 28, 1945, after just three days in northern Germany, Speer visited Dönitz at his Plön headquarters.[17] He visited Dönitz again on April 30. While the grand admiral, Speer, and Admiral-General Kummetz (naval commander in chief of the Baltic Sea) were having supper,[18] the wireless telegraph receiver started ticking in a nearby room. A telegram in the secret naval code was being sent from the Führer's Berlin bunker. A few moments later, Dönitz's aide, Commander Walter Lüdde-Neurath, hurried over to his superior and handed him the decoded message:

> FRR Grand Admiral Dönitz. Instead of former Reich Marshal Göring, the Führer names you, Grand Admiral, as his successor. Written authorization on the way. As of now, you are in charge of all measures necessary in the present situation. Bormann.[19]

All the people present were dumbstruck. Speer was the first to break the silence: He congratulated the grand admiral, but his words were embarrassing and "had little effect . . . given the gravity of the situation."[20]

The appointment of Dönitz as Hitler's successor brought an end to all the struggles for that position—struggles that had been fought behind the scenes of the collapsing German Reich until Hitler's suicide. On April 23, Hitler had dismissed Göring, his official successor, from all his capacities. A few days later, Hitler also ousted Heinrich Himmler, his loyal SS-Reichsführer, who had his own crown-prince ambitions. The Führer's secretary, Martin Bormann, who had been Speer's opponent in the power struggle, was unable to act, since Berlin was surrounded. And the Armaments Minister, still driven by his ambition to become the ruler of Germany, had his "Winnetou plans"—which, to be sure, would be supplanted by other intentions during the next few weeks. Dönitz's appointment amid the chaos of the crumbling Reich is one of the mysterious events that will probably never be completely cleared up. During the final days, the Führer, intent on suicide, was greatly influenced by the insinuations of Goebbels and Bormann. These two men might have shed light on the mystery of that appointment; but they did not survive. Those who did survive Hitler's death in the Berlin bunker are unable to help, since they were not present when he made his final decisions.

In his memoirs, Speer reports that when he paid his last visit to the bunker of the Reich Chancellery, Hitler asked him his opinion of Dönitz. "I had the distinct feeling that he was not asking about Dönitz by chance; the question involved his successor."[21] Speer said positive things about the grand admiral, but did not try to "influence him in Dönitz's favor for fear that this would drive him in the opposite direction."[22]

What this means is that Speer's ploy did, in fact, influence Hitler's decision; it steered him away from Bormann and Himmler. On that evening of April 30, 1945, when Dönitz was suddenly burdened with Hitler's legacy, Speer said nothing about his conversation in the bunker[23]—a conversation that may have swayed Hitler in his decision to make Dönitz his successor. However, Bormann may have had some influence on Hitler's decision. At least, this is conjectured by Reimer Hansen, the chronicler of the Dönitz regime, for "Bormann's behavior after Hitler's death fully bears out this interpretation."[24]

Bormann had absolutely no intention of becoming a Wagnerian hero à la Goebbels and taking his own life on the Nazi sacrificial altar. On the contrary: After Hitler's suicide, Bormann attempted to get through the Russian lines, escape from Berlin, and make his way to Dönitz. His goal, evidently, was to take office as Party minister, a position to which he had been appointed by Hitler in his last will and testament. The grand admiral had no experience in government or Party politics, and Bormann probably saw "a chance not only to maintain his position of power, but also to increase it," says Hansen.†[25]

But the new Party minister never reached the admiral. Speer, in contrast, moved into Dönitz's headquarters at Plön that very day.[26] Here a remnant of the former Greater German Reich was still somewhat operational. Speer, as he explained his change of residence to his friend Baumbach, wanted to make sure that Dönitz would "not do anything foolish."[27]

However, something else seems to have drawn the restless minister to Plön. Dönitz, as head of state, represented power—albeit power that was shrinking steadily. The "great" decisions would now be made in the grand admiral's headquarters, and Speer, banking on their friendship, could hope to be involved in those decisions. Even the surrender needed its organizer.

Dönitz, as successor to the Führer, immediately had an assignment for Speer: He was to compose a telegram to the Reich bunker in response to the grand admiral's appointment. In order to have a choice of texts, Dönitz also ordered naval

---

†Shortly after the war, Field Marshal Milch (although unaware of the conversation between Hitler and Speer) said that Bormann had played an essential part in Dönitz's appointment as Hitler's successor. "The appointment looks more like Bormann's handiwork," Milch speculated. "He was looking for a figurehead who could be compliantly eliminated at any time. If Hitler made the choice himself, then he virtually declared the complete bankruptcy of the Party and the regime—an action that could only have been caused by mental illness." (Ifz, Erhard Milch, *op. cit.,* p. 41.)

captain Von Davidson to draft a telegram. Davidson formulated two sentences that were sober and to the point.[28] Dönitz's adviser Speer, however, penned some deep-purple prose:

> Mein Führer, my loyalty to you will be everlasting and unconditional. I will therefore first make every effort to rescue you from Berlin.
>
> If, however, Destiny nevertheless forces me to rule the German Reich as your appointed successor, then I shall perform this task with dignity and decency to the very end, as is demanded by this unique heroic struggle of the German people.[29]

The grand admiral preferred Speer's text, and, after making some minor revisions,[30] he had the message sent to Berlin early on the morning of May 1, 1945.[31]

At 10:35 A.M., a new message from the Berlin bunker arrived in the grand admiral's headquarters, informing him that Hitler's last will and testament was in effect.[32] Now it was clear to Dönitz that the Führer of the German Reich was dead. It never occurred to Germany's highest-ranking naval officer that Hitler could have taken his own life. "I did not think that [suicide] was possible [for Hitler], given my knowledge of his personality," Dönitz wrote in Nuremberg several months later. "I was certain that he had sought and found death in the battle of Berlin."[33] Dönitz's staff shared this opinion.[34]

Still, there was someone very close to the grand admiral who could have enlightened him about Hitler's death. One week earlier, when Speer was saying good-bye to his former patron, Hitler had told him how he wanted to die. "I shall not fight personally. There is always the danger that I would only be wounded and fall into the hands of the Russians alive. I don't want my enemies to disgrace my body, either." The Führer, determined to commit suicide, announced to his Minister of Armaments: "I have given orders that I be cremated."[35]

During the first few days of May, Speer seldom left Dönitz's side, taking part in conferences, discussions, and decisions. Yet he never uttered a word about what the Führer had told him. As Dönitz's adviser, Speer, utilizing the best Greater German vocabulary, diligently drew up the announcement with which the new head of state intended to inform the German people that their Führer and Reich Chancellor had died.

> To the German Nation:
> The Führer has perished in Berlin in the struggle against Bolshevism. With this voluntary decision, he has once again indelibly set down for all time the meaning of his entire life, the substance of his activities, and his indefatigable labors. The Führer may be the subject of controversy today. But someday his historic personality will be recognized in a fair history.

Speer wanted to put more words into the grand admiral's mouth:

> We hope that after his death, not only his personality, but also his prophetic realization of the danger from the East now threatening all mankind will be recognized in time for Europe and the entire world.[36]

The principle guiding all future decisions, according to Speer, was to save as many Germans as possible from the Bolshevist floodtide. Therefore the Germans were to keep fighting in the East with all their energy. In the West, however, the fight was only a protective cover. Speech-writer Speer demanded that a "united people" do its duties and show discipline and comradeship. He concluded his draft with an appeal to a higher power: "God protect Germany."[37]

Dönitz used little of Speer's draft. However, his obituary in honor of Hitler, with which the grand admiral began his May First appeal, was very much the kind of hymn that Speer had composed in the style of the *Götterdömmerung.*[38]

Hitler's successor realized that he would "soon . . . [have to] put himself into contact with the enemy."[39] He therefore needed a Foreign Minister. He did not bother to consider whether Ribbentrop (whom Hitler had once called a "second Bismarck"[40] and in whom Goebbels, on the contrary, had found nothing worth praising[41]) might be the suitable man. Dönitz recalls: "I needed someone . . . to whom foreigners would be responsive in the context of the coming negotiations."[42]

The grand admiral would actually have preferred to assign this post to Ribbentrop's predecessor, Baron Von Neurath, but the former Foreign Minister was nowhere to be found. Speer than suggested giving the job to the Reich Minister of Finance, Count Schwerin von Krosigk.[43] The aristocratic minister asked for twenty-four hours to think it over and then accepted the position on May 2. Dönitz, as he himself admits, could not have made a better choice. "It turned out that we agreed on all fundamental issues."[44]

Schwerin von Krosigk soon convinced the grand admiral that it was necessary to form an "acting government"[45] And Speer, still keeping a watchful eye on Dönitz to make sure he did "nothing foolish,"[46] could be certain of receiving a portfolio in this government. After all, Dönitz, Schwerin von Krosigk, and Speer formed the triumvirate that met on May 3 and 4 to discuss the possible members of the new cabinet.[47]

At the very time that they were forming this new, if limited, "acting government," Speer, interestingly enough, gave up his bizarre Greenland plans. In his diary-like jottings about those turbulent days, the last mention of the project is dated May 2.[48] There were new things for Speer to do: He was assigned the duties of Reich Minister of Economy and Production.[49]

On May 5, the grand admiral signed an edict drafted by Speer; it prohibited any immobilization or demolition—even in territories occupied by the enemy.[50] Speer's earlier efforts to undermine Hitler's Nero-like orders had become superfluous. Hitler was no longer in command.

On May 5, Speer had no sooner become Minister of Economy

and Production in the Dönitz cabinet than he began his peculiar dissociation from the government that he had so actively helped to set up. He wrote Count Schwerin von Krosigk, head of the "acting cabinet," that he intended to perform his duties only in the areas not yet occupied by the enemy: "I refuse to fulfill my obligations in the territories occupied by the foe." However, he was willing to make himself available for an office to settle government affairs if the enemy so wished. Speer was thinking of participating "within the framework of an armistice commission." After the surrender of both occupied and unoccupied territories, he intended to resign from the Reich government.[51]

He made similar statements in a letter of May 7 to Dönitz;[52] and one week later, he even asked Schwerin von Krosigk "to ask the grand admiral to release me from the duties of Reich Minister of Economy and Production." The reason, Speer explained, was that he did not have the qualifications to perform the duties of a Reich Minister of Economy. "I am an architect," Speer reminded the head of the cabinet, "and it is as thankless an enterprise to put an artist in charge of settling debts as it was to put a champagne dealer in charge of the Reich Foreign Ministry." However, in the very same breath, the "architect" stated that, as Dr. Todt's successor, he had gathered knowledge in the area of production; furthermore, he said, he was acquainted with the staffers who were capable of rebuilding German industry and coping with the major construction tasks to come: "Making this knowledge available for the benefit of the German people even under the most dishonorable circumstances would be a task with which I could end my three-year activity."[53]

The sentences thus formulated hints that Speer had special reasons for wanting to leave a government made up of men who more or less had Nazi backgrounds. By that time, members of the United States Strategic Bombing Survey had discovered Speer at Glücksburg Castle near Flensburg (the entire Dönitz team had already moved to Mürwik, near Flensburg). These Americans were discussing the possibilities, effects, and mistakes of aerial warfare, and they hoped that Speer would supply the key to what they saw as the enigma of the German armaments miracle.[54] The resulting situation was grotesque: From May 10 to May 25, a still officiating minister of the German Reich, "at liberty" (Speer),[55] was divulging secrets of the German armaments industry to the enemy. Just a few months earlier, Speer would no doubt have regarded such conduct by any of his staffers as high treason. In his memoirs, he writes about those conversations: "An almost comradely tone prevailed in our 'university of bombing.' "[56]

The American interrogator soon realized that Hitler's favorite minister was using a "well-considered ploy of self-justification and the wish to survive." John Kenneth Galbraith was one of the Americans who was attempting an academic analysis of aerial warfare with the former organizer of armaments. He recalls:[57] "The first part of [this] strategy [Speer's] was to qualify himself as a brilliant technician and administrator. He could guess that his enemies admired brains and technical ability. . . . The second part of his strategy was to appear completely unconcerned over his own fate." Because, according to interviewer Galbraith, "No one admires a coward; Speer wanted us to know that he realized his danger and did not care."[57]

Speer's efforts to make an impression worked. His curious interrogators soon noticed that they were dealing with a highly intelligent man who had perfected the arts of organization and improvisation. Galbraith: "No one could doubt it. Here was a personality."[58]

During the hours that Hitler's clever protégé chatted amiably and casually about the German armaments miracle, the Americans or Britons might very well have offered him the prospect of making his talents available for the reconstruction of a demolished Germany. In any case, Speer told Herbert Backe, Minister of Food, Agriculture, and Forestry, that he, Backe, ought to resign from the Dönitz government. "The two of them, Speer and Backe, he said, had the only active posts in the new government, and they would be better off not incriminating themselves by remaining in their positions. Because of statements made by the Englishmen and Americans questioning him, Speer was convinced that he would become Minister of Reconstruction in Germany within six months at the latest."[59]

Driven by this faith in a new career, Speer missed no opportunity to dissociate himself from the Dönitz government, even though he was still a member of its cabinet. Every afternoon, when Speer returned to Glücksburg Castle from the daily cabinet meeting, the interviewers, who then questioned him for hours, could be certain of hearing his opinion on the latest session of the Dönitz team. "A bad movie comedy" or "poor theater" were some of his barbs.[60]

Hence, it is not surprising that the Minister of Economy and Production made a strange impression on the head of the cabinet in the Dönitz administration. Schwerin von Krosigk later wrote: "When Speer was Minister of Economy during the few short weeks of the Dönitz administration, he showed how strongly his decisions were contingent on momentary impressions. Speer was one of the people who, after the [German] surrender, urgently advised Dönitz to vacate his office with a grand gesture. But then the very next day, he saw himself as the [re]builder of the demolished cities or as the negotiator of commercial treaties with the Soviets, and he requested staffers for these tasks."[61]

Nor did British and American disorganization, to which Speer once fell victim, shake the composure of the minister, who felt he was sailing toward new shores. One day, he was apprehended by American intelligence officers who released him only when he explained that he had an appointment with their colleagues. Speer was gracious enough to overlook this faux pas: "Under Hitler, the chaos was even worse."[62]

It is understandable that the acting Minister of Economy and Production, who was chock-full of new ambitions, advocated the resignation of Dönitz's entire government after the German surrender.[63] The grand admiral's administration, as anyone could see, was merely an instrument to wind up Hitler's estate;

it offered no opportunity for the new beginning that Speer had in mind. So it is obvious why Speer asked to be let go when Dönitz refused to resign voluntarily with his cabinet.[64] And it is equally obvious why he made a generous offer concerning his employees: "To the extent that my staff have acted in accordance with my instructions, [I am prepared] to defend their activities during the past three years and to shield them from any possible reproaches made by the enemy."[65] Evidently encouraged by the British and the Americans, Speer assumed he would become German's "Minister of Reconstruction" within six months. He probably failed to reckon that this "commitment to the activities of his employees" would cost him dearly.

It was clear that Minister Speer could hardly wait for the Dönitz government to exit from the "world stage." One day, he even asked his American interrogators to "put an end to that wretched joke."[66]

And the end came very quickly for the Dönitz administration, albeit not at Minister Speer's urging. The British Prime Minister, Winston Churchill, wanted to reorganize Germany under Allied control and with the help of a "Dönitz administration," but he was being vehemently opposed, chiefly by the Soviets but also by the Americans, who insisted on terminating the Dönitz government.[67]

The liquidation of the acting government by the British was carried out in an embarrassingly undignified and ultimately unsuitable manner. On May 23, 1945, at 10 A.M., Schwerin von Krosigk opened the usual brief meeting of his cabinet. All at once, "British soldiers, armed to the teeth with drawn tommy guns and hand grenades,"[68] burst into the room and shouted, "Hands up!" The members of the acting administration had to lower their trousers and undergo an examination that, according to Dönitz's aide-de camp Walter Lüdde-Neurath, "left nothing to the imagination."[69]

Meanwhile, Dönitz had been arrested on the passenger ship *Patria,* which was occupied by Anglo-American forces.[70] Speer had been taken into custody at Glücksburg Castle.[71] Later, the members of the Dönitz government all met again in a Flensburg police station. "A melancholy mood prevailed," Speer writes in his memoirs. "One by one we were summoned to an adjoining room to be registered as prisoners. Depending on their dispositions, the new prisoners returned angry, insulted, or depressed. When my turn came, I too was affronted by the embarrassing physical examination to which I was subjected."[72] For no sooner had all the members of the Dönitz government been interned at the Flensburg police station than the Britons and Americans evidently felt that a new examination was necessary. Nor was the baggage excluded from thorough inspection. Lüdde-Neurath recalls: "Jodl coined a term for what happened: 'organized plunder.' "[73]

Yet none of this appeared to dim Speer's hopes for the future. Even weeks later, when the former armaments organizer was behind bars at Dustbin Camp, he still assumed that he would shortly take office as "Minister of Reconstruction." A former employee of Speer's remembers that "he scheduled something like 'meetings with section heads,' and he wanted to collect names and addresses of people who were not politically incriminated."[74]

However, Speer had long since been cast in a different role: His name had been placed on the Allied list of major German war criminals.[75]

10

THE NUREMBERG TRIAL

"One morning, shortly after six o'clock, one of my former assistants roused me from sleep. 'I've just heard on the radio that you and Schacht are going to be tried at Nuremberg!' " The incarcerated ex-Minister of Armaments tried not to lose his composure, for he had never dreamed that he too would be tried as a war criminal. In his memoirs, Speer recalls: "The news hit me hard."[1]

His reaction was understandable: The former dictator of Greater Germany's armaments empire had become more and more deeply caught up in his plans for the future. The ex-minister had just penned a memorandum at the idyllic setting of Kransberg Castle, which he had revamped in 1939 for use as Göring's headquarters. Now the Americans had converted it into a prison camp, and they had given it a telling name: Dustbin. In his memorandum, Speer had settled accounts with the recent German political past and discussed in detail the "reshaping" of a destroyed Germany. The title of his thirty-page exposition was "The Further Development of the German Problem in Europe."[2]

In it, among other things, Speer passes a devastating judgment on the "sub-Führers" of the Third Reich; this was yet another step in dissociating himself from his former colleagues. He dogmatically declared: "The man who preached an unconditional struggle in this war, obligated his subordinates to wage that struggle and sent them to their death, while he himself avoided all danger and then worried about his ruined life at the tragic end of that struggle—that man will be despised by the German people as well as by his closest followers."[3]

Nevertheless, at the same time (June 1945), Albert Speer provided an unimpeachable certificate of good conduct for his dead Führer: "Adolf Hitler was rooted in the people. His irreproachable life-style and his persevering labor have become widely known, so that his memory cannot be so easily wiped away."[4] With these words, the history-writing ex-minister may have proclaimed the death of the Nazi Party. Nevertheless, with his characteristic ambivalence, he managed not to condemn the perished dictatorship in toto. "National Socialism too must have had a good core."[5]

After coping with the Nazi past in this way, he then launched into a detailed discussion of the political reconstruction of Germany. He looked forward to organizing the new state along the lines of the mammoth ministry that he had once directed. The result was a semi-utopian blueprint for a restoration of the Reich. Small districts were to be created in "comradely togetherness"[6] and centrally run by "experts." For the time being, said the futurist, there were to be no elections according to political principles, and "no professional politicians."[7] Speer also clearly postulated a Western orientation for his new *res publica*. During the rapid advances of the Allies, the Germans, he said, had hoped that the territories east of the Elbe would also be occupied by the Americans or the British. "A silent election took place among the Germans, a clear-cut demonstration in favor of the West and against the East."[8]

But, as fate would have it, just when Speer was exercising his political theory and advocating a westward shift for the Germany of the future, the Americans placed him on their list of the sixteen top war criminals.[9] (The British had already entered him in their list in 1944.) This put an end to all the plans and unrealistic ambitions nurtured by prisoner Speer.

Nevertheless, although declared a major war criminal, Speer once again displayed his extraordinary flexibility. He adjusted to the new situation with astonishing ease and set about finding a lawyer. Reasoning that the best possible attorney would have to come from the ranks of his former enemies, Speer asked George Ball, one of the Americans interrogating him at the Dustbin camp, to defend him at the Nuremberg Trial. Speer told him that young American lawyers often made a name for themselves by "defending notorious evildoers. . . . Where could you find a better-known client?"[10] George Ball refused.[11]

In October 1945, Speer was brought to Nuremberg, where he was handed a copy of the long indictment by the Allied Tribunal.[12] The Allies were accusing him of participation in a "joint plan of conspiracy" (Charge I); "crimes against peace" (Charge II); "war crimes" (Charge III); and "crimes against humanity (Charge IV)."[13] In his memoirs, Speer writes: "After reading it I was overwhelmed by a sense of despair."[14] Previously, he had assumed that "each of us would receive an individual indictment. Now it turned out that we were one and all accused of the monstrous crimes that this document listed."[15] Shorn of all his illusions, the ex-minister may not have realized that the imminent mammoth trial (which lasted 218 days) was to be a life-and-death struggle.

About two weeks before the trial began, Albert Speer was brought to the visitors' room of the Nuremberg prison, where a slender, bespectacled man awaited him: Dr. Hans Flächsner, a lawyer from Berlin.[16] Speer found him likable and "unhistrionic,"[17] and he retained him as his attorney, setting two conditions: Flächsner was not to present anything in court that would compromise the dignity of a former minister of the Reich (this would also hold for the other defendants); and none of Speer's former employees were to be incriminated.[18]

Speer then told his new attorney the ideas that had already gone through his mind about his defense. The ex-Minister of Armaments had long since realized that a "flight from responsibility"[19] could only make his position worse. He intended to do the exact opposite. He wanted to assume "collective responsibility" as one of the leaders of the Third Reich. Flächsner sharply disagreed; he was afraid his client would literally lose his head.[20] The lawyer from Berlin failed to see that this stance, which he regarded as a fundamental mistake, would become a tactical, indeed strategic ploy used by his client. Flächsner also advised Speer not to mention his plan to assassinate Hitler. The lawyer had altogether different ideas on how to proceed at the Allied Tribunal. He wanted to present his client as a man who had simply done his professional duty according to objective professional standards. Flächsner thought that this line of defense would separate the ex-organizer of German armaments production from the officials within the Nazi dictatorship who had determined the "top-level policies" of the Third Reich.[21] Dr. Flächsner must be credited with hatching the legend of "Albert Speer, the apolitical minister." The lawyer, of course, was hardly thinking of future historians; his only goal was to defend the former Armaments Minister as best he could.

Finally, the lawyer and his client agreed on a plan that was shaped largely by Speer's ideas. And so, at the Nuremberg Tribunal, Hitler's favorite minister defended himself with admirable dexterity and strategical genius. He completely dissociated himself from Hitler and his system; but, as one of the leading figures of the Nazi state, he untheatrically assumed "collective responsibility." He presented himself as a minister who had always been careful to keep aloof of politics. He acted contrite, but not submissive. With virtually pretentious modesty, he stylized himself as the final, albeit frustrated assassin of the Third Reich. He defended himself stubbornly, though cordially, whenever the prosecutors accused him of direct involvement in atrocities. And, as in the interrogations of the past few months, he showed absolutely no fear of what might hap-

n. His cultivated manner, emphasized by his charac-
ısualness, did not fail to have its effect: Speer was the
gentleman in the prisoners' dock at Nuremberg.

However, Speer was not only defending himself; he also had to
fight against one of his co-defendants, who regarded Speer's
behavior in the courtroom as treason against the dead Führer
and a conquered Germany.

Hermann Göring, Reich Marshal of Greater Germany and
now Major Defendant Number 1, had been a drug addict during the war and had grown apathetic and lethargic from over-
weight. However, after a drug-withdrawal treatment and then
weight loss in Nuremberg,[22] he had regained his old bellicose
élan. He had no illusions about the outcome of the trial, although in his virtually dichotomous thinking he did nurture
other illusions. "Yes," he told prison psychiatrist Douglas M.
Kelley, "I know the Americans will hang me, and you too know
they will hang me. I am ready. However, I am determined to
enter German history as a great man. If I cannot convince the
tribunal, then I will at least convince the German people that
everything I have done was done for the Reich. In fifty or sixty
years, Germany will put up monuments to Hermann Göring."[23]

Driven by his sense of a historic mission, Göring wanted to
prepare the soil for a renaissance of National Socialism in the
"ultimate battle" with the Allies. And although he knew what
the outcome of the trial would be, he struggled with impressive
energy for his hopeless cause.

In his self-assigned mission, Göring used the same tactics as
Hitler's favorite minister. Like Speer, Göring generously took
responsibility whenever he thought he could afford to do so:
"[I] have no intention of hiding behind the Führer's orders in
any way."[24] Göring assumed a theatrical pose. And in his
grandstand testimony, Göring, all too often taking responsibility for Hitler's orders, seriously incriminated himself. The chief
American prosecutor, Robert H. Jackson, later admitted that
it would have been difficult to prove Göring's complicity in

conspiring to wage a war of aggression. However, Göring, "in his boastfulness, provided valuable evidence himself."[25]

Major Defendant Number 1 did not want to fight this feud all by himself. As "commander in chief," he felt he had the right to commit all his fellow defendants to his concept of the "ultimate battle" for National Socialism. This was probably the main reason for the rivalry between the former Reich Marshal and the former Armaments Minister at Nuremberg. Göring was striving for a rehabilitation of National Socialism in the eyes of Germany and the rest of the world; with no consideration for his own head, he turned the Nuremberg Tribunal into a forum for intelligent and quick-witted Nazi propaganda. Speer, however, felt called upon to pronounce the death sentence on the Nazi ideology—a judgment that had already been delivered by the outcome of the war. Working strategically, the ex-Minister of Armaments took every precaution to save his head from the noose, which was getting tighter and tighter because of the evidence presented by the prosecution.

In 1977, the German historian Werner Maser speculated that Speer had made his plans to survive the trial even before the opening session took place.[26] And the American historian Bradley Smith had a difficult time "not feeling . . . some skepticism" when he analyzed the Speer case.[27] Such critical reactions were triggered by a letter that Speer wrote on November 17, 1945, to the chief American prosecutor, Robert H. Jackson. In his letter, Speer said that before his arrest in Flensburg on May 23, 1945, and also during his incarceration, he had had detailed discussions with Americans and Englishmen "on the effects of strategic aerial warfare on the German production that I was in charge of." Because of his vantage point and because of his partly successful three-year struggle against the effects of air raids, he had gained sound knowledge of tactics, antiaircraft defense, and industrial precautions. "I would feel . . . wretched," said Speer, "if others forced me to divulge this knowledge once again."[28] Bradley Smith interprets the letter as follows: "In plain speech, this meant that the American prose-cutor should not ask [Speer] any questions on the witness stand if the answers might give the Soviet Union useful military infor-mation."[29]

This letter, which might be taken as evidence of a secret agreement between Speer and Jackson, was not made public until several decades after the Nuremberg Trial. Speer's expla-nation for his letter was scarcely satisfactory: "We had been told that if the defendants sabotaged the trial, it would simply be halted, and the defendants would be turned over to the Russians without further ado. The 'others' I speak of in my letter to Jackson are, of course, the Russians, to whom I did not wish to be handed over."[30]

No historian can be content with Speer's claim that he feared being turned over to the Russians. It is more than improbable that the Americans or the British would have done so "without further ado," since unity between the Western Allies and the Soviets was being openly demonstrated now only in the court-room. Behind the scenes, the Cold War had already begun.

Not even David Irving, a successful tracker of original docu-ments of modern history, has been able to solve the riddle of Speer's letter. While investigating Robert H. Jackson's papers after the prosecutor's death, Irving stumbled on further letters written by Speer to Jackson. They were "printed in the obliga-tory capital letters with a pencil. . . . [These letters] reveal Speer's mysterious fear of making any sort of deal with the Americans, of favoring them over the other Allied powers."[31]

Although the documents supply no evidence of any secret written deal between Speer and Jackson,[32] the two men seemed to have made some sort of verbal arrangement. Thomas Dodd, the American prosecutor originally assigned by Jackson[33] to cross-examine Speer, had had intensive conversations with the defendant.[34] Dodd believed he had figured out the actual mo-tives behind Speer's conduct: vanity and ill-will toward Göring. Furthermore, as Dodd reported to the chief American prosecu-tor, Speer was offended at not being personally interrogated by

Jackson—as Göring was to be. Dodd advised Jackson to cross-examine Speer himself. "It will raise his spirits, he will feel important, and therefore be a much more honest witness."[35]

Jackson, accepting these arguments, decided to take Dodd's advice. He unofficially informed Speer that he would be cross-examining him personally. And Speer showed his gratitude by promising to tell everything.[36]

We can assume that all these actions were part of Speer's carefully planned strategy for survival. But this is obvious only if we examine individual aspects of his case and largely ignore the chronological course of the trial.

No sooner had Speer taken the witness stand on the afternoon of June 19, 1946, to be questioned by his attorney, Dr. Flächsner, than he zeroed in on his position in the Third Reich. He made it clear to the Allied Tribunal that he was no ordinary person among the VIPs of the Nazi state. "If Hitler had ever had any friends," said the Führer's favorite minister, "then I would certainly have been one of his close friends."[37]

Having described his special position at Hitler's court, he must have impressed the judges even more a short time later, when, as the Führer's "almost-friend," he made his fundamental statement on the theme of "responsibility." "This war brought an inconceivable catastrophe upon the German people, and also a catastrophe upon the whole world. . . . It is my obvious duty to take responsibility for this disaster even in regard to the German people. This is all the more my duty because the head of the [Nazi] government has eluded his responsibility toward the German people and to the world. As an important member of the leadership of the Reich, I therefore bear collective responsibility as of 1942."[38] The next day, Jackson, whose cross-examination was hard but strikingly polite in its tone, asked the witness to be more precise about this "collective responsibility." Speer managed to nuance it and skillfully modify it.

"You have previously said," Jackson told the defendant, "that you as a member of the [Nazi] government have a certain responsibility. I would like you to tell us what responsibility you meant when you said that you assumed responsibility as a member of the government."

Speer asked back: "You mean the statement I made yesterday that I . . . ?"

Jackson: "Your collective responsibility. What do you mean by 'collective responsibility' together with others?"

"Well, in my opinion, there are two kinds of responsibility in politics," Speer began his lengthy explanation. "One responsibility is for one's own sector; here, needless to say, one bears full responsibility. Beyond that, I personally feel that there is and has to be such a thing as collective responsibility for crucial things, if one is one of the leaders; for who else should bear responsibility for the course of events if not the people working closest to the head of state? But—" and this is where the defendant Speer began his qualification, "this collective responsibility can pertain only to basic things. It cannot pertain to the handling of details in the offices of other ministries or other responsible agencies; otherwise, the entire discipline of political life would become chaotic, for no one would know who in particular . . ." Here Speer faltered, and then went on: "Individual responsibility in one's own area of work must nevertheless be clearly and plainly reserved for the individual."[39]

For the ex-Minister of Armaments, this qualifying definition was necessary. Although willing to accept an abstract and theoretical collective responsibility (however he may have formulated it), he refused to have anything to do with cruel and bloody "details," which had also existed in his former area of responsibility.

Thus he defended himself stubbornly when Jackson confronted him with documents of inhuman practices which had occurred in "individual parts" of the armaments empire that he had once ruled. The American prosecutor introduced an affidavit in which a former armaments worker revealed the dreadful conditions in a labor camp and the barbaric treatment dealt out by the head of the camp. "L. [the head of the camp] was rather brutal toward the foreigners," Jackson quoted. "He confiscated food belonging to the prisoners of war and took it to his apartment. Every day, he mistreated eastern European workers, Russian, French, and Italian prisoners of war, as well as other foreign civilians. He built a steel box that was so small one could barely stand in it. He would lock foreigners in it, even women, for as long as forty-eight hours, without giving them any food. They were not allowed out to relieve themselves. Other people were not permitted to help these prisoners or release them. Once, during a raid on a secret camp, he fired at fleeing Russian civilians without hitting them. One day, during food distribution, I saw him hit a French civilian in the face with the ladle, so hard that the blood gushed down his face."

"It goes on like that for a while," Jackson said, "but I do not want to enter any more of it in the court record."[40]

Such incriminating documents might have bloodied Speer's declaration of collective responsibility. When confronted with them, he did what his co-defendants did in similar instances: He challenged the authenticity of the affidavit. "I view this affidavit as mendacious. I would like to say that such things do not occur in the German people."[41]

However, this response did not satisfy the American prosecutor. "What about these steel boxes? Were these steel boxes not built?" he pressed the defendant. "Or do you not believe this story?"

"No." Speer stood his ground. "I do not believe it, I mean I do not believe that it is true. I mean after the collapse in 1945, a great number of people must have signed affidavits that were not quite truthful. That is not your fault," he apologized to Jackson and grew more and more uneasy, "that is because of . . . that is after a . . . after a defeat, it is quite possible that there are people who resort to this sort of thing."[42]

The chief American prosecutor presented photographs of such torture chambers, adding a detailed description: "Photograph A shows an iron closet specially manufactured by the Krupp firm to torture Russian civilian laborers in a way that is impossible to describe with words. In a compartment of the closet, in which a man can barely stand for a long time—it is five feet high and sixteen or twenty inches deep and wide—men or women were often locked up for a long time, frequently two together, kicked and shoved in." And thus it went: "Photograph B shows the same closet locked. Photograph C shows the closet open. . . ."[43]

However, the presiding magistrate, who felt that Jackson had neglected an important detail, asked him to mention it. So Jackson went into further particulars: "On the top of the closet, there are a few sieve-like holes, through which cold water was poured on the unfortunate victim in the ice-cold winter."[44]

However, Speer had a different interpretation of this photograph. These were clothing lockers, he explained: "Any expert in Germany can tell you that these are not special closets. This is a standard manufactured object. Further proof is offered by the fact that the air holes are on the top, for every clothes closet has air holes on the top and on the bottom."[45]

Whatever the purpose of these closets, which Justice Jackson saw as torture chambers, Speer's reaction is crucial: He skirted the problem of responsibility by disputing the authenticity of the documents presented to him. Simply said, he wanted nothing to do with them.

All these details of human cruelty with which Jackson confronted the ex-Minister of Armaments were consequences of a wartime program that Speer had participated in and profited from, namely the system of forced labor.

Fritz Sauckel, a former worker and seaman, had advanced to the position of Gauleiter of Thuringia under Hitler. On March 21, 1942, a Führer edict had appointed him Commissioner of Labor.[46] In this capacity, he brutally shanghaied more than five million foreigners into forced labor during the war.[47] Speer urgently needed these laborers to increase his output and maintain his armaments industry. He would tell Sauckel how many workers he needed, and Sauckel would draft and deport manpower in order to meet the Armaments Minister's quota. Of course, Speer had no authority over Sauckel; the Labor Commissioner was not subordinate to him. Furthermore, the two men kept squabbling about the problem of foreign laborers. Their cooperation was marked by mutual antipathy and was sustained only by the requirements of their positions.

Speer was enough of a realist to see that his involvement in the Sauckel actions could cost him his head. The prosecutor had stated on December 11, 1945, "We will prove that the defendant [Albert] Speer, as Reich minister of armaments and munitions, as head of the Todt Organization, and as a member of [the] Central Planning [Committee], was responsible for establishing the number of foreign slaves needed for the German war machine, that he was responsible for the decision on forced recruitment and for the use of foreign civilians and prisoners of war in the armaments and munitions industry, for the construction of fortifications as well as active military enterprises, and under brutal, inhuman, and degrading conditions."[48]

Evidently, Speer had realized shortly after the war that it might save his life if he retrospectively drew a sharp distinction between his and Sauckel's areas of jurisdiction. But he handled this problem very emotionally during the months before the trial. Whenever Sauckel's name was mentioned during the interrogations, Speer's animosity, still smoldering after the war, flared up. Sauckel, Speer told the Americans, ought to be placed at the top of every list of war criminals;[49] and "if anyone in the Third Reich deserves his just reward, it is Sauckel."[50]

The former Labor Commissioner was being questioned in a different camp, and every time Speer's name was mentioned, it triggered an explosion: "There is a man you should hang."[51]

On a different occasion, Speer once again gave free rein to his anger at Sauckel—whose recruitment methods he had known and tolerated because he had been intent on getting as many laborers as possible to produce as many weapons as possible for his Führer's war. "As my subordinates reported," Speer stated, "Sauckel was one of the few who succeeded in misinforming

A[dolf] H[itler] so systematically about me that his [Hitler's] decisions almost always went against me. In his personal attitude [toward me], Sauckel was often quite hateful."[52]

Still, Speer did admit that the former Labor Commissioner had taken great pains to "assure decent treatment and food for the foreign workers in Germany. He always fully committed himself to this."[53]

Twenty-three years later, in his memoirs, Speer claimed that Sauckel had "said a good deal . . . about me on the principle of 'incriminate the absent.' "[54] The pot was calling the kettle black; Speer had done nothing but pass the buck during the preparations for his defense.

During his interrogations, Sauckel (who was eventually condemned to death at Nuremberg and hanged) did his share in incriminating Speer. The latter found out about it at the Nuremberg Prison, where he was taken for questioning in October 1945. Speer recalls: "A young American officer awaited me. He pleasantly invited me to sit down and then began asking for explanations of various matters. Apparently, Sauckel had tried to make a better case for himself by branding me as solely responsible for the importation of foreign workers."[55] However, the Americans obviously were more benevolent to Speer than to Sauckel, for, according to Speer's autobiography, "the officer proved to be well-disposed and of his own accord composed an affidavit which straightened out this matter. This eased my mind somewhat."[56]

However, having exploited the forced-labor program, the ex-minister was far too clever to make an attempt at eluding all responsibility. On the contrary, during an interrogation on October 18, 1945, he categorically declared: "I do not wish to make it seem as if I did not urgently demand manpower and foreign manpower from Sauckel."[57] Speer was shrewd enough not to dissociate himself from this—as he emphasized—"voluntary statement" when he was being questioned by his attorney Flächsner at the Nuremberg Tribunal in June 1946.[58]

It was far more important to make it clear to the court that he was not responsible for any of the barbaric conditions in the labor camps. Flächsner addressed this problem directly when he cross-examined his client: "The prosecution accuses you of complicity in the labor conditions of foreign workers, prisoners of war, and the manpower from the concentration camps. What do you have to say on this matter?" Speer replied, "Neither I nor the ministry was responsible [for any of these things]."[59] The defendant could also prove that he had frequently tried to better the conditions of the workers and obtain adequate food for them.[60]

The court went along with this. "Speer's position was such that he had nothing to do directly with the cruelties in the implementation of the forced-labor program, although he knew about them," the verdict read. "However, Speer did insist on adequate food and working conditions for the forced laborers, so that they could work properly."[61]

Flächsner also achieved his goal of presenting Speer to the court as an artist who had become a politician in spite of himself. The lawyer said that Speer had been reluctant to exchange his profession as architect for a minister's portfolio; and Flächsner documented his assertion by quoting from the speech that Speer had given to the Gauleiters and Reichleiters two weeks after becoming minister. Speer had described it as a personal sacrifice that he could no longer be an architect, and he had made it clear to the Nazi potentates: "After all, I can maintain that my personal contribution is a large one. Until recently, I moved in an ideal world."[62]

Of course, Flächsner avoided quoting anything else from that highly revealing speech given by the newly appointed minister. For two sentences later, we hear how Speer intended to tackle his new work, which was vital to the war effort: "I have given up my professional activity and thereby my true vocation in order to commit myself relentlessly to the task of war." Those were Speer's words to the gathering of sub-Führers.[63]

Flächsner tried to prove that Speer had been an apolitical minister by quoting a passage from the memorandum that the armaments organizer had sent to Hitler on September 20, 1944. A large number of historians regard this text as strong enough evidence to accept the thesis of the "apolitical minister Speer." "The task," Flächsner quoted, "that I have to perform is an apolitical one. I have felt good in my work so long as I and my work have been evaluated purely on the basis of my professional performance."[64]

In his summing-up, Flächsner again went into this topic. He pointed out that Speer's name had been put on the list of ministers drawn up by the leaders of the putsch of the Twentieth of July; he was the only minister included from Hitler's cabinet. Flächsner concluded his arguments with a rhetorical question: "Is it possible that this group would have selected Speer if he had not been regarded for a long time as a decent, apolitical professional both in Germany and abroad?"[65]

The highlight of Speer's defense strategy was probably the way he presented himself to the court as the last rebel of the Third Reich. During Dr. Flächsner's first few meetings with his client, when they tried to work out the best defense tactic, the lawyer opposed mentioning Speer's assassination plan. This plan, Flächsner argued, had been simply an intention that had never even been acted on;[66] besides, Speer could cite only one witness. His lawyer feared a negative reaction from the tribunal, but he and his client agreed that Speer would bring up his plan during his testimony.[67]

"In court I intended merely to mention my plan to assassinate Hitler," says Speer, offering a rather weak explanation, "chiefly in order to show how dangerous Hitler's destructive intentions had seemed to me."[68]

Yet something he did does not fit in with this statement: He sought a very early opportunity to bring up his assassination plan, thereby virtually stealing the courtroom scene. His chance came on January 3, 1946, when Otto Ohlendorf took the stand. Ohlendorf had been in charge of the SD (Sicherheitsdienst = Security Service), the SS-organization that had spread an invisible network throughout the Nazi Reich, eavesdropping in order to ferret out everything taking place day or night. Ohlendorf, as head of the SD, was the right man to ask whether he knew of any plan to assassinate Hitler toward the end of the war. In this way, it was possible to start a rumor about the very existence of such a plan. Furthermore, Dr. Flächsner was on Christmas holiday and not informed of his client's intention to reveal the assassination plan at such an early point.[69] Speer did it with the help of Dr. Egon Kubuschok, who was the defense attorney for Papen and the Reich government and who also proxied for Flächsner whenever the latter was absent.

"Are you aware," Kubuschok asked Ohlendorf on the witness stand, "that the defendant Speer was preparing to assassinate Hitler in mid-February of this year?"[70] Naturally, Ohlendorf had to say no;[71] for had he known about this plan in the spring of 1945, the would-be assassin could scarcely have eluded the clutches of the SD.

However, the very asking of the question got Speer what he was after. The courtroom was electrified. The defendants exchanged astonished gazes. Göring even had a fit. In the brief recess that followed, he dashed over to Speer and furiously asked him "how he could have dared to make such a treasonable admission in an open court proceeding, thus destroying their unified front."[72]

Speer's "admission" was indeed a heavy blow for Göring. He not only saw that Speer could thus improve his position as a defendant, he also immediately realized that Speer had torpedoed Göring's plan of an "ultimate battle" with a unified front under his leadership.

On the evening of that January 3, 1946, Göring, in his cell, seemed tired and dejected, according to Gilbert, the prison psychologist. "That damn fool Speer!" Göring raged. "Did you see the way he completely humiliated himself in the courtroom today? God in heaven! Damn it all, how could he humiliate himself like that, do something that miserable, just to save his filthy neck! I nearly died of embarrassment! To think that a

German can act that vile in order to prolong his lousy life—to say it openly—in order to keep pissing in front and shitting in back! Goddamn it, damn it to hell—Do you think," he snapped at Gilbert, "I give a hoot about this lousy life? I don't give a tinker's damn whether I'm executed, drown, die in a plane crash, or drink myself to death! But there's such a thing as a sense of honor in this accursed life! Assassinate Hitler! Ha! God in heaven! I could have sunk into the ground!"[73]

The next day, during the lunch recess, the furious ex-Reich marshal told Baldur von Schirach, the former Reich youth leader and then Gauleiter of Vienna, to talk to Speer and order him back into the "unified troop" of defendants. Schirach did his best to carry out his mission. He nagged Speer vehemently in the vestibule of the canteen, telling him that he, Speer, had covered himself and his good name in Germany with shame. But Speer, who had never allowed the Reich marshal to order him about, had only scornful words for Defendant Number 1: "As the second man in the Reich, he had the obligation . . . to do something, but he was too big a coward! Instead, he numbed his mind with drugs and looted art treasures all over Europe. . . . Göring still thinks of himself as the 'great man,' and even now, as a war criminal, he still thinks he can steal the show."[74]

When Speer took the witness stand on June 20, 1946, and was questioned by Flächsner, he used the opportunity to offer the court a detailed presentation of his abortive plan to assassinate Hitler. His attorney skillfully maneuvered the questions to this topic: "Herr Speer! The witness Stahl testified in his written interrogation that in mid-February 1945 you asked him for a supply of the new poison gas in order to assassinate Hitler, Bormann, and Goebbels. Why did you intend to do so?"

Speer replied: "In my opinion, there was no other way out. I wanted to take this step in my despair, for as of early February I had come to realize that Hitler would continue the war against his own nation with all means [at his disposal] and with no consideration. It was clear to me that if the war were lost, he would confuse his fate with that of the German people and that he saw his end also as the end of the German people. It was also clear that the war was so thoroughly lost that even unconditional surrender had to be accepted."

Dr. Flächsner: "Did you want to carry out this assassination yourself? Why did your plan fail?"

Speer: "I prefer not to go into the details; I could carry it out myself only because after July 20, only a small group still had access to Hitler. I encountered various technical difficulties. . . ."[75]

Speer could be certain that the judge would not be satisfied with such hints and that he would ask for particulars of the assassination plan hatched by a defendant who, just several days earlier, had described himself as one "of Hitler's few possible friends." Speer's calculation was correct. "The court would like to hear the details," announced Lord Justice Lawrence, "but we will hold our recess now."[76]

During the ten-minute interval, the defendants were tense and nervous. "Göring seemed to exercise great self-control," Gilbert noted, "to keep from saying anything out loud."[77]

When the recess was over, the former Minister of Armaments described his assassination designs in detail. "Herr Speer," his attorney asked him, "would you please tell the court what circumstances prevented you from carrying out your plans?"

Speer: "I hesitate to describe details, because such things are unpleasant. I am doing so only because the court has requested it."[78]

In his memoirs, Speer quotes these statements from the records of the Nuremberg Tribunal; however, these almost embarrassingly modest words are joined by a further sentence: "I do not intend to cite my role during this phase as part of my defense."[79]

Speer the litterateur has given free rein to his imagination here. That last sentence was never uttered during the Nuremberg Trial; it is not to be found in either the German- or the English-language records.[80]

Speer then gave a fluent and coherent description of his assassination plan. His glibness showed that he had counted on being able to speak his piece, that he had prepared himself and was anything but "unwilling."

During that period, Hitler often had discussions of the military situation with Ley, Goebbels, and Bormann in his bunker. These men were especially close to him then, because they supported and went along with his radical course. Since the Twentieth of July, it has been impossible for even Hitler's closest collaborators to enter his bunker without having their pockets and briefcases searched for explosives by the SS. As an architect, I was thoroughly familiar with this bunker. It had a fresh-air device, like the one installed in this room. It would not have been difficult to introduce gas into the intake valve of the fresh-air mechanism, which was in the garden of the Reich Chancellery. [The gas] would have spread quickly through this facility, throughout the entire bunker.

In mid-February 1945, I then sent for Stahl, head of my Main Committee of Munitions, a man who was very close to me. Since I had already worked closely with him during the demolitions, I openly revealed my intention to him, as he has testified, and I asked him to get me modern poison gas from the munitions factory. He asked his colleague, Lieutenant Colonel Soika of the Army Ordnance Office, how one could get at this poison gas, and it turned out that this new poison gas is effective only if exploded, since that brings about the high temperature necessary for gassing. (I don't know if I am going too much into detail.) An explosion was not possible, however, since the fresh-air mechanism was made of thin metal, which would have been torn apart by an explosion. I then had several discussions with Hänschel, head maintenance man of the Reich

Chancellery after mid-March 1945, and in the course of our conversations, I learned that the gas filter was no longer switched on all the time. I thus could have used a normal sort of gas. Naturally, Hänschel had no knowledge of why I was having these talks with him. When I was ready, I, together with Hänschel, inspected the intake valve in the garden of the Reich Chancellery. I found out that, a bit earlier, at Hitler's personal orders, a thirteen-foot chimney had been constructed on this intake valve. It can still be found there today. This made it impossible for me to carry out my plan.[81]

The next day, Jackson, the chief American prosecutor, brought up Speer's assassination plan when he was cross-examining him: "There were other plots besides the ones you told us about, weren't there?"

Speer replied: "During that period, it was extremely easy to hatch a plot. You could stop almost anyone in the street and tell him what the situation was like, and he would then say, 'Why, that's sheer madness,' and, if he had any courage at all, he would agree to go along with it."[82]

With these words, the former Minister of Armaments showed the absurdity of his testimony of the previous day, when he had claimed that he had been the only one who could have personally carried out his assassination plan. Now, he presented the situation in such a way as if countless people during the period of collapse would have been willing to join a plot against Hitler. However, the chief American prosecutor appeared not to notice this contradiction; in any event, he did not go into it.

"[I] agreed with my defense attorney," Speer writes in his autobiography, "that he was not to use this part of my testimony in his final summation."[83] Still, Flächsner would have been a poor lawyer had he not touched upon the "plot" in his grand defense speech. After all, contrary to his expectations, the "plot" had been counted in the defendant's favor by the prosecution. "As of the end of February 1945, the defendant

Speer, by planning plots, tried to bring about a faster end to the war. Both the witness Stahl and the witness Von Poser[84] have testified that Speer was also planning other violent measures. Chief Justice Jackson has also determined in his cross-examination that the prosecution is familiar with other plans that were to be carried out under Speer's leadership."[85]

Speer's detailed depiction of his assassination plan rekindled the old rivalry with Göring. After Speer's testimony, Göring mumbled dire threats and curses against Hitler's former protégé[86] and conjured up the specter of a kangaroo court, the old Germanic *Fehmegericht,* which would make short shrift of the "traitor" if he managed to get out of this trial alive.[87] Yet it was not really Speer's alleged treason that infuriated Göring. The former Reich Marshal felt personally offended by Speer's testimony, for Speer had gone against his original resolution not to say anything incriminating or humiliating about his fellow defendants. In the courtroom—and thereby in front of the international press—Speer had quoted Hitler, who had made no bones about his opinion of Göring during the last days of the war. The Führer had called him a corrupt drug addict and a failure.[88] Speer had thus greatly insulted his arch rival. Even Göring had to realize that no German monuments would be put up to a drug addict and failure with the title of Reich Marshal —even fifty years hence.

Von Papen was gratified to hear Speer's attack on Göring: "That should polish off the fat man!"[89] Baldur von Schirach, who had been under Göring's influence at the beginning of the trial, and Hans Fritzsche, the former radio commentator, summed up the effect of Speer's testimony in a terse sentence: This would be the end of the Göring/Hitler saga.[90] And Hjalmar Schacht, the Führer's financial wizard, enthused about his co-defendant's performance: "That was a masterful defense!"[91]

Speer's cultivated manners, his intellectually fashioned aura of remorse did not fail to make an impression on the observers, the prosecutors, and the judges. A short time after the trial, one of the journalists commented: "Even at the risk of being misunderstood, I would like to state that Speer is the only one of the defendants whom I respect for his personal honesty and courage."[92] Nor was Jackson, the chief American prosecutor, sparing with his praises: "Tell your client," he said to Flächsner, "that he is the only one of the defendants whom I respect."[93] And even Justice John J. Parker admitted that Speer had made an impression on him. Noticing that Jackson had treated Speer respectfully, Parker said "that one must be indulgent with him if he aroused sympathy even in the prosecution."[94]

Given these manifestations of goodwill, the defendant Speer never appeared to be profoundly contrite.[95] ("I didn't have to be.")[96] Hans Frank, the former governor-general of Poland, suffered the torments of crime and punishment at Nuremberg and returned to Catholicism, but such responses did not fit in with the mentality of the man who had been number two in the Greater German Reich. He shielded himself against such deeply spiritual struggles by using the method of planned mental repression that he had successfully practiced during the Nazi regime.

One evening, Dr. Flächsner visited his client in order to discuss the day's sessions. They had important things to talk about, since Speer had been confronted with a wealth of incriminating documents; but this time, Speer didn't want to go into them. "Let's forget about the trial for today, Dr. Flächsner." Speer waved him off. "I would rather know whether you have ever looked at my Reich Chancellery in Berlin? How did you like it?" Flächsner replied that he liked the building; but then he sketched one of the gigantic doors of the New Reich Chancellery and added a human figure in the proper ratio. Because of the enormous size of the construction, Flächsner told his client, man was no longer "the measure of all things." Hitler's former master builder mused for a while and then said, "I don't think I would do that a second time."[97]

Interestingly enough, when Dr. Flächsner tried to bring out

"Tyrolean Reminiscences," drawn by Speer during the Nuremberg Trials. Speer's caption dedicates the drawing to Hans Fläschner.

167

the special nature of the Speer case during the hours he spent summing it up in the Nuremberg courtroom, his client flaunted a superior casualness in the prisoners' dock. He was sketching a castle at the foot of a steep mountain: "Tyrolean Reminiscences"—an utterance of perfected repression.

While the judges of the International Military Tribunal were negotiating their verdicts behind the scenes,[98] the thirty-two American journalists had already cast their lots in regard to the fate of the defendants. In the press room, the reporters had recorded their conjectures about the coming judgments by making crosses in the columns next to the names of the defendants to indicate "guilty," "not guilty," "prison," or "death penalty." The correspondents were unanimous in expecting the death penalty for Göring, Ribbentrop, and Kaltenbrunner; but only eleven predicted capital punishment for Speer.[99]

After protracted discussions behind closed doors, the court found Speer guilty of charges III (war crimes) and IV (crimes against humanity). The debate about his sentence was equally heated. J. T. Nikichenko, the Russian, demanded the supreme penalty as in all other cases; but Norman Birkett, the Englishman, felt that ten years' imprisonment would fit the crime.

The judges did not reach an agreement until early in the morning of September 11, 1946.[100] On October 1, Albert Speer learned his fate. He was sentenced to twenty years in prison.[101]

Hitler's favorite architect and armaments organizer had played a sovereign game of roulette at Nuremberg. His willingness to accept collective responsibility could have also led him to the gallows. However, in assuming this stance he manifested —for whatever motives—insight and remorse, even in regard to crimes in which he had no demonstrable complicity. After carefully thinking out his tactics, he presented himself to the prosecutors and judges as the very embodiment of honorableness among the National Socialists. His gamble paid off. The gentlemanly defendant in the prisoners' dock at Nuremberg escaped the noose.

11

SPANDAU

"My cell is 3 meters long and 2.7 meters wide," noted the prisoner Albert Speer on October 3, 1947. He also measured the height: 4 meters.[1] The cell was located in a colossus of red and black brick at 24 Wilhelmstrasse in Spandau, on the outskirts of Berlin. Constructed during the reign of Kaiser Wilhelm, the prison was supposed to house six hundred inmates. But on October 3, 1947, it contained only seven. These were the notables of the "Thousand-Year Reich" who had managed to escape the gallows at Nuremberg; the court of the victorious Allies had handed down sentences ranging from ten years to life imprisonment.

The roster of prisoners was as follows: Karl Dönitz, former commander in chief of the German navy and, as Hitler's successor, the last head of state of the Third Reich; Konstantin von Neurath, former Foreign Minister under Hitler (until he was replaced by the diplomatic outsider, Joachim von Ribbentrop); Baldur von Schirach, former Reich youth leader and Gauleiter of Vienna; Albert Speer, former Reich Minister of Armaments and War Production; Walter Funk, former Minister of Economy; Rudolf Hess, Hitler's deputy until

1941; and Erich Raeder, head of the German navy until 1943.

These seven prisoners were guarded by four hundred soldiers and fifty guards; four physicians watched over their health, and four wardens made sure that the prison rules were obeyed. In the eyes of the Americans, British, French, and Russians, a force equal in strength to a batallion guaranteed that the seven former Nazi celebrities would never even dream of trying to escape.

After being sentenced, Albert Speer had spent the first nine months of his imprisonment—from October 1, 1946, to July 17, 1947—in the Nuremberg Prison. Here, he had realized that even incarceration required organization. "I already know that a life plan is important if I am to keep going,"[2] he noted after six weeks in prison. And the former organizer of the Greater German armaments industry, who now lived as Prisoner Number 5 in Spandau's Allied Prison for War Criminals, decided to organize his survival. His method of tackling this problem was described nine years after his release, when his *Spandau Diaries* was offered for literary consumption to millions of readers.

In order to survive physically, Speer became an obsessed gardener. He made a kind of park out of the giant garden that had been running wild for years. And he ran several miles every day with impressive discipline. In order to give some meaning to his daily run, he began to count the miles as he took an imaginary trot around the globe.

However, Speer also had to survive mentally; and so Prisoner Number 5 decided to turn his cell into a scholar's den. To keep abreast of his real profession, he systematically read architectural journals. He also set about studying history, from ancient to modern—excluding the contemporary period, since prison rules prohibited the seven inmates of Spandau from reading about "their history." The former Minister of Armaments also soared into the metaphysical spheres of theology and philosophy; and from time to time, belles lettres helped him to forget his bleak surroundings. Speer the autodidact brushed up on his English and French, which he had acquired at school and then forgotten while organizing the German war machinery.

Inevitably, the passionate mathematician kept a numerical record of his studies. After his release,[3] he proudly announced that he had read five thousand books in prison. Yet this number would appear too high even to a mathematical layman, for the former Armaments Minister spent some 7,300 days in prison (not counting the months of the Nuremberg Trial). Had he actually read five thousand books, then, theoretically, he could not have devoted more than an average of a day and a half to each. However, Speer passed several hours a day gardening and more than one hour a day "globe-trotting" (7.3 kilometers, about 4.4 miles).[4] Furthermore, he wrote thousands of pages at Spandau. Given these occupations, he could not have spent more than a few hours on each book. Yet this brief time span would not have sufficed for works like Karl Barth's *Doctrine of Creation.* Nor could authors like Karl Jaspers, Jean-Paul Sartre, or Houston Stewart Chamberlain[5] be covered in such a short time.

In October of 1947, a "new dimension" was added to Speer's prison life.[6] Toni Vlaer, one of the guards, told him that he would be willing to smuggle his mail, uncensored, from the heavily guarded institution. From then on, Speer could maintain unsupervised contact with the outside world. At first, the secret messages were transmitted via Speer's former secretary, Annemarie Kempf, and immediate members of his family in Heidelberg. But then, in 1951, Rudolf Wolters' architectural office in Coesfeld became Speer's secret post office. His former comrade-in-arms took on the task of organizing his ex-boss's imprisonment from the outside. And Wolters did such a good job of organizing it that life became more bearable for the prisoner in Spandau. Of course, in his best-selling *Diaries,* Speer made sure not to tell his readers about the improvement; it would not have fitted in with the "infinite monotony of those years"[7]—as Speer depicted his time in Spandau. Speer also had a good reason for concealing his friend's name in the published

Diaries and for "transferring" him from Coesfeld to Coburg: He wanted to shield Wolters from the scrutiny of the historians. Too many documents—indeed, too many revealing ones—had passed through his helper's hands.

Wolters had been aiding his incarcerated friend even before 1951. The most important thing, he felt, was to take care of Speer's family, especially his six children, who were still in school. Since the family fortune had been confiscated, Wolters sent requests for money to former staffers of Speer's who had become successful in architecture or industry. Soon, small and then larger sums of money began arriving regularly in a bank where Wolters had opened a "tuition account." Every deposit or withdrawal was meticulously entered in a ledger; and three voluminous ledgers now testify to a brisk financial activity between 1948 and 1966. During this period, Speer had at his disposal a total of over 154,183.34 Deutschmarks.

Through the secret mail, Speer determined which helpers should be rewarded, which relatives or friends should receive presents.[8] Then, in late 1953, there was good news: The West German government released Speer's considerable family fortune. Overnight, the prisoner became a prosperous man. Wolters hoped that Speer could act more generously with the aid of this money. But Speer, who had thriftier aims, told Wolters that this fortune was to be left intact.[9] Nevertheless, the prisoner continued to make generous use of the "tuition account."[10]

Within a very short time, the architectural office in Coesfeld had become a general agency for the "Spandau Outside Organization." A flood of letters began pouring out of the Allied War Criminals' Prison—far more than Wolters would ever have dreamed. "At times, [the mail] kept two of my secretaries busy full-time."[11] The secret correspondence, which continued, unchallenged, until Speer's release from prison, ran to thousands of pages. "In emergencies," Wolters recalls, "the communication lines between the inside of Spandau and the outside world operated as swiftly as the hot line between the White House and the Kremlin."[12]

172

Labels of the three ledgers of the "tuition accounts." The figures show how much money Speer had at his disposal during the years of his imprisonment.

The well-organized office of Speer's zealous helper was very useful for the prisoner when he was writing his memoirs in 1953–54. In early years, he had been accustomed to writing notes, letters, or speech drafts in oversized script; but now, in prison, he had to employ a minute penmanship in order to get as much use as possible out of the available paper. For untrained eyes, the resulting miniature manuscripts were difficult, sometimes even impossible to decipher. Nevertheless, one of Wolters' assistants became so practiced in reading the tiny handwriting of the highly productive prisoner that for fifteen years she was the real "translator" of the secret pages.

Speer recorded his memoirs on all kinds of paper, and the material, under the code name "Aria," was then smuggled piecemeal from Spandau to Coesfeld. The autobiographer seemed to realize what inestimable help he was getting from his former fellow-student and comrade-in-arms. He wanted to express his gratitude in a dedication: "To the true friend of myself and my family."[13]

Fifteen years later, when Speer was reworking his memoirs with the German publisher Wolf J. Siedler and the writer Joachim C. Fest, he must have sensed that such a dedication would hardly appeal to his friend. Speer sidestepped the problem neatly: He published his memoirs with no dedication.

However, when Speer had completed his memoirs in prison, he appointed Wolters administrator of his historigraphic estate —thus repeating something he had done ten years earlier.[14] Dr. Wolters was to get the memoirs published, and the prisoner offered him a number of suggestions. The structure, content, and diction were not to be altered in any way; only the worst stylistic mistakes were to be smoothed out. The reader, Speer felt, should notice that this book had been written under special conditions. Furthermore, Speer wanted his friend to ask the British professor Hugh R. Trevor-Roper of Christ Church College, Oxford, whether he would care to pen a foreword to the memoirs. Speer had a special reason for his choice. In 1945, Trevor-Roper had interrogated Speer at Kransberg Castle.

Later, he had used Speer's statements for his book *Hitler's Last Days*,[15] because he viewed them as a highly objective source. Having secretly read this book in Spandau, Speer felt that Trevor-Roper was the first historian to shed some positive light on him.[16] He no doubt hoped for a benevolent foreword from the renowned Oxford don.

Naturally, for Speer, the passionate calculator, it was imperative that he deal with the problem of the royalties that his memoirs might possibly reap. He generously promised percentages of the profits to everyone involved in the "Aria" enterprise.[17] Subsequently, however, only a few of the prison guards actually enjoyed Speer's magnanimity. When his autobiography became an international best-seller, Hitler's former protégé made generous contributions to *Aktion Sühnezeichen*,[18] an organization striving for the reconciliation of Germans and Jews. Such noble gestures must have been more consistent with his plan of organized self-rehabilitation.

Dr. Wolters felt that anything was justified if it made the prisoner's life easier behind the walls of Spandau. Eventually, when he managed to smuggle not only letters, but also bulkier objects into his friend's cell, he exploited this possibility in order to "add to the supplies sent by the four trustee powers."[19] Pâté de foie gras found its way into the ex-minister's cell, as did splits of French champagne. Russian caviar could likewise be found in the "bulkier deliveries" from Coesfeld. Wolters was astonished that his friend, who ultimately grew accustomed not only to his Coesfeld bank account but also to these luxury articles, became picky. Once, when Wolters sent him pressed caviar, a somewhat less expensive kind, Speer asked him to send only beluga in the future—and it had to be fresh.[20]

The Spandau inmates zealously indulged in a pipe cult, as Speer informed his helper, and this too was supported by the latter. "I've procured unusual [pipes] made of English root woods."[21] "[I've] bought a small Dunhill (145!!!)," Wolters once announced a new "wood delivery": "Looks to be about 3 marks 50. Name removed, gone up in smoke."[22]

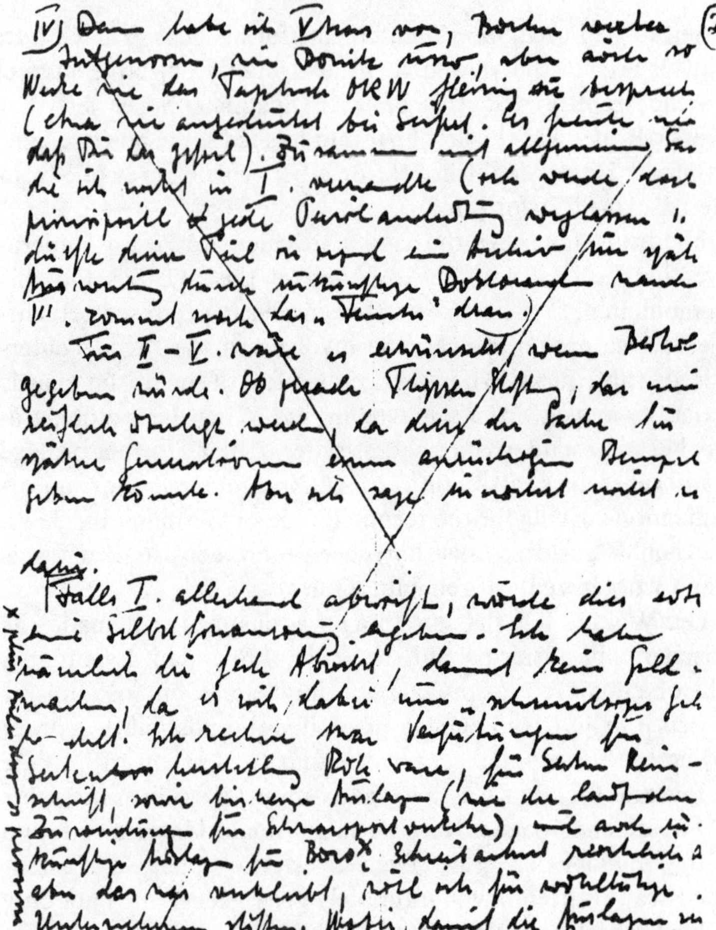

A secret message sent by Speer from Spandau Prison; it contains a detailed discussion of his plans for his complete memoirs. About the money he might receive from their publication, he wrote: "I am determined to make no money from this, since it would be 'dirty' money."

Eventually, the two letter writers got to enjoy their secret correspondence so much that it became a true pleasure for them to encode both major and minor things in such a way that no outsider could understand what was meant. As the volume of mail and freight increased, so did the number of camouflage words. If Speer was planning to send a secret letter, he would indicate the date as follows: "The next astrological [point] is the. . . ."[23] The word "Aria," as already explained, stood for the memoirs. The Spandau diary entries reached Coesfeld as "chips" *(Späne).* Spandau itself was called "Spain," and the prison was euphemistically referred to as a "hotel." And if Speer celebrated yet another holiday with French bubbly, he would laconically confirm its receipt with the onomatopoeic symbol "plöpp."[24]

Generally, their peculiar situation inspired the prisoner and his helper to view many things with black humor, occasionally even with cynical glosses. Once, when Speer complained about the moles and rabbits plaguing his prison garden, Wolters gave vent to ironic and humorous thoughts: "You could certainly get rid of the rabbits," he wrote to his friend in Spandau. "Can't you get hold of a rifle? Or even better, a machine gun. I'm surprised you haven't thought of it yourself. [Once], sixteen inmates of Ivy Bluff [an American prison] went for a walk with such an instrument—they still haven't caught the last one. . . . One might also ask the mole how it managed to get into that well-guarded courtyard. These animals know their business."[25]

Of course, the main goal was to obtain Speer's early release from prison. Efforts in this direction were especially intense during the early nineteen fifties. Wolters contacted Dönitz's lawyer, Dr. Otto Kranzbühler, who was on excellent terms with Konrad Adenauer, Franz Josef Strauss, and other political celebrities. The grand admiral was to be released on October 1, 1956. Speer, and also Wolters, pinned their hopes on this date: "If Speer and Dönitz could be seen as parallel cases, then there was a possibility of having Speer get out of prison together with Dönitz. At least, that was what we believed."[26]

However, the expectations shared by the prisoner and his helper were disappointed. Moreover, Kranzbühler subsequently drew away from them because of certain differences in opinion and also because he—and also Wolters—disagreed with the former Minister of Armaments on how to use his "plan to assassinate Hitler." The lawyer's view, to some extent shared by Wolters, was that it would be wiser if the prisoner dissociated himself from that episode—at least partially. Kranzbühler, who, according to Wolters, was always as terse as he was lucid, explained, "There were other people in the bunker."[27]

The attempts to get Speer "paroled" are documented in a voluminous correspondence. But all efforts failed; and Prisoner Number 5 had to continue his globe-trotting and complete his twenty years. By the time the prison gates opened, at exactly twelve midnight on October 1, 1966, he had figuratively circled almost three quarters of the globe: 31,816 kilometers—about 19,000 miles.[28] He instantly wired his "whereabouts" to his friend: "Please call [for me] thirty-five kilometers [twenty-one miles] south of Guadal[a]jara, Mexico."[29]

In Coesfeld, shortly after his release, Albert Speer was able to receive a kind of "reparation for imprisonment": there were still 25,000 marks left in the tuition account, and Wolters handed him the balance in cash.[30] Eventually, however, the largest "reparation for imprisonment" was organized by Speer himself. Working closely once again with German publisher Wolf J. Siedler, Speer published *The Spandau Diaries*. This book, carefully edited, was a sure-fire hit.[31] After the success of *Inside the Third Reich,* Speer's *Diaries* were a further step in his efforts to make an international name for himself as a decent National Socialist who had seen the light and turned over a new leaf. For Wolters, however, the new book spelled the end of a friendship that had lasted for more than fifty years.

The publication of Speer's memoirs in 1969 had already

rubbed Wolters the wrong way, for he had barely recognized his friend in this book. And he was then extremely indignant at Speer's 1971 interview in *Playboy,* which was excerpted in the German Magazine *Quick.* [32] The man who knew Speer so intimately could not endure witnessing the metamorphosis: After his confessions of guilt in *Inside the Third Reich,* his friend kept presenting himself more and more radically as a criminal, for whom twenty years in prison had been too little. Wolters saw a profound discrepancy between his friend's confessions of guilt and his actual life-style. He knew Speer as a "cheerful person, taking one lovely trip after another . . . and enthusiastically talking about his literary and financial triumphs." [33]

Then, Wolters read parts of *The Spandau Diaries* in the German newspaper *Die Welt am Sonntag,* which had bought the first serial rights for 600,000 marks. [34] Wolters was dumbstruck. After all, he had read the "chips" in the original. It was obvious that his friend, for tactical reasons, kept confessing his guilt for all to hear in order ultimately to confirm his irreproachable past.

When Speer, who never mentions Wolters in any of his books, sent his friend a copy of *The Spandau Diaries,* he offered flimsy excuses for it and speculated that Wolters would put it in his bookcase unread. [35] Wolters reacted with sovereign composure. His letter to Speer was both ironic and humorous:

> I thank you for your book . . . and, . . . as you have understandingly conjectured, I will put it in my bookcase. There, it can stew for a while and prevent me from nit-picking and moralizing.
>
> Needless to say, I forgive you for not "localizing" me in the diaries after your modest restraint in the memoirs. The author of the Journal, the temporary "best friend," and the indefatigable contact for Spandau remains nonexistent. I also accept my "disciplinary transfer" to Coburg. It's a fine town, smacking of parliamen-

tary business committees and [royal] majesties. After all, you might just as easily have picked Kotzenau.†

Chance often makes peculiar leaps. So, someday, we could very possibly run into one another—goodness knows where or how. We should then behave toward each other as you suggested in a letter to Bormann concerning Giesler—i.e., for the Führer's sake, act as if nothing had happened. . . .

And, bristling with sarcasm, Wolters signed the letter "Duke of Coburg."[36]

Wolters probably knew Speer better than anyone else did; and a revealing comment by the friend of Hitler's favorite architect and Minister of Armaments makes it unnecessary for the historian to pass any judicial verdict. "Had I been forced to become the administrator of Speer's literary estate," says Dr. Wolters today, "the true facts would have produced an entirely different picture of Speer in the eyes of history."[37]

---

†"Kotzenau" (the name of the imaginary town) contains the German word "kotzen," a vulgar expression for "vomit."

12

SPEER AND THE FINAL SOLUTION —A NECESSARY CORRECTION

"I shall never forget the account of a Jewish family going to their death: the husband with his wife and children on the way to die," writes Albert Speer in his memoirs.[1] "[They] are before my eyes to this day." He claims he knew nothing about the truth and the details of the Final Solution, although he does admit that "one could have known if one wanted to know."[2] Speer explains, "I had only a vague notion."[3]

Sentences of this kind are supposed to indicate that he had nothing to do with the terrible things for which the terms Final Solution, Holocaust, and concentration camp are now used synonymously. Yet Speer is not quite hewing to the truth, for when he was Inspector General of Buildings for the Reich capital, he was already implementing anti-Semitic policies of the Nazi state. In his last book, *Infiltrations,* Speer devotes an entire chapter to the fate of the Jews in Berlin.[4] Naturally, he conceals the part he played in these events. Thus his statements, as so often, do not merely sound apologetic, they become an outright farce.

After "Reich Crystal Night," on November 9, 1938, the government's anti-Jewish measures intensified. A new law gave the Nazi authorities an instrument, created at the highest level, to forge ahead with the separation of Jews from Germans of Aryan blood. On April 30, 1939, the government promulgated the so-called Law Concerning Rental Situations of Jews.[5] One of the signatories was Reich Chancellor Adolf Hitler.[6]

From then on, a Jewish tenant evicted by his landlord could not fall back upon the Tenant Protection Law if his landlord could prove that the Jew could find lodgings elsewhere.[7] Paragraph 2 of the law made it possible for anyone to break a lease by giving normal legal notice if any of the parties was Jewish.[8] Such a lease could be broken (and this must have been why this paragraph was included) even if it had been worked out for a specific length of time or "stipulated a period of notice longer than the legal one." All that the landlord had to do to press his eviction (according to Paragraph 1 of the law), was to prove that the tenant in question could find lodgings elsewhere.

The passage of this dryly worded law was followed by a forced resettlement of Jews within German cities; their relocation was carried out by the regional housing authorities. It soon took on such vast proportions that these agencies had to set up special "resettlement divisions."[9]

But not in Berlin. Here, the housing offices did not have to assume the burden of resettling Jews. The task was performed by an agency that evidently hoped to profit from the action; this agency was the office of the Inspector General of Buildings for the Reich Capital.[10]

Speer's office created a "Main Resettlement Division" as early as spring 1939; it was headed by Dietrich Clahes, former prime minister of Brunswick. The task of this division was to register all apartments occupied by Jews within the Reich capital, to evict the Jewish tenants, and to allocate these apartments to non-Jewish tenants who would lose or had already lost their own apartments because of Speer's urban renewal project.[11]

The scope of this relocation was such, however, that no single office in the Speer agency could implement it, for, at that time, Berlin had over 23,000 Jewish apartments[12] and over 82,000 Jews.[13] And then there was another problem: Official measures against Jews were actually under the aegis of the SS, in this case its Secret State Police, or Gestapo.[14] Consequently, Speer and the Gestapo had to coordinate their activities in the "Jewish Apartment Eviction Actions."[15]

The arduous labor of registering the Jews and the Jewish apartments was thrust upon the Jewish Congregation Office. "The head of the community was willing to cooperate, since he justifiably assumed that [his office] could mitigate many harsh aspects," reports Dr. Martha Mosse, who was on the staff of the Jewish Congregation Office. "The Congregation Office established . . . a so-called Housing Advisory Service to assist Jewish tenants who were forced out of their homes to find suitable lodgings elsewhere."[16]

Since the outbreak of the war, British airplanes had also been bombing civilian homes. As a result, Speer's Resettlement Division had to do more than reassign formerly Jewish apartments to Gentile tenants who had lost their homes because of Speer's urban renewal. Now the apartments occupied by Jews were "vital to the war effort." Speer made them available for emergencies. Bombed-out Aryans in Berlin could, if they were lucky, move into formerly Jewish apartments. But this necessitated a preliminary measure—as described in the original Speer Journal during the period of January 1 to April 15, 1941. "At the beginning of the year, [we] began to increase the rate of evacuating areas slated for demolition and to move the inhabitants of those areas into Jewish apartments. The Jewish apartments rented by those resettled tenants were cleared and the Jewish tenants crammed into Jewish housing owned by Jews."[17]

There was more and more evicting and cramming, as the holes left by enemy bombs in civilian residential blocks grew bigger and bigger. From January to mid-April 1941, the Inspector General of Buildings took advantage of his Jewish apartment potential to "allocate some thousand rooms for the war effort" to fifty agencies and government offices.[18] But then the Führer requested that one thousand apartments be made available to "Germans who have lost their homes."[19] And Speer ordered more evictions. The evicted Jews were "assigned housing with other Jews by the Jewish Congregation Office."[20] And just six weeks later, the Speer Journal could report that Speer had carried out the Führer's wish one hundred percent. The entry of May 31, 1941, said: "As a result of the Jewish Apartment Eviction Action, 940 apartments were made available to the city of Berlin for emergency purposes, i.e., for lodging members of the German nation made homeless by air raids."[21]

Nevertheless, these resettlements within cities were merely a preliminary stage for measures that became a topic of discussion at the Reich Propaganda Ministry on March 20, 1941. The participants at this meeting were Leopold Gutterer (on Goebbels' staff), Adolf Eichmann (from the Reich Main Security Office), and a representative of Albert Speer (presumably Dietrich Clahes, head of his Resettlement Division). This conference was prompted by information that Goebbels, the intellectual outrider of Nazi anti-Semitism, had just received while lunching with the Führer: There were still 60,000 or 70,000 Jews left in Berlin and, he had been told, it simply would not do "for the capital of the National Socialist Reich still to contain such a high number of Jews."[22]

Goebbels' representative, Leopold Gutterer, got down to business: "Now the Führer did not decide during this conversation that Berlin should be instantly cleared of Jews; however, Dr. Goebbels says he is convinced that a suitable suggestion for their evacuation will certainly be accepted by the Führer."[23] Such reflections seemed consistent with the ideas of Speer's representative, who remarked that "at the moment, twenty thousand apartments in Berlin are being used by Jews. These apartments are needed by Speer as a reserve for relocations caused by major bombing damage and for later relocations from apartments that will have to be torn down as part of the urban renewal of Berlin."[24]

The upshot of this conference was that Eichmann was "asked" to "work out a proposal for evacuating the Jews from Berlin for Dr. Goebbels."[25] However, during the next few months, neither Goebbels nor Eichmann initiated their evacuation plans—as yet. Speer, however, did not remain idle. He got hold of all Jewish properties that were put up for sale in Berlin's western section, an exclusive area for prosperous citizens since the turn of the century. No vacated Jewish house or its lot could be sold until the "Inspector General of Buildings had first checked to see if it fitted in which his program."[26]

However, in the summer of 1941, the Führer's architect needed apartments far more urgently than he needed one-family houses. So, in August, "in accordance with Speer's directives . . . a further evacuation of five thousand Jewish apartments began."[27] This large number of apartments "had to be speedily prepared and then occupied by tenants relocated from condemned apartments. To carry out this task, the Speer agency had to enlarge the apparatus of its Resettlement Division.[28] "As a result of these measures," we read in the Speer Journal, "the Jewish apartments will be used for their specified purposes, and . . . more empty apartments are being made available for emergencies."[29]

Shortly after the war, Hildegard Henschel, the wife of the last head of the Jewish Congregation Office, recalled that a new "resettlement" was scheduled for the end of September 1941. At first, as far as the Jews were concerned, this resettlement seemed to be following the pattern of the previous ones. "[The officials] announced the Christian-owned buildings in which Jews were to be evicted from their apartments; the Congregation Office was supposed to tell the tenants to give up their apartments. The Congregation Office was [also] ordered to make housing available for the evicted tenants or else relocate them to other apartments in Jewish buildings."[30]

But this forced resettlement never took place. October 15, 1941, became a day of horror for the Jewish tenants who had been told to move. The moment darkness fell, two Gestapo men

Speer je eine Stunde lang durch die Ausstellung ge-
führt.

Der Besuch der Ausstellung war ein außerordentlich
reger bereits am ersten Tage, so daß festgestellt
werden konnte, daß das Interesse hier weitaus stärker
war, als es bei den bisherigen Ausstellungen des Generalbauinspektors der Fall war.

In Lissabon war Herr Speer während seines Auf-
enthaltes am 8. und 9. November Gast des Deutschen
Gesandten Freiherr v. H o y n i n g e n - H u e n e.

Am 10. November fuhr Herr S p e e r mit Professor B r u g m a n n und Dr. W o l t e r s im Wagen
von Lissabon zurück nach Berlin. Der Weg führte durch
Portugal und Spanien über Coimbra-Bussaco-Salamanca
und Burgos in drei Tagen nach Biarritz. Von hier aus
fuhr Herr Speer mit Professor Brugmann nach Nevers, um
Major B r ü c k n e r zu besuchen. Am folgenden Tage
ging die Fahrt bereits weiter über Heidelberg nach
Berlin, wo er am 15. November nachmittags eintraf.

Inzwischen war Dr. W o l t e r s weiter nach
Paris gefahren, um dort mit dem Verleger F l a m a r i o n
über ein Speer-Buch und mit der Propagandastaffel über
die für das nächste Jahr geplante Speer-Ausstellung
zu verhandeln.

In der Zeit vom 18. Oktober bis 2. November wurden
in Berlin rund 4 500 Juden evakuiert. Dadurch wurden
weitere 1000 Wohnungen für Bombengeschädigte frei und
vom Generalbauinspektor zur Verfügung gestellt. Die
Wohnungen werden später wieder zur Unterbringung von
Kriegsmietern bereitgestellt.

Am 7. November waren von den Schadenstellen, die
vom 1. November 1940 ab in Berlin gemeldet waren, rd.
77% wiederhergestellt.

Am Dienstag, dem 18. November lud Herr S p e e r
seine gesamte Gefolgschaft in das Kleine Haus des
Staatstheaters ein, wo unter großer Begeisterung das

Entry in the original Office Journal about the first deportation of
Jews from Berlin.

186

~~Nachdem der Generalbauinspektor die Umsied-~~
lungsangelegenheiten abgegeben hatte, berichtete
Vizepräsident C l a h e s abschliessend über die
Arbeiten der Hauptabteilung Umsiedlung für die Zeit
vom 1.Februar 1939 bis zum 15. November 1942.
In diesem Bericht heisst es u.a.: Aufgabe der Um-
siedlungsabteilung war es, sämtliche im Gebiet der
Reichshauptstadt vorhandenen Judenwohnungen zu er-
fassen, sie zu räumen und den Mietern zuzuweisen, die
durch Maßnahmen der Neugestaltung ihre Wohnungen ver-
loren hatten. Insgesamt wurden erfasst 23.765 jüdische
Wohnungen. Der Kreis der zu Betreuenden wurde auf Vor-
schlag des Generalbauinspektors durch Führerbefehl er-
weitert auf kriegsversehrte Soldaten, Ritterkreuzträger
und mit dem EK I ausgezeichnete Mannschaften und Unter-
offiziere. Von den erfassten Judenwohnungen wurden 9000
Wohnungen vergeben. Die Zahl der umgesiedelten Personen
betrug 75 000. 2600 Wohnungen wurden dabei völlig
neu instandgesetzt. Für die Unterbringung etwaiger
Bombengeschädigter wurden 3700 teilmöblierte Wohnun-
~~gen bereitgestellt.~~

    Baudirektor H e l m c k e meldete, daß sämtliche
Operationsbunker für die Städtischen Krankenanstalten
der Reichshauptstadt übergeben wurden.

    Am 26. Oktober berichtete Oberst K o l l , der
Chef für das Instandsetzungswesen beim neuen General
für Motorisierung, über das Nebeneinander der ver-
schiedenen Dienststellen, die sich mit Angelegenheiten
der Kraftfahrzeugindustrie befassten. Anschliessend
trugen General L e e b und Oberst L ö h r über
die Vereinfachung des Heereswaffenamtes vor. General
T h o m a s kam mit Generalleutnant B a r k h a u -
s e n , Generalmajor T h ü n i s s e n und den
Oberstleutnanten v. N i c o l a i und W a g n e r
zum Minister, um über den Abzug von Arbeitskräften
aus französischen Rüstungsbetrieben vorzutragen.

A report to Speer on the evictions and resettlements of Jews
ordered by his agency.

suddenly appeared in each apartment to be evacuated and ordered the family to pack necessities and follow them.[31] These Jews were taken to a gathering place that, at the orders of the Gestapo, had been set up in the synagogue on Levetzowstrasse. After remaining there for three days, they were marched in a long procession through the city to Grunewald railroad station. Children and the feeble were brought there in trucks.[32] Some of the Jews may have sensed what lay in store for them—rumors about an evacuation had been circulating for several days—but no one had expected it to come this soon. According to Hildegard Henschel, "the Jews were all the more surprised; they did not resist, but many people put an end to their despair by taking Veronal."[33]

On October 18, 1941, the first trainload of Berlin Jews left Grunewald Station and headed east. Countless trains were to follow.[34] The Propaganda Minister's deportation plans, which had been merely discussed in his office seven months earlier, had now become a reality.

Speer too was informed of the evacuations. Moreover, he profited from them. "From October 18 to November 2, some 4,500 Jews were evacuated from Berlin," says the original Speer Office Journal. "As a result, one thousand more apartments for bombed-out [Germans] are vacant and are being made available by the Inspector General of Buildings."[35] Evidently, these places were quickly occupied—often by Party members who asked Speer to get them large apartments.[36] Indeed, more and more people were given Jewish apartments by Speer, since, at Hitler's orders, he had "to find housing for people who had been seriously injured in the war, and for highly deserving soldiers of this war."[37]

In any case, Inspector General of Buildings Speer needed more housing. While trainloads of Jews were rolling from Berlin to Lodz, Minsk, Kaunas, and Riga,[38] Speer "initiated the third major eviction [of Jews] from the Jewish apartments at the end of November." The results of this action were considerable: three thousand apartments.[39]

In his last book, Speer claims he had little knowledge of what was happening to the Jews of Berlin: "When I recall the fate of the Jews of Berlin, I am overcome by an unavoidable feeling of failure and inadequacy. Often, during my daily drive to my architectural office and, after February 1942, en route to my ministry on the city highway, I could see . . . crowds of people on the platform of nearby Nikolassee Railroad Station. I knew that these must be Berlin Jews who were being evacuated. I am sure that an oppressive feeling struck me as I drove past. I presumably had a sense of somber events."[40]

These lines do not express merely an apologia by a man who evaded the truth because he simply did not care to know it.[41] Clahes had seen to it that Speer was informed of the activities of his Resettlement Division.[42] Speer's later claims that he had no precise knowledge of those things sound hollow when we read a document submitted to him in November 1942. Clashes was resigning from the Resettlement Division because of overwork, and this was his final report to his superior.[43] It states among other things that "a total of 23,765 Jewish apartments have been vacated. . . . Of these Jewish apartments, 9,000 have been reassigned. The number of resettled persons runs to 75,000."[44]

In Nuremberg, to be sure, Albert Speer had already forgotten his resettlement activities. He testified—and this was quite in keeping with the facts—that in 1941 and 1942 the Jews had been transferred to armaments factories "in order to have work vital to the war effort, an occupation vital to the war effort, and with this occupation vital to the war effort they could escape the evacuation that was already operating full force."[45] However, Speer, applying a bit of historical cosmetics, described their situation as follows: "These Jews were completely free, and their families were still in their apartments."[46]

When he was Minister of Armaments, Speer's jurisdiction became so vast that he must have had more than hearsay knowledge about the places to which the Jews were being sent and where these prisoners—in part—helped manufacture armaments items. He must have had direct knowledge since he kept himself informed about the conditions of the concentration camps. His interest, it seems, was prompted by his dismayed observation when he personally inspected the Mauthausen concentration camp on March 30, 1943.[47] Here, where the inmates were laboring for his armaments machinery, housing and other constructions were being built with a generous use of material. Yet, since construction material was growing ever scarcer because of the war, Speer was having terrible problems getting hold of material for agencies whose construction projects were vital to the war effort. Hence, the generous use of construction material at Mauthausen struck him as sheer waste.

Minister Speer instantly notified SS-Reichsführer Himmler: "We now have a shortage of not only iron and wood but also manpower for building armaments factories for the immediate needs of the front lines; yet, on the occasion of my inspection of the Mauthausen concentration camp, I was forced to see that the SS is implementing projects that strike me as more than lavish under present-day conditions."[48] He certainly did not— Speer went on—underestimate the task assigned to the concentration camps within the framework of the war effort. But he felt that the SS could not continue its constructions along the same lines. "We must therefore carry out a new planning program for the construction of concentration camps in terms of utmost efficiency, the use of the least possible amount of [material and labor], and the greatest success for the *present-day* demands of the armaments industry; i.e., we must immediately switch to a primitive construction method."[49] In order to learn about the situation in the other concentration camps, Speer proposed that one of his assistants, together with a representative of Himmler's, "should inspect all concentration camps *in situ.*"[50]

Speer's letter to Himmler also passed through the hands of SS-Obergruppenführer Oswald Pohl, who, as manager of the SS-factories, was an ambitious competitor of the Minister of

Armaments. Pohl regarded Speer's letter as "a bit much." The agitated Pohl went on: "Reich Minister Speer is acting as if we were building on a large scale in the concentration camps without his knowledge and without any awareness of the times. He is concealing the fact that *every* construction project in the concentration camps has been registered in accordance with regulations and that he himself issued his authorization on February 2, 1943. . . . The SS-Reichsführer can therefore see that Reich Minister Speer has been informed in detail about all construction projects and that he has also authorized them."[51] Pohl felt it would be a big mistake to adopt primitive building methods. With 160,000 prisoners, they were already struggling against epidemics and a high mortality rate "because the housing for inmates, including sanitary facilities, is completely inadequate."[52]

There is no telling what negative consequences the more primitive constructions would have had for the prisoners. In any event, Speer issued an edict in March 1943, ordering that no more permanent structures were to be put up. The inmate housing had to be makeshift. The outer and inner walls were to be lightweight, and there was to be no plastering inside or outside.[53]

However, Speer changed his mind when he read the report on Auschwitz by his two assistants,[54] who must have found catastrophic sanitary conditions there. Speer quickly wrote to Himmler and made building material available—iron, cast-iron pipes, water pipes, and round bar steel—especially for construction at Auschwitz.[55] However, conditions in other concentration camps must have been presented to him in a more favorable light. For, in a handwritten addendum to his letter to Himmler, Speer remarked: "I am delighted that the inspection of the other concentration camps resulted in a highly positive picture."[56]

This episode is described in Speer's final book, *Infiltration.* Granted, a historian must allow an active witness of contemporary events to depict them from his vantage point. However, it

Perſönlicher Stab Reichsführ
Schriſ : wo ung
Akt. Nr. Geh. / **101/23**

Berlin-Charlottenburg 2
~~BERLIN XX~~, den 3o. 5.43
~~XXXXXXXXXX~~verl. Jebensstr.

DER REICHSMINISTER
FÜR
BEWAFFNUNG UND MUNITION
GB 26/1-1oo27 g

𝔊𝔢𝔥𝔢𝔦𝔪!

An den
Herrn Reichsführer ₷₷ und Chef
der Deutschen Polizei H i m m l e r

B e r l i n   SW   68
Prinz-Albrecht-Str. 8

Betr.: Baueisenkontingent für ₷₷, insbesondere KZ-
         Lager Auschwitz.

Lieber Parteigenosse   H i m m l e r !

Auf Grund der vorliegenden Berichte und der
Besichtigung des KZ-Lagers Auschwitz durch meine Herren
Desch und Sander bin ich bereit, über die im III/43
zur Verfügung gestellte Baueisenmenge in Höhe von
450 moto für den Bedarf im Reichsgebiet und 18o moto
für den Bedarf in den angeschlossenen und besetzten Ge-
bieten einmalig folgende Mengen zuzuteilen:

1.) 1 ooo t Baueisenbezugsrechte.

2.) 1 ooo t Gußrohre, für die die ₷₷ aus ihrem
     Gesamtkontingent 3oo t Eisenbezugsrechte zur
     Verfügung stellt.

3.) Rd. 1oo t Wasserleitungsrohre 1/2 " aus
     dem Verfügungslager des GB-Bau in Hamm.

4.) Rundstahl 8 - 2o mm aus Hartstahl in der
     erforderlichen Menge.

A letter from Speer to Himmler concerning the concentration camp at Auschwitz. In his last book, *Infiltrations,* Speer describes this letter as a report by SS-Obergruppenführer Pohl and claims that his own handwritten addition—including his signature—was made by Pohl (cf. p. 194).

192

- 2 -

Diese Baueisenmengen sind nur für den Ausbau
der KZ-Lager, insbesondere Auschwitz, zu verwenden.
Für zusätzliche Behelfsbaumaßnahmen für die Aufstel-
lung neuer Divisionen der Waffen-ꜩ kann ich leider
keine weitere Baueisenmengen zuteilen. Der Bedarf
muß aus den im Rahmen des Gesamtbaueisenkontingentes
des GB-Bau an die ꜩ zugeteilten Mengen entnommen werden. Die Einzelfragen der Zuteilung werden zwischen
Ihren Dienststellen und meiner Rohstoffstelle gere-
gelt. Die Beschaffung der Bezugscheine für 1 ooo t
Gußrohre, sowie der Versand der Wasserleitungsrohre
ist bereits in die Wege geleitet.

Hei H tler!

193

is more than disconcerting to find that documents have been falsified. Probably to ward off any suspicion that he knew too much of the truth, Speer writes: "As revealed in a handwritten addendum in Pohl's report to Himmler, I was told at the same time that the inspection of the other concentration camps resulted in a highly positive picture."[57] Speer the "historian" has misquoted his own handwritten comment from one of his own letters, and he identifies his letter as a report penned by his rival Pohl. Speer does not even recognize his own penmanship. What are we to think?

Once the concentration camps had been inspected, Speer was given a "detailed report" by his assistants, as he told the SS-Reichsführer.[58] In Nuremberg, however, he forgot this, just as he forgot his "Jewish apartment eviction actions." In 1946, Speer claimed that he had known as little about the concentration camps "as any other minister [had known] about the V-2."[59]

Decades later, when Speer set about writing his memoirs, he obviously had a hard time dealing with the problem of the Nazi atrocities. He had forgotten and repressed too many things. His publisher, Wolf Jobst Siedler, combed the manuscript in vain for some position on Crystal Night, November 9, 1938, when blazing fires and shattered windows had announced an ominous future for the Jews. Speer, who had been in Berlin that day, said nothing about the event in his memoirs. Siedler told Speer: "You have to write something about it. You *must* have felt something! And even if you felt nothing, then at least say so!"[60] Speer committed to paper what he had seen—charred beams, collapsed portions of facades, burned-out walls—and felt: "The smashed panes of shop windows offended *my sense of middle-class order* [author's emphasis]. . . . But I accepted what had happened rather indifferently."[61] Still, Speer manages to compensate for this avowal of indifference. He says that his old friend Karl Hanke came to him in summer 1944 and warned him not to inspect a certain concentration camp in Upper

Silesia. For Hanke had seen things there about which he could not and dared not speak.[62] Speer writes: "I did not investigate —I did not want to know what was happening there. Hanke must have been speaking of Auschwitz."[63] Speer called his failure "deliberate blindness," and he announced: "Because I failed at that time, I still feel, to this day, responsible for Auschwitz in a wholly personal sense."[64] This was nothing more than a literary gesture that was bound to arouse his readers' sympathy. What could be more honorable than taking responsibility for crimes one knew nothing about?

Nevertheless, Speer realized that the foundation of his honorableness as a contrite and converted National Socialist was his ignorance of "what was really beginning on November 9, 1938, and what ended in Auschwitz and Majadanek" (Speer).[65] Consequently, the ex-Minister of Armaments never once accused himself of anything without simultaneously asseverating that he had ultimately known nothing.

This verbal tightrope walk between self-accusal and apologia sometimes became grotesque. In 1968, Speer was subpoenaed as a witness in the trial of former SS-guards of the Dora concentration camp. The court had established that in this underground factory for A-4 rockets, prisoners had been hanged "as a warning measure" to discourage sabotage. Speer had visited Dora on December 10, 1943,[66] a time when preparations were being made to execute inmates "as a warning measure." The capo of the crematory, who was also a witness at the trial, testified that Speer had prevented the planned executions. Speer, however, could not remember his good deed—he dared not remember it, for that would have been tantamount to admitting that he had indeed been directly confronted with the atrocities of the Nazi regime.[67] His honorable stance required that he forget his good deed.

In 1977, Speer took a further step within the framework of his self-accusations when he stated: "I still see my guilt as residing chiefly in the approval of the persecution of the Jews and the murder of millions of them."[68] When asked how he could have approved of something he knew nothing about, he elucidated the matter in this way: His had been "approval through ignorance."[69]

Once, however, Speer's foundation of honorableness seemed to quake seriously, and his white cloak of ignorance about the Holocaust nearly turned pitch-black. In 1971, the American historian Erich Goldhagen appeared to be able to prove that the former Minister of Armaments and now world-famous author of best-sellers had known more than he was willing to admit.[70] On October 6, 1943, Heinrich Himmler had addressed a meeting of the Gauleiters and Reichsleiters in Poznan; the SS-Reichsführer specifically discussed the topic of the Final Solution, even though it was taboo. One of the passages that Goldhagen quoted from that speech went as follows:

> I must ask you only to listen to what I tell you in this group and never to speak about it. We were asked: What about the women and children? I made up my mind to find a clear solution here too. You see, I did not feel I had the right to exterminate the men—i.e. kill them or have them killed—while allowing the children to grow up and take revenge upon our sons and grandsons. We had to reach the difficult decision of making this nation vanish from the face of the earth.[71]

Goldhagen comments: "One of the men to whom Himmler revealed the 'great secret' was Albert Speer." For, the American professor concludes, Speer attended this conference of the Gauleiters and Reichsleiters. Speer talks about it in *Inside the Third Reich,*[72] but omits any mention of Himmler's speech. Yet Himmler actually addressed Speer directly:

> I have cleared out large Jewish ghettoes in the rear areas. In Warsaw, we had four weeks of street fighting in a Jewish ghetto. Four weeks! We destroyed about

seven hundred bunkers there. This entire ghetto was producing fur coats, dresses, and the like. Whenever we tried to get at it in the past, we were told: Stop! You're interfering with war production! Stop! Armaments factory! Of course, this has nothing to do with Party Comrade Speer. You can do nothing in this connection. It is this portion of alleged armaments factories that Party Comrade Speer and I intend to clean out together during the next few weeks and months. We will do this as unsentimentally as all things must be done in the fifth year of the war—unsentimentally but with a large heart for Germany.[73]

Speer, as Goldhagen points out, does not deny participating at this meeting, but "he says nothing, simply nothing, about Himmler's speech, much less about Himmler's presence. He secretly washed his hands clean of the blood of those to whose deaths he contributed, and he remorsefully beats his breast with seemingly clean hands: 'I am a murderer, even though I neither saw, nor heard, nor knew about, the deaths of my victims.' It is, to put it mildly, a despicable spectacle."[74]

When Speer read this apparently cogent accusation, he was "horrified."[75] He promptly set to work rebutting Goldhagen's charges—though not without first reaffirming his "responsibility for these events," i.e., the "final solution."[76]

In his refutal, he offered a wealth of data, facts, and figures, of which only the most important can be cited here. He and his staffers, says Speer, gave their speeches in the morning of that day; Himmler did not speak until the afternoon. Since Speer had annoyed the Gauleiters with his own speech, and since he and his people were only guest speakers anyway, "there was no reason to ask Bormann to let us be present that afternoon."[77] Speer claims that he left the conference in the afternoon. It was quite customary, Speer goes on, for speakers to apostrophize fellow party members, even if they were not present. Furthermore, says Speer, some seventy people were sitting in the large room, so that "a speaker [could] not really tell who the individual participants were."[78] Hence, Himmler could not have seen whether or not Speer was in the audience.

Apparently, however, Speer did not feel that his rebuttal in "Reply to Erich Goldhagen" was adequate; he seems to have required a greater catharsis in his own eyes and the eyes of the public. This time he was aided by his former assistant, Walter Rohland ("Panzer-Rohland"). The latter could remember precisely that during the afternoon of October 6, 1943, he and Speer had left Poznan before Himmler's speech and driven off to Rastenburg. Speer explains: "There is no possibility of a mistake [says Rohland], since this was his only visit to Poznan; besides, [Rohland says that] the drive with me was unforgettable."[79] Rohland confirmed these details in a sworn affidavit.[80] And Ministerial Councilor Harry Siegmund, who was "involved in the protocol and organization of the conference," stated in an affidavit: "I remember precisely that Albert Speer drove off in his car shortly after lunch."[81]

The thus exonerated ex-Minister of Armaments published both affidavits in "Addendum to Reply to Erich Goldhagen."[82] His honorable character was saved; it once again rested on a solid foundation.

As Albert Speer writes in *Inside the Third Reich:* "Those who ask me are fundamentally expecting me to offer justifications. But I have none. No apologies are possible."[83]

AFTERWORD

Speer's books, especially *Inside the Third Reich,* lay claim to describing history. More precisely, Hitler's former friend and protégé wanted to depict the history of the Third Reich in terms of his own history. One must admit that, with his efforts, he has made history.

However, Albert Speer's intention lay elsewhere. He wanted to warn future generations and also, as a writer, prevent a recurrence of what had happened in Germany between 1933 and 1945. In 1954, when he believed he had completed the first full-length version of his memoirs, he asked his friend and former assistant Rudolf Wolters: "Will people realize that my aim was not so much to write history as to warn them of the future?"[1]

In the foreword to the published version of *Inside the Third Reich,* Speer tells his readers: "I have set forth what I experienced and the way I regard it today."[2] He thus virtually gave himself carte blanche to depict himself and all the others who together with him had created the physiognomy of the Third Reich—depict them as he saw them from a hindsight of twenty-five years and as he wanted to see them. His self-assigned "moral task" has nothing to do with historiography.

For two years, he was assisted in his work by the publisher Wolf Jobst Siedler and the writer Joachim C. Fest, who guided his ideas and his pen by asking "urgent questions."[3] The result was an image of the Nazi dictatorship and the part that Speer had played in it—a picture that historians had been sketching for years under the influence of Speer's self-portrait at the Nuremberg Tribunal.

This picture appealed to everyone. It appealed to Speer's publisher and to his adviser, who wanted to solidify the image of the past in terms of accessible and customary historiography; and what could be more solid than testimony by a witness who had demonstrated his own integrity! Speer's picture also appealed to many historians because it confirmed their view of the Nazi past—even though other historians were disappointed, since *Inside the Third Reich* did not turn out to be much of a factual source. The book delighted the reading public, which, hungry for sensation, eagerly awaited the inside report by a crony of Hitler's. Speer was pleased that his legend had received an expert's (Joachim Fest's) blessing and was accepted by the broader public.

The success of the memoirs put their author and his helpers in the right—even though (or precisely because?) in many respects Speer's actual role in the Nazi state was misrepresented. Many things were embellished, a few essential facts were omitted or retrospectively interpreted in such a way that Albert Speer could present himself to the German public after cleansing himself of the factual fallout of the Nazi regime.

However, Hitler's friend looks quite different to a historian who does a thorough job of research and checks the sources critically. If we carefully investigate Hitler's unique relationship with his favorite architect, if we comb the relevant documents and listen to eye witness accounts, we learn that things were not quite as Speer depicts them today. Throughout his life, Speer could not escape the spell that Hitler had cast upon him. And the Führer himself appeared to be so deeply involved with his protégé that he could not shake off the fascination, even up to the point of his suicide. True, most historians, along with their chief witness, Speer, believe that they can discern cracks in this friendship. Yet no true breach ever really developed. Even after Hitler's death, his minion maintained his peculiar love-hate ambivalence toward him. This was felt very keenly by

Wolters, a man who knew Speer very well, when he read what his friend wrote about his relationship to Hitler in his memoirs. Wolters then reproached Speer: "Hitler? One can feel him on almost every page as the gravitational mass dominating you."[4]

Speer's favorite role—as Hitler's master builder—comes across somewhat differently in the sources, documents, and eyewitness accounts than in *Inside the Third Reich.* Nothing could be further from the truth than the image of Speer as an architect with purely artistic ambitions, absorbed in his work, wearing a white smock, perched at his drawing board, designing one project after another for his supreme client. On the contrary: Speer very quickly realized that his position as Hitler's special architect involved practicable power as well, and Speer quickly learned how to wield it. Everyone who tried to curb his ambitions learned about Speer's power the hard way. They had to experience his methods first-hand: his skillful use of intrigues and machinations to make his way to the top. Speer's position as Hitler's premier architect was his novitiate for higher orders, and ultimately the highest orders in the Nazi hierarchy.

His consecration came sooner than he himself thought possible. The sudden death of Fritz Todt, Hitler's first Minister of Munitions, placed Speer at the top of an apparatus that soon performed crucial military functions. Perhaps, on that fateful February 8, 1942, Speer hesitated briefly before laying aside his architectural ambitions for his new office. However, the facts show that, once in office, he unhesitatingly grabbed the full wealth of power that his patron Hitler was willing to give him.

In his inconspicuous but coldly grasping way, Speer swiftly managed to fortify the vast authority he gained as weapons-maker of the Third Reich. He nonchalantly cleaned up the chaos of rivalries in the armaments industry and rearranged the areas of responsibility within the bureaucratically structured war industry. In order to put his credo into action—i.e., to supply his Führer with the weapons necessary for the ultimate German victory—Speer gradually got his hands on all parts of the armaments industry and reorganized them in terms of his vision of total efficiency.

To implement his plans, Speer—eschewing sentimentality—employed any means and methods that the dictatorial system gave him. Forced laborers from the Nazi-occupied territories were thrust into the factories along with inmates of concentration camps; and the millions of laborers were pushed to absolute discipline and utmost productivity by threats of the most severe punishments.

It was with such draconic management that the minister created what was known inside and outside Germany as the "German armaments miracle"—and it brought him a reputation that made his position within the Nazi leadership well-nigh unassailable. It comes as no surprise that this successful man, who was also certain of his Führer's tacit friendship, dared to believe that he could reach the highest rung in the Nazi state as Hitler's legitimate successor; or that the portrait, drawn by most historians and especially by Speer himself, of an unpolitical man who was "only a technocrat," does not stand up to critical scrutiny.

Speer's hopes were not fulfilled. Nevertheless, he did not surrender his claim to power even when the collapse of Nazi Germany became inevitable. One cannot reject the thesis that Speer could picture a Germany without Hitler, but only with Speer in a leading position. Speer clung hard to his claim, even when a new beginning lay ahead for Germany after the end of the war.

And the end also came for the powerful Minister of Armaments, despite all his stick-it-out speeches and his sermons of confidence in an ultimate German victory. Something that he had never even dreamed of happened: Speer found himself being tried in a court of law for his participation in the Nazi dictatorship—a complicity that had been active in more ways than one.

Even in this almost hopeless situation, Speer once again proved to be a pragmatist and tactician of the first rank by exploiting entirely on his own behalf the unique and gigantic legal spectacle created by the victors. Many of his colleagues were still fighting a long-lost battle, blaming others for their own crimes and clinging blindly to their historical missions. But Speer not only dissociated himself from these men, he even switched sides in his *mea culpa* stance—and he did so before a worldwide audience—one that failed to notice that he had reduced it to witnessing a shrewdly calculated change of positions. The public was astonished to see—and not without sympathy—that an accomplice and witness had achieved critical insight, especially since he was able to convince the world that he had known nothing about the atrocities of the Nazi regime, including the Final Solution.

Speer was sentenced to twenty years in prison, and his pilgrimage to Spandau was as demonstratively penitential as his earlier assumption of responsibility. However, the insignificance thereby thrust upon him was something that he could not and would not harmonize with his claim to his lifetime goal— a new and suitable role in the eyes of the public. And so, shortly after entering Spandau, he began to prepare for his rebirth.

Perhaps this unswerving pursuit of a goal explains how he was able to achieve something inconceivable: his endurance of two decades in prison with no physical or mental damage. Of course, we should not forget that he was given an enormous amount of outside help, such as none of his fellow inmates received.

Partly because of this assistance, Speer was able, just three years after his release, to establish a position whose foundation he had already laid during the Nuremberg Trial. By the time his memoirs were published, Speer was recognized as a reliable informant about the history of the Third Reich—by the media, by historians, and by scholars in other disciplines.

Under the most disparate conditions, a chameleonlike opportunism enabled Albert Speer to pursue three extraordinary careers and to achieve success in each one: as an architect, as Nazi Minister of Armaments, and as a witness writing for posterity.

During these three careers, he hogged the limelight more and more, manipulating it as effectively as the massed searchlights in the "cathedral of light" that he invented. If we look at his achievements, setting aside moral considerations, then we would have to credit Speer with genius—a genius motivated by his drive to become and remain a historic figure.

In the long run, however, historians will not and cannot be satisfied with Albert Speer's self-portrait: Too much of it is myth, legend; too little of it historical truth. We have no choice but to call Speer's writings the most cunning apologia by any leading figure of the Third Reich.

SPEER AND THE HISTORY OF
THIS BOOK

This book describes history and, like any book, it also has a history. Usually, the story of a book's publication has little bearing on its value. This time, however, the author feels that he should not hold back at least one part of the history of his book that will clarify the methods Albert Speer employed to maintain his public image.

While doing the research necessary for this volume, the author came upon the original copy of the so-called *Speer Chronik* (Office Journal) in the private archive of Speer's former staffer, Dr. Rudolf Wolters. Wolters had maintained the Journal from 1941 to 1944. In 1964, as detailed in the first chapter of this book, Wolters made a number of important deletions. He by no means intended to manipulate history forever; he only wanted to save former colleagues from possible criminal proceedings and his former superior from further prosecution. Such possibilities were not out of the question, since, as we can glean undeniably from the document revised by Wolters, Speer and one of his assistants were directly involved, in Berlin from 1939 to 1942, with the beginnings of the process that ultimately ended in the Holocaust. Furthermore, the correspondence between Speer and Wolters—described in the first chapter of this book—could also be found in these files. Speer's letters indicate that shortly after the German publication of *Inside the Third Reich,* he wanted to prevent any surfacing of the original Office Journal in a public archive.

Wolters, from the very first, planned to release the documents for publication as soon as none of the people therein mentioned could be harmed by them. By coincidence, Wolters felt that the time for their release had come in 1980, when this author was to interview him.

Dr. Wolters handed the author these documents for evaluation—with the justifiable stipulation that their overall context and background be presented in unadulterated form. The author felt it was absolutely necessary to hear Speer's side of the story, because, during a detailed interview in 1979, Speer, for obvious reasons, had said nothing about the original Office Journal or the correspondence pertaining to it. When the author questioned him about the original documents in 1980, Speer claimed to know nothing about the existence of the original text of the Office Journal or about the letters. Nevertheless, he offered no objections to an evaluation of these documents. When the author then asked him, for caution's sake, whether Speer might take legal action against Dr. Wolters, Speer replied that he would do nothing of the kind: "How could I? After all, Dr. Wolters helped me for twenty years."[1]

But Speer changed his mind. A short time later, he threatened to sue his friend Wolters. He even went so far as to announce his alleged rights to the documents in an advertisement that he placed in the German publishing newspaper, *Börsenblatt des Deutschen Buchhandels.* Apparently, Speer was trying to prevent publication of this book. The author and his publisher had the matter checked by lawyers, who concluded that Speer had no legal grounds for any such lawsuit.

Speer's sudden death in London on September 1, 1981, saved him from the necessity of taking a position on the picture of Speer that is offered in this book.

NOTES

ABBREVIATIONS

BA	Bundesarchiv = Federal Archives of West Germany
BDC	Berlin Document Center
CC	Concentration Camp
D	Diary
DAF	Deutsche Arbeitsfront = German Labor Front
DAZ	*Deutsche Allgemeine Zeitung*
FHQ	Führer Headquarters
GBA	Generalbevollmächtigter für den Arbeitseinsatz = Commissioner of Labor
GB Bau	Generalbevollmächtigter für die Regelung der Bauwirtschaft = Commissioner of Construction
GBI	Generalbauinspektor für die Reichshauptstadt = Inspector General of Buildings for the Capital of the Reich
GWU	*Geschichte in Wissenschaft und Unterricht*
HZ	*Historische Zeitschrift*
IfZ	Institut für Zeitgeschichte = Institute of Modern History
IMT	International Military Tribunal (Nuremberg)

KTB	Kriegstagebuch = War Diary
NPL	Neue politische Literatur
NSDAP	Nationalsozialistische Deutsche Arbeiterpartei = National Socialist German Workers' Party
NSDStB	Nationalsozialistischer Deutscher Studentenbund = National Socialist German Student Alliance
OKW	Oberkommando der Wehrmacht = Supreme Command of the Wehrmacht
OT	Organization Todt = Todt Organization
RGBl	*Reichsgesetzblatt*
R	Retaliatory Weapon
SA	Sturm-Abteiling = Storm Division
SD	Sicherheitsdienst = Security Service
SS	Schutzstaffel
TH	Technische Hochschule = Technical School
VB	*Völkischer Beobachter*
VSWG	*Vierteljahrschrift für Sozial- und Wirtschaftsgeschichte*
VHZG	*Vierteljahrshefte für Zeitgeschichte*
ZfdGJ	*Zeitschrift für die Geschichte der Juden*
ZS	Zeugenschrifttum = Testimonies
ZS SP	Zeugenschrifttum Spandau = Testimonies, Spandau

The call numbers of some microfilms at the West German Federal Archives in Koblenz and the Institut für Zeitgeschichte, Munich, as well as several other documents have not been listed individually in the bibliography or in the list of sources.

The quoted passages are in the following section of notes.

1. Birth of a Myth

1. BA R 3/1557. Speer's speech to the Gau leaders in Munich, 2/24/42.
2. BA R 3/1551, fol. 14. Speer's appeal to the men in German technology, New Year's 1945.
3. BA R 3/1557, fol. 13, 14. Speer's memorandum on the armaments situation, 1/30/45.
4. Sworn affidavit by Hermann Giesler, 4/22/81.

5. Cf. pp. 103–105 and 132–138.
6. Albert Speer, *Inside the Third Reich* (New York: Macmillan, 1970), p. 538 (henceforth cited as *ITR*).
7. *Ibid.,* p. 579.
8. IfZ Ed 99/13. Albert Speer, *Die weitere Entwicklung des deutschen Problems in Europa.*
9. Cf. Albert Speer, *ITR.*
10. A good survey of the variety of opinions about the Speer case is provided by Adelbert Reif's collection of source material and essays: *Albert Speer. Kontroversen um ein deutsches Phänomen* (Munich, 1978; cited henceforth as *Kontroversen*).
11. John Kenneth Galbraith, *Economics, Peace and Laughter* (New York: New American Library, 1981), p. 290.
12. *Ibid.*
13. *Ibid.,* p. 293.
14. *Ibid.,* p. 295.
15. *Ibid.,* p. 294.
16. Cf. pp. 123ff.
17. IMT, Vol. XVI, p. 479.
18. J. C. Fest, "Albert Speer und die technische Unmoral," *Das Gesicht des Dritten Reiches* (Munich, 1963), pp. 271–285.
19. *Ibid.,* p. 272.
20. *Ibid.*
21. Cf. M. Broszat, *Der Staat Hitlers: dtv Weltgeschichte des 20. Jahrhunderts,* Vol. 9 (1969), p. 439; also S. Haffner, *Anmerkungen zu Hitler* (Munich, 1978), pp. 57ff.
22. Cf. Viefhans, "Zwischen Technokraten und Bürokraten." Afterword to H. Kehrl, *Krisenmanager im Dritten Reich* (Düsseldorf, 1974), p. 533.
23. Cf. K.-H. Ludwig, *Technik und Ingenieure im Dritten Reich* (Düsseldorf, 1974), p. 38.
24. J. C. Fest, *op. cit.,* p. 272.
25. H. R. Trevor-Roper, *The Last Days of Hitler* (New York: Macmillan, 1947), p. 240.
26. *Ibid.*
27. Speer's letter to Dr. Wolters, 8/10/46.
28. *Ibid.*
29. In the following passage, the author draws on Rudolf Wolters, *Kurzer Lebensabriss* (Coesfeld, 1966; unpublished).

30. Among his many assignments, Dr. Wolters had the task of planning Berlin's north-south axis. He was also responsible for hiring and overseeing free-lance architects, painters, and sculptors for the urban renewal of Berlin. In 1939, he took office as exhibition commissioner for the exhibition of New German Architecture. In 1942, he became head of the Staff for the Reconstruction Planning for Bombed-Out Cities. He was also head of the Culture, Press, and Propaganda Division in the Todt Organization.
31. Cf. pp. 16ff.
32. Rudolf Wolters, *Albert Speer* (Oldenburg, 1943).
33. Speer's letter to Dr. Wolters, 8/10/46.
34. *Ibid.*
35. *Ibid.*
36. Cf. Speer, *ITR,* p. 356.
37. Speer's letter to Dr. Wolters, 8/10/46.
38. *Ibid.*
39. Cf. Speer, *Spandau: The Secret Diaries* (New York: Macmillan, 1976), p. 6 (henceforth cited as *SPDI*).
40. *Ibid.,* pp. 221 and 263.
41. *Ibid.,* p. 264.
42. *Ibid.,* p. 263.
43. Speer's letter to Dr. Wolters, 10/28/64.
44. Speer, *SPDI,* p. 398.
45. Personal information from Dr. Wolters.
46. Speer's letter to Dr. Wolters, 10/28/64.
47. *Ibid.*
48. *Ibid.*
49. *Ibid.*
50. *Ibid.*
51. Personal information from Dr. Wolters.
52. Speer's letter to Dr. Wolters, 10/28/64.
53. Speer: *SPDI,* p. 398.
54. Personal information from Dr. Wolters.
55. Speer's letter to Dr. Wolters, 10/28/64.
56. *Ibid.*
57. Gregor Janssen, *Das Ministerium Speer* (Berlin, Frankfurt am Main, Vienna, 1968).
58. Personal information from Speer. Cf. also Speer, *ITR,* p. 620.

59. G. M. Gilbert, *Nürnberger Tagebuch* (Frankfurt am Main, 1962), p. 142.
60. Cf. Speer, *SPDI,* p. 95.
61. *Ibid.,* p. 137.
62. Personal information from Wolf Jobst Siedler.
63. Personal information from Wolf Jobst Siedler.
64. Speer: *ITR,* p. 621.
65. Personal information from Albert Speer.
66. *Albert Speer, Technik und Macht.* Introduced and edited by Adelbert Reif (Stuttgart, 1979).
67. Cf. Erich Fromm, *Anatomy of Human Destructiveness* (New York: Holt, Rinehart and Winston, 1973), p. 396ff.
68. ZS 23.
69. Dr. Wolters' letter to Speer, September 1969.
70. Cf. Erich Fromm, *op. cit.,* p. 396, note 11.
71. Cf. *FAZ,* 3/19/80.
72. Speer, *SPDI,* p. 33; cf. also IMT, Vol. XVI, p. 529.
73. Cf. pp. 49–52.
74. Cf. pp. 189–191.
75. Speer, *SPDI,* p. 32.
76. BA R3/1549, fol. 57 and 59. Reich Minister Speer on the first awarding of the Dr. Fritz Todt Prize on 2/8/44. Mayor Liebel was head of the Central Office in Speer's ministry.
77. In the following passage, the author relies on a letter from Dr. Wolters dated 3/19/80.
78. Two copies of the 1942/43 period were burned at the Berlin Zoo and on Viktoriastrasse during the confusion of the final weeks of the war. A complete original text, together with all the pertinent documents, printed texts, and speeches, was stored in the Harz region. There, all the material vanished. (Personal information from Wolters to the author.)
79. Speer Office Journal page numbers (without index)

	original	new version
1941	99	78
1942	128	97
1943	276	232
1944	200	294

The fact that the new version of the year 1944 has ninety-four pages more is due to the circumstance that in 1964 Dr. Wolters inserted the post-August 1944 entries into the text.

80. Cf. BA R 3, catalog of files of Speer's ministerial office, p. iv.
81. Personal information from David Irving.
82. Speer's letter to Dr. Wolters, 1/3/70. Irving evidently found only the year 1943, in which Dr. Wolters had made only slight changes.
83. Cf. *ibid.*
84. Dr. Wolters' letter to Speer, 1/10/70.
85. *Ibid.*
86. *Ibid.*
87. *Ibid.*
88. *Ibid.*
89. Speer's letter to Dr. Wolters, undated, ca. late January 1970.
90. *Ibid.*
91. Dr. Wolters' letter to Speer, 2/10/70.
92. Personal information from Dr. Wolters.
93. Speer's letter to Dr. Wolfgang Mommsen, 2/13/70.
94. Speer's letter to Dr. Wolters, 2/13/70.
95. Speer, *ITR,* p. xxv.

2. The Road to Hitler

1. Cf. Speer, *ITR,* p. 4.
2. *Ibid.*
3. Information from the Central Office of the German Weather Bureau.
4. Cf. H. Wältin, *Christuskirche Mannheim, 1911–1961,* p. 15.
5. Speer, *ITR,* p. 4.
6. Dr. Wolters' jottings (unpublished).
7. Cf. Speer, *ITR,* p. 5.
8. Gitta Sereny, "Hat Speer alles gesagt?" *Zeitmagazin,* No. 43 (10/20/78), p. 12.
9. *Ibid.*

10. *Ibid.*
11. *Ibid.* Also Speer, *ITR,* p. 6.
12. Speer, *ITR,* p. 6.
13. Cf. Gitta Sereny, *loc. cit.,* p. 14.
14. *Ibid.*
15. Cf. Speer, *ITR,* p. 8.
16. Cf. Gitta Sereny's comment, *loc. cit.,* p. 14.
17. Written information from Dr. Theo Hupfauer to the author, 2/14/79.
18. Quoted by Gitta Sereny, *loc. cit.,* p. 12.
19. Cf. Speer, *ITR,* p. 10f.
20. Quoted in Gitta Sereny, *op. cit.,* p. 12.
21. Cf. Gitta Sereny's comment, *op. cit.,* p. 12.
22. Cf. William Hamsher, *Albert Speer. A Victim of Nuremberg?* (London, 1970), p. 31.
23. *Ibid.*
24. Cf. Speer, *ITR,* pp. 11ff; also G. Sereny, *loc. cit.,* p. 16. In regard to Speer's cultural ambitions, cf. *ITR,* p. 10.
25. Quoted in Gitta Sereny, *loc. cit.,* pp. 14f.
26. According to a former student of Tessenow's in a letter to the author. In regard to Heinrich Tessenow, see Gerda Wangerin and Gerhard Weiss, *Heinrich Tessenow—Ein Baumeister 1876–1950. Leben, Lehre, Werk.* (Essen, 1976).
27. Quoted in W. Hamsher, *op. cit.,* p. 39.
28. Written information from Professor Peter Koller to the author, 3/29/80.
29. *Ibid.*
30. Quoted in Speer, *ITR,* p. 12.
31. *Ibid.,* p. 13.
32. Dr. Wolters' jottings (unpublished).
33. *Ibid.*
34. *Ibid.*
35. *Ibid.*
36. Quoted in W. Hamsher, *op. cit.,* p. 41.
37. In regard to Baldur von Schirach, cf. J. C. Fest's portrait in *Das Gesicht des Dritten Reiches,* pp. 300–318; also Anselm Faust, *Der Nationalsozialistische Deutsche Studentenbund. Studenten und Nationalsozialismus in der Weimarer Republik* (Düsseldorf, 1973), pp. 76ff. In regard to the problem of German students and

the Third Reich, cf. Michael H. Kater, *Studentenschaft und Rechtsradikalismus in Deutschland 1918 bis 1933. Eine sozialgeschichtliche Studie zur Bildungskrise in der Weimarer Republik* (Hamburg, 1975); also Hans Peter Bleuel and Ernst Klinnert, *Deutsche Studenten auf dem Weg ins Dritte Reich. Ideologien— Programme—Aktionen 1918 bis 1935* (Gütersloh, 1967).

38. K. D. Bracher; *Die Auflösung der Weimarer Republic. Eine Studie zum Problem des Machtverfalls in der Demokratie* (Villingen, 1971), p. 133.

39. Code of the National Socialist German Students' Alliance, § 3. Quoted from A. Faust, *op. cit.,* p. 153.

40. *Ibid.,* p. 9.

41. *Ibid.*

42. Cf. K. D. Bracher, *op. cit.,* p. 133, note 85.

43. A. Faust, *op. cit.,* p. 10.

44. Speer, *ITR,* p. 16.

45. *Ibid.,* p. 17.

46. *Ibid.*

47. Written information from Peter Koller to the author, 3/19/80.

48. Cf. Speer, *SPDI,* p. 77.

49. Cf. *Der Angriff* (12/5/30). December 4, 1930, was the only date on which Hitler spoke to the students during the period indicated by Speer. Cf. *VB* (July 1930–January 1931); cf. *Der Angriff* during the same period.

50. Speer, *ITR,* p. 18.

51. Cf. *Der Angriff* (December 2 and 3, 1930).

52. *Ibid.* (12/5/30).

53. *Ibid.*

54. *Ibid.*

55. According to *Der Angriff,* in its report on the speech. Cf. *ibid.* (12/5/30).

56. M. Domarus, *Hitler. Reden und Proklamationen 1932–1945,* 2 vols. (Würzburg, 1962–63), p. 1. In regard to this problem, cf. also R. Binion, . . . *dass ihr mich gefunden habt. Hitler und die Deutschen. Eine Psychohistorie* (Stuttgart, 1978), pp. 163f.

57. Quoted in John Toland, *Hitler* (Bergisch-Gladbach, 1977), p. 317.

58. *Ibid.*

59. Cf. R. Binion, *op. cit.,* p. 164.

60. Speer, *ITR,* p. 19.
61. *Ibid.*
62. *Ibid.*
63. *Ibid.,* p. 20.
64. Cf. BDC. Letter from the government of Thuringia, 6/30/38, to the Reich Treasurer of the Nazi Party in Munich. Cf. also reply: "Albert Speer, engineer, born on March 19, 1905, in Mannheim, now residing in Berlin, was accepted into the National Socialist German Workers' Party on March 1, 1931, as member Number 474,481."
65. Written information from Peter Koller to the author, 3/19/80.
66. In regard to the periodical *Die Tat,* cf. Karl Sontheimer, "Der Tatkreis," in *VHZG,* Vol. 7 (1959), pp. 228–260.
67. Roswitha Mattausch, *Siedlungsbau und Stadtneugründungen im deutschen Faschismus* (Frankfurt am Main, 1981), p. 72.
68. Speer, *ITR,* p. 20.
69. Cf. Speer, *ITR,* p. 23. These remarks are not in the German edition. Speer evidently got them from a letter that he had written to his daughter Hilde in 1953 while in Spandau Prison. Cf. W. Hamsher, *op. cit.,* pp. 62ff.
70. Speer, *ITR,* p. 24.
71. Speer, *ITR,* p. 19.
72. Quoted in W. Hamsher, *op cit.,* p. 52.
73. Personal information from Dr. Wolters to the author.
74. Cf. Speer, *ITR,* p. 20.
75. Rudolf Wolters, *Albert Speer,* p. 63.
76. BA R3/1547, fol. 152. Speech by Reich Minister Speer. Demonstration at the Berlin Sports Palace, 6/5/43.

3. The Führer's Architect

1. BA R 43 II/1181. Minutes of a meeting with representatives of the city of Berlin with Hitler on 9/19/33. Date of the document: 9/25/33. In this chapter, the author is not trying to deal with Speer's architecture or that of the Third Reich. In regard to Speer's architecture, cf. Albert Speer, *Architektur. Arbeiten 1933 bis 1942* (1978). Cf. also the positive critical contributions by

Karl Arndt, pp. 113–135; Georg Friedrich Koch, pp. 136–150; Lars Olof Larsson, pp. 151–175. In regard to Speer's Berlin designs, cf. Lars Olof Larsson, *Die Neugestaltung der Reichshauptstadt. Albert Speer's Generalbebauungsplan für Berlin* (Stuttgart, 1978). In regard to urban planning in the Third Reich, cf. Jost Dülffer, Jochen Thies, Josef Henke, *Hitlers Städte. Baupolitik im Dritten Reich* (Cologne and Vienna, 1978).

2. *Adolf Hitler: Monologe im Führerhauptquartier 1941–1944. Die Aufzeichnungen Heinrich Heims,* ed. by Werner Jochmann (Hamburg, 1980, referred to hereafter as *Monologe*), p. 101. Hitler did not say this until 1941, but it is quite legitimate to quote him in this context, since these were his thoughts as of 1933. In regard to the continuity in Hitler's ideas on urban planning, especially in Berlin, cf. Dülffer, Thies, Henke, *op. cit.,* p. 85.

3. *Monologe,* p. 404.

4. *Ibid.*

5. BA R 43 II/1028. Letter by the mayor of Berlin to Lammers, 12/5/33.

6. Cf. Dülffer, Thies, Henke, *op. cit.,* p. 21.

7. Speer, *ITR,* p. 29.

8. *Ibid.,* pp. 26f.

9. *Ibid.,* p. 27.

10. *Ibid.,* p. 26.

11. *Ibid.,* pp. 31f.

12. *Ibid.,* p. 32.

13. Cf. picture in Albert Speer, *Architektur,* p. 82.

14. The construction on Tempelhofer Field, Berlin, for May 1, 1933. By Albert Speer. Cf. Anna Teut, *Architektur im Dritten Reich 1933–1945* (Berlin, Frankfurt am Main, Vienna, 1967), p. 187.

15. Cf. Speer, *ITR,* p. 32.

16. Cf. Rudolf Wolters, *Albert Speer,* p. 8.

17. Cf. Speer, *ITR,* p. 32.

18. Adolf Hilter, "Die Reichskanzlei," in *Die neue Reichskanzlei* (Munich, no date), p. 7.

19. *Ibid.*

20. In regard to Hitler's first architect, Paul Ludwig Troost, cf. K. Arndt, *op. cit.,* pp. 116f.

21. Cf. Speer's own description in *ITR,* p. 34.

22. *Ibid.,* p. 36.

23. From a letter by Heinrich Tessenow to Frau Speer, 1950. Quoted in Speer, *ITR* (Germ. ed.), p. 531, note 3.
24. *ITR,* p. 36.
25. Joachim C. Fest, *Hitler* (Frankfurt am Main, Berlin, Vienna, 1973), p. 716.
26. Personal information from Dr. Theo Hupfauer, Hans Kehrl, Dr. Rudolf Wolters.
27. Cf. Speer, *SPDI,* p. 3.
28. Cf. the chapter entitled "Illness and Crisis," p. 85.
29. Cf. IMT, Vol. XVI, p. 476.
30. Speer, *ITR,* p. 40.
31. Cf. Jochen Thies, *Architekt der Weltherrschaft. Die "Endziele" Hitlers* (Düsseldorf, 1976), p. 89; G. Janssen, *op. cit.,* p. 35. Frau Gerdy Troost told the author that Adolf Hitler and her husband never discussed the question of whether the latter should design the Nuremberg project.
32. Personal information from Frau Gerdy Troost.
33. Cf. Karl Arndt, "Architektur und Politik," in Albert Speer, *Architektur,* p. 120.
34. Cf. M. Domarus, *Hitler,* pp. 347f.
35. Speer, *ITR,* p. 58.
36. R. Wolters: *Albert Speer,* p. 9.
37. Personal information from Frau Gerdy Troost, quoted also in John Toland, *Hitler,* pp. 549f.
38. Personal information from Dr. Wolters.
39. Albert Speer, "Die Bauten des Führers," in *Bilder aus dem Leben des Führers* (Altona: Cigaretten-Bilderdienst, 1936), p. 34.
40. Cf. Speer, *ITR,* p. 134.
41. Albert Speer, "Die Bauten des Führers," p. 34. Cf. in this connection Hitler's statement at the cornerstone ceremony of the Wehrtechnische Fakultät, Berlin, 11/27/37. "The grandeur of this project and this construction should not be measured in terms of the needs of the years 1937, 1938, 1939, or 1940. They are based on the realization that for a thousand-year-old nation with a thousand years of historical and cultural past, it is our duty to build an equally worthy thousand-year future for the unforeseeable future lying ahead of [us]." Quoted in Dülffer, Thies, Henke, *op. cit.,* p. 30.
42. BDC. Albert Speer's questionnaire for the Party's statistical sur-

vey of 1939. In regard to Hitler's "religious belief," cf. *int. al. Monologue,* pp. 40, 85, 105, 301–303.

43. BA R 3/1573, fol. 158 RS. Speer's letter of 10/3/44 to Bormann. Bormann had asked Speer about the activities of his Reconstruction Planning staff in regard to destroyed churches; Speer had thereupon told the head of this agency "not to negotiate with representatives of ecclesiastic agencies."

44. Cf. pp. 37–38 of this book.

45. Cf. R. Wolters: *Albert Speer,* p. 9.

46. G. Janssen, *op. cit.,* p. 36, erroneously indicates 1938 as the year. Speer himself told the author that he was made a professor in 1936. This is very probable, since, starting in 1937, letters to him addressed him as "Herr Professor." Speer was not particularly proud of this title, nor did he ever use it himself. It does not appear on any of his stationery. One reason why Speer did not set much store by this title was that he received it together with people like Hitler's court photographer Heinrich Hoffmann. Personal information from Albert Speer to the author.

47. Quoted by J. Thies, *op. cit.,* p. 22.

48. Cf. Dülffer, Thies, Henke, *op. cit.,* p. 22.

49. *VB* (1/31/37).

50. Cf. *RGBl* (1937), p. 103. In regard to the Führer edicts, cf. K. D. Bracher, *Die deutsche Diktatur* (Cologne, 1976), p. 376.

51. Cf. § 2 of the edict of 1/30/37.

52. Cf. § 4 of the edict.

53. BA R 43 II/1187a, fol. 137. Speer's letter to Lammers, 3/18/37.

54. BA R 43 II/1187a, fol. 139. Lammers' letter to Speer of 4/6/37.

55. BA R 43 II/1187a, fol. 140. Speer's letter to Lammers of 4/16/37.

56. *Ibid.*

57. *Ibid.,* fol. 140, 141.

58. BA R 43 II/1187a, fol. 145. Lammers' memorandum of 6/22/37.

59. BA R 43 II/1187a, fol. 146 and RS. Lammers' letter to Speer of 6/28/37.

60. BA R 43 II/1187a, fol. 144 RS.

61. BA R 43 II/1187a, fol. 146 RS. Lammers' letter to Speer of 6/28/37.

62. BA R 43 II/1187a, fol. 144 RS.

63. *Ibid.*

64. Cf. Speer's own information, *ITR*, p. 75.
65. *Ibid.*
66. BA R 43 II/1187a, fol. 87–90.
67. BA R 43 II/1187b, fol. 9. Lammers' letter to Schwerin von Krosigk of 4/29/37.
68. K.-H. Ludwig, *op. cit.*, pp. 414f.
69. Speer, *ITR*, p. 109.
70. Dr. Wolters' jottings (unpublished).
71. Cf. Speer, *ITR*, p. 178; the picture between pp. 324 and 325.
72. Cf. Speer, *Architektur*, pp. 22ff.
73. *Die Neue Reichskanzlei*, p. 8.
74. Dr. Wolters' jottings (unpublished).
75. G. Janssen, *op. cit.*, p. 36.
76. Cf. BA R 3/1602, fol. 4f. Speer's letter to Fritz Tamms; BA R 3/1594, fol. 70f. Speer's letter to Caesar Pinnau of 2/6/41. Also cf. Speer Journal, 2/6/41.
77. Dr. Julius Lippert's biography in Wilhelm Kosch, *Biographisches Staatshandbuch der Politik. Lexikon der Politik, Presse und Publizistik* (Berne and Munich, 1963), p. 775.
78. This can be gleaned from Speer's letter to Lippert, 7/1/40. BA NS 19 new/2046.
79. *Ibid.*
80. *Ibid.*
81. *Ibid.*
82. *Ibid.*
83. *Ibid.*
84. BA NS 19 new/2046. Edict issued by the Inspector General of Buildings for the Reich capital on his agency's cooperation with the mayor of Berlin.
85. BA NS 19 new/2046. Dr. Lippert's letter to Speer of 6/24/40. Lippert cited § 6 of the Führer edict of 1/30/37 concerning the Inspector General of Buildings: "I reserve the right to issue special implementation rules by way of an edict." Speer had used the edict of 1/31/37 to justify his edict of June 31, 1940: "In cases of differences of opinion, the Inspector General of Buildings will issue the necessary orders."
86. BA NS 19 new/2046. Dr. Lippert's letter to Speer of 6/24/40.
87. BA NS 19 new/2046. Speer's letter to Dr. Lippert of 6/28/40.
88. BA NS 19 new/2046. Dr. Lippert's letter to Speer of 7/9/40.

89. *Ibid.*
90. BA NS 19 new/2046. Speer's letter to Dr. Lippert of 7/16/40.
91. BA NS 19 new/2046. Speer's memorandum of 7/16/40.
92. *Ibid.*
93. Speer, *ITR,* p. 87.
94. BA NS 19 new/2046. Memorandum from the personal staff of the SS Reichsführer, 1/11/41.
95. J. Thies, *op. cit.,* p. 92.
96. In regard to Hermann Giesler, cf. Hans Peter Rasp, *Eine Stadt für tausend Jahre. München—Bauten und Projekte für die Hauptstadt der Bewegung* (Munich, 1981). This is the first work that attempts to do justice to the controversial figure of Hitler's "second" architect, since the author tries to avoid political polemics against the inveterate National Socialist, which permits him to reach an objective judgment—to the extent that this is possible for a historian. Because of their prejudice against Hermann Giesler, other historians have come to grossly erroneous conclusions, if only because they have used Albert Speer as an informant, *e.g.,* J. Thiess, *op. cit.,* pp. 92f; Dülffer, Thies, Henke, *op. cit,* pp. 22f; *ibid.,* p. 22, note 60, and p. 23, note 61. The page numbers of Speer's *SPDA* given in note 61 do not document the statements made in the text. Joachim C. Fest also believed Speer more than Giesler in regard to the controversy over Hitler's grave site. Cf. J. Fest, *Hitler,* p. 1023, and note 126.
97. Giesler found this out after the war from a member of Speer's staff. Handwritten note by Hermann Giesler, undated (copy in author's possession).
98. BA R 3/1733. Draft of an organizational plan for a Führer deputy for architecture and urban planning of the Nazi Party.
99. *Ibid.*
100. *Ibid.*
101. Cf. Speer Office Journal, 1/17/41.
102. Personal information supplied by Hermann Giesler.
103. Hermann Giesler, *Ein anderer Hitler* (Leoni, 1977), p. 342.
104. *Ibid.,* p. 344.
105. Cf. Speer Office Journal, 1/17/41.
106. *Ibid.,* 1/20/41.
107. BA R 3. Speer's memorandum of 1/20/41.
108. BA R 3. Speer's letter to Hermann Giesler, 2/2/41.

109. Cf. BA R 3/1573, fol. 40. Speer's letter to Bormann, 1/2/42.
110. *Ibid.,* fol. 40f.
111. *Ibid.,* fol. 41.
112. Speer, *ITR,* p. 105.
113. BA R 3/1573, fol. 42. Speer's letter to Bormann, 1/2/42.
114. BA R 3/1585, fol. 82. Speer's letter to Hermann Giesler, 3/26/42.

4. The Minister of State

1. BA R 43 II/1157, fol. 66. Lammers, head of the Reich Chancellery, was present when Speer took his oath of office.
2. Speer: *SPDI,* p. 442.
3. Statements by Dr. Todt (unpublished).
4. In regard to Fritz Todt, cf. A. Milward, "Fritz Todt als Minister für Bewaffnung und Munition," *VHZG,* Vol. 14 (1966), pp. 40–58. Cf. also the laudation in honor of Todt's fiftieth birthday in *Deutsche Allgemeine Zeitung* (9/4/41), which includes a detailed biography.
5. Cf. A Milward, *op. cit.,* p. 44.
6. Statements by Dr. Todt (unpublished).
7. Cf. *DAZ* (9/4/41).
8. BA R 43 II/1157 and *RGBl* I (1940), pp. 513–515. Edict of the Führer and Reich Chancellor about the appointment of a Reich Minister of Armaments and Munitions, 3/17/40.
9. Cf. *DAZ* (9/4/41).
10. *Ibid.*
11. Only Todt's three most important offices are mentioned here. He was, among other things, head of the Todt Organization, head of the Office of Technology, administrator of the National Socialist Alliance of German Technology, and Inspector General of Special Assignments in the Four Year Plan. Cf. A Milward, *op. cit.,* pp. 44–46; also *DAZ* (9/4/41).
12. Cf. A. Milward, *op. cit.,* p. 45.
13. IfZ MA 441/5, fol. 5858. "Reports from the Reich" (2/12/42). In regard to the background of the "Reports from the Reich," which render the mood of the population and were compiled by

the SD, cf., Heinz Boberach, ed., *Meldungen aus dem Reich. Auswahl aus den geheimen Lageberichten des Sicherheitsdienstes der SS 1939–1944.* (Neuwied and Berlin, 1965), pp. ix–xxviii. However, the documents mentioned here are not available in this compilation.

14. Statements by Dr. Todt (unpublished).
15. Speer, *ITR*, p. 232.
16. Speer Office Journal, 2/7/42.
17. Speer, *ITR*, p. 230.
18. Cf. IfZ Ed 99/9, Speer Interrogation. Written statement by Walter Rohland about Todt's and Speer's positions on the war.
19. Statements by Dr. Todt (unpublished).
20. Cf. IfZ Ed 99/9, Speer Interrogation. Written statement by Walter Rohland.
21. *Ibid.*
22. Cf. ibid.
23. Cf. *ibid.*
24. Speer, *ITR*, p. 230.
25. In regard to Hitler's unusual daily schedule, cf. W. Maser, *Adolf Hitler,* pp. 398–401.
26. Speer, *ITR*, p. 231.
27. Cf. Speer Office Journal, 2/8/42.
28. Quoted from the report on the causes of the accident of the commanding general in Luftgau I, Königsberg, 3/8/43. BA Zentralnachweisstelle.
29. Cf. Hans Baur, *Ich flog Mächtige der Erde* (Kempten, 1962), p. 214.
30. Speer voiced this conjecture to the author.
31. Cf. M. Domarus, *Hitler,* p. 1834, note 55.
32. Cf. Speer, *ITR*, p. 235.
33. Cf. also Max Müller, "Der plötzliche und mysteriöse Tod Dr. Fritz Todts," *GWU,* Vol. 18 (1967), pp. 602–604; also R. Hansen, "Der ungeklärte Fall Todt," *ibid.,* pp. 604–605.
34. Quoted in M. Domarus, *Hitler, loc. cit.,* p. 1834.
35. Cf., IfZ MA 441/5, fol. 5817. Reports from the Reich, 2/9/42.
36. *Ibid.*
37. IfZ MA 441/5, fol. 5861. Reports from the Reich, 2/12/42.
38. Udet's suicide was turned into a "serious accident . . . during the testing of a new weapon." Cf. David Irving, *Die Tragödie der*

Deutschen Luftwaffe (Frankfurt am Main, Berlin, Wien, 1970), p. 204.

39. IfZ MA 441/5, fol. 5859. Reports from the Reich, 2/12/42.
40. Speer: *ITR,* p. 235.
41. Goebbels Diaries. *Tagebücher aus den Jahren 1942–1943. Mit anderen Dokumenten,* ed. by Louis P. Lochner (Zurich, 1948). Quotation in 2/9/42.
42. Milch's diary, 8/2/47. Quoted in D. Irving, *op. cit.,* p. 435, note 28.
43. Cf. A. Milward, who quotes Speer, *Die Deutsche Kriegswirtschaft 1939–1945* (Stuttgart, 1966), p. 68. Concerning Milward's book, especially his one-sided use of sources, cf. W. Birkenfeld, *VSWG,* Vol. 53 (1966), pp. 570–573.
44. Quoted in David Irving, *Hitler und seine Feldherren* (Frankfurt am Main, Berlin, Wien, 1975) p. 374.
45. Speer indicates two different times: In the minutes quoted by Milward, he says it was eleven o'clock; in *ITR,* p. 233, he says it was one o'clock.
46. In regard to the following, cf. Speer, *ITR,* pp. 233–235; A. Milward, *op. cit.,* p. 68, and BA A11. Proz. 2, FC 1818, fol. 1f. During a conversation with the author, Speer once again offered a detailed description of his appointment as Todt's successor.
47. Cf. A. Milward, *op. cit.,* p. 71.
48. Cf. David Irving, *Die Tragödie der Deutschen Luftwaffe,* p. 435, note 28. Irving refers to the Speer Office Journal.
49. Speer, *ITR,* p. 237.
50. IMT, Vol. XVI, p. 477.
51. Speer Office Journal, 2/9 and 2/10/42.
52. BA R 43 II/1157, fol. 53.
53. BA R 43 II/1157, fol. 67.
54. BA R 43 II/1157, fol. 55.
55. Personal information from Speer.
56. BA R 3/1660, fol. 3.
57. Personal information from Dr. Wolters.
58. David Irving, *Die Tragödie der Deutschen Luftwaffe,* p. 213. Cf., also Speer, *ITR,* pp. 234f.
59. Cf. Alan Milward, "Fritz Todt als Minister für Bewaffnung und Munition," *loc. cit.,* p. 46.
60. Cf. BA A11. Proz., FC 1818, fol. 2; also Speer, *ITR,* p. 235.

61. BA A11. Proz., FC 1818, fol. 2. Original in English.
62. A. Hitler. *Monologe,* p. 119.
63. BA R 43 II/1157, fol. 49.
64. *VB* (2/10/42).
65. BA R 43 II/1157, fol. 50.
66. BA R 43 II/1157, fol. 56.
67. Cf. "Edict of the Führer and Reich Chancellor on the Appointment of a Minister of Armaments and Munition" (3/17/40). BA R 43 II/1157, fol. 30 and RGBl 1940, I, p. 513.
68. BA R 43 II/1157, fol. 50.
69. *Ibid.*
70. BA R 43 II/1157, fol. 71.
71. Cf. *ibid.*
72. BA R 43 II/1157, fol. 72.
73. Cf. RGBl I, 1942. Published on 2/20/42.
74. BA R 43 II/1157, fol. 64.
75. BA R 43 II/1157, fol. 76.
76. Cf. A. Hitler, *Monologe,* p. 140.
77. Cf. *VB* (2/10/42).
78. Cf. int. al., *Westfälische Tageszeitung* (2/10/42).
79. *Ibid.*
80. VB (2/10/42).
81. IFZ, MA 441/5 5859. Reports from the Reich, 2/12/42.
82. *Ibid.*
83. Goebbels' Diary (2/10/42). Quoted in David Irving, *Die Tragödie der Deutschen Luftwaffe,* p. 216.
84. Speer Office Journal, 2/12/42.
85. In regard to this frequently depicted conflict, cf. G. Janssen, *Das Ministerium Speer,* pp. 38f; A. Milward, *Die deutsche Kriegswirtschaft 1939–1945,* pp. 70–71; cf. also Speer's own description in *ITR,* pp. 239–241.
86. Speer, *ITR,* p. 238.
87. Cf. *ibid.,* p. 177.
88. BA R 3/1571. Speer's letter to the Foreign Office of the Teachers of German Universities and Institutions of Higher Learning.
89. Speer Office Journal 2/14/42.
90. BA R 3/1547, fol. 4–7. Speer's speech of 2/14/42.
91. *Ibid.*
92. H. Kehrl, *Krisenmanager im Dritten Reich,* p. 245.

93. Cf. W. A. Boelcke, ed., *Deutschlands Rüstung im Zweiten Welt-krieg. Hitlers Konferenz mit Albert Speer 1942–1945* (Frankfurt am Main, 1969). Meeting of 2/9/42, item 5, p. 64.
94. Speer Office Journal, 2/24/42.
95. BA R 3/1547. Minister Speer's speech, given at the conference of Reichsleiters and Gauleiters of the Nazi Party, 2/24/42, Munich.
96. Speer Office Journal, 2/24/42.
97. H. Kehrl, *op. cit.,* p. 244.
98. *Das Reich* (4/19/42).
99. In regard to the problem of demarcating a Todt Era and a Speer Era, cf. K.-H. Ludwig, *Technik und Ingenieure im Dritten Reich,* pp. 415 ff.
100. Cf. Speer, *ITR,* p. 236.
101. Cf. Trevor-Roper, *The Last Days of Hitler,* p. 110.
102. *Die Neue Reichskanzlei,* p. 8.
103. Cf. also Speer's statements in *ITR,* p. 237.
104. K.-H. Ludwig, *op. cit.,* p. 407.
105. Cf. IMT, Vol. XVI, p. 477.

5. The Successor to the Throne

1. IfZ, Field Marshall Erhard Milch, *Persönlichkeiten, Hitler* (9/1/45), p. 39.
2. Cf. M. Domarus, *Hitler,* p. 1316.
3. General Bodenschatz regards 1943 as the latest point in time for a cooling of the relationship between Göring and Hitler. Cf. Charles Bewley, *Hermann Göring and the Third Reich* (Toronto, 1962), p. 385.
4. Cf. Rolf Wagenführ, *Die deutsche Industrie im Kriege,* 2nd edition (Berlin, 1963), p. 66. Index number of German armaments output in February 1942: 97; July 1943: 229.
5. Quoted in Speer, *ITR,* p. 257.
6. BA R 3/1548, fol. 11. Speer's speech of 7/3/43 at the Babelsberg Works for Machine-Building and Railroad Needs, Inc.
7. Goebbels' speech of 6/5/43, in *Goebbels-Reden 1939–1945,* ed. by Helmut Heiber (Düsseldorf, 1972), p. 519. Speer had spoken before Goebbels' speech. Cf. BA R 3/1547, fol. 157ff. Reich

Minister Speer's speech. Demonstration at the Berlin Sportpalast, 6/5/43. In regard to the argument about the lengths of the speeches, cf. Speer, *ITR,* p. 319. Cf. also Heiber's critical comment, *op. cit.,* p. 219, note 3.

8. IfZ Ed 83/2, Goebbels' Diary, 9/29/42.
9. IfZ Ed 83/1, Goebbels' Diary, 6/23/43.
10. Cf. Rudolf Wolters, *Kurzer Lebensabriss,* p. 23.
11. *Ibid.*
12. Cf. Speer, *ITR,* p. 306.
13. Rudolf Wolters, *op. cit.,* p. 24. In regard to the "separate peace with Russia," cf. L. Gruchmann, *Der Zweite Weltkrieg* (Munich, 1975), pp. 242ff., etc.
14. Rudolf Wolters, *op. cit.,* p. 24.
15. *Ibid.*
16. Cf. Speer, *ITR,* p. 306.
17. Cf. Jochen von Lang, *Der Sekretär: Martin Bormann, der Mann, der Hitler beherrschte* (Stuttgart, 1977), p. 166.
18. Cf. Ernst K. Bramsted, *Goebbels und die nationalsozialistische Propaganda 1925–1945* (Frankfurt am Main, 1971), p. 462. Cf. also Jochen von Lang, *op. cit.,* p. 228.
19. Cf. Jochen von Lang, *op. cit.,* p. 230.
20. Cf. Speer, *ITR,* p. 301.
21. Goebbels' Diary, 3/18/43, p. 279.
22. Speer, *ITR,* p. 303.
23. *Ibid.,* p. 307.
24. The Ministerial Council for the Defense of the Reich had been established by Hitler on August 30, 1938. Cf. RGBl 1939, Part I, p. 1539.
25. IfZ Ed 83/1, Goebbels' Diary, 2/19/43.
26. Cf. Goebbels' Diary, 3/1/43, p. 237. Cf. also Speer Office Journal, 2/28/43.
27. Cf. Speer Office Journal, 3/1/43.
28. Cf. Goebbels' Diary, 3/2/43, p. 238.
29. *Ibid.*
30. *Ibid.,* p. 243.
31. *Ibid.,* p. 244.
32. *Ibid.*
33. *Ibid.,* p. 239.

34. Speer, *ITR*, Germ. ed. (*Erinnerungen;* Berlin: Verlag Ullstein, 1969), p. 273.
35. *Ibid.*
36. Speer, *ITR*, p. 312.
37. Cf. Speer Office Journal, 3/5/43.
38. Cf. Speer, *ITR*, p. 313.
39. Goebbels' Diary, 3/9/43, p. 253.
40. *Ibid.*, p. 254.
41. *Ibid.*
42. Speer, *ITR*, p. 312.
43. Cf. Supreme Army Command Report of 3/9/43; cf. also Goebbels' Diary, 3/9/43, p. 264.
44. *Ibid.*
45. Goebbels' Diary, 3/18/43, p. 279.
46. *Ibid.*
47. *Ibid.*
48. Cf. Jochen von Lang, *op. cit.*, p. 463.
49. *Monologe*, p. 273. On a different occasion, Hitler said: "It will be the finest day of my life when I leave political life and leave all the worries, anxieties, and concerns behind me. I want to do this as soon as I have completed my political tasks after the war." *Ibid.*, p. 234.
50. BA All. Proz., FC 1818, fol. 3.
51. *Ibid.*
52. IfZ, Field Marshal Milch, *Persönlichkeiten, Hitler* (9/1/45), p. 39.
53. Speer, *ITR*, p. 329.
54. Cf. Speer Office Journal, 10/14/43.
55. This was how Kehrl was described by one of his former collaborators in *Krisenmanager im Dritten Reich*, p. 9.
56. *Ibid.*, p. 334.
57. In the following passage, the author uses Kehrl's description in his memoirs *Krisenmanager im Dritten Reich*, pp. 33ff. In a 1979 interview, Kehrl gave the author detailed elucidations.
58. H. Kehrl, *op. cit.*, p. 334.
59. *Ibid.*, pp. 306–309.
60. *Ibid.*, p. 335.
61. *Ibid.*

62. IfZ, Field Marshal Milch, *op. cit.,* p. 39.
63. Affidavit signed by Gerhard Klopfer, Bormann's state secretary, 7/7/47. Quoted in Speer, *ITR,* p. 329, note 2.
64. IfZ, Field Marshal Milch, *op. cit.,* p. 39.
65. Speer, *ITR,* p. 329.
66. The portrait that Speer generally drew of himself as a "pure technocrat" is not modified when, in his description of this episode (*ITR,* p. 308), he concedes that, faced with this situation, he left his corner as a technocrat and was forced to involve himself in politics.

6. Illness and Crisis

1. The author is grateful to Herr Otmar Katz, Munich. Herr Katz, who is working on a book about Hitler's personal physician, allowed the author to see the detailed medical reports on Speer. This information is used here purely to correct Speer's statements. As a historian, the author does not have the necessary medical knowledge to assess the qualifications of the doctors who treated Speer. In regard to evaluating Speer's disease symptoms and the treatment prescribed by his doctors, the author is grateful for assistance rendered him by the internist Dr. Jürgen Klamroth, Berlin. Dr. Klamroth studied with Professor Koch, who treated Speer in 1944.
2. Cf. Gitta Sereny, "Hat Speer alles gesagt?" *Zeitmagazin,* No. 43 (1978). Cf. also Speer, *ITR,* p. 5.
3. Cf. Sereny, *op. cit.,* No. 44.
4. In regard to Dr. Theo Morell, cf. W. Maser, *Adolf Hitler,* Chapter VIII; also David Irving. *Wie krank war Hitler wirklich.* (1980).
5. Speer, *ITR,* p. 126.
6. Cf. *Amtliches Telefonbuch* [official telephone book], 1936.
7. Speer, *ITR,* p. 126.
8. Cf. *Amtliches Telefonbuch,* 1936.
9. Cf. Speer, *ITR,* p. 126.
10. *Ibid.,* p. 127.
11. Ibid., p. 127.
12. Professor Chaoul's letter to Dr. Morell, 7/2/41. This letter ex-

plicitly says that Speer originally planned to have Morell examine him and consulted Professor Chaoul only because of Morell's absence.

13. *Ibid.*
14. Dr. Morell's letter of 7/7/41 to Speer.
15. Cf. Speer, *ITR,* p. 126.
16. Cf. Dr. Morell's letter of 7/7/41 to Speer.
17. Cf. *ibid.* It is not clear why Morell prescribed piperazine for Speer. This medicament is used today for worm diseases of the intestinal tract. Cf. *Allgemeine und spezielle Pharmakologie und Toxikologie,* ed. by W. Farth, *et al.* (Mannheim, Vienna, Zurich, 1977), p. 549.
18. Dr. Wolters' manuscript (unpublished).
19. Hilde Speer's medical record, 8/2/43.
20. Speer Office Journal, 1/18/44.
21. Telephone record of 1/26/44. Conversation between Morell and Gebhardt.
22. A. Mitscherlich, in Reif, *Controversies,* p. 469.
23. Cf. Speer, *ITR,* p. 389.
24. Speer Office Journal, 1/18/44. Cf. *ibid.,* 2/2/44: "The great length of the meeting and the late hour are very irritating for Professor Gebhardt. The provisional anteroom had to put up with the physician's anger, impotently—but at least with the aid of an alcoholic restorative."
25. Cf. the Reports to the Führer, 1–4, 1/25/44. BA R 3/1515.
26. Cf. telephone record of 1/26/44 of Morell-Gebhardt conversation.
27. Speer Office Journal, 1/18/44.
28. Cf. Speer Office Journal, 2/10/44.
29. Cf. Speer, *ITR,* p. 393.
30. Cf. Gebhardt's intermediate report to Dr. Morell, 2/15/44. Speer maintains that Gebhardt attempted to oust Professor Koch by writing to Hitler's personal physician, Professor Morell, and asking him to act as consultant in the internal treatment. However, the available documents do not bear out Speer's claim. Cf. Speer, *ITR,* Germ. ed. *(Erinnerungen),* p. 566, note 6.
31. Cf. Gebhardt's intermediate report to Morell, 2/15/44.
32. Morell's note: Conversation with Prof. Koch, 2/14/44.
33. Cf. Speer, *ITR,* p. 393, note 1.

34. Cf. H. Auterhoff, *Lehrbuch der Pharmazeutischen Chemie* (Stuttgart), 1980, p. 594.

35. Dr. Morell's prescription for Speer, 2/11/44. In regard to sulfonamide ultraseptyl, cf. David Irving, *op cit.*, pp. 75f.

36. Cf. Speer, *ITR*, p. 393, note 1.

37. *Ibid.*, p. 394.

38. *Ibid.*, p. 395.

39. Affidavit by Professor Koch: Doc. NO-2602. Cf. also Speer, *ITR*, p. 643, note 4.

40. Morell's note about his telephone conversation with Prof. Koch, 2/13/44.

41. Cf. Speer Office Journal, 2/12/44.

42. IfZ, MA 302, fol. 7231. Gebhardt's letter to Himmler, 2/21/44.

43. *Ibid.*

44. Doc. NO-2602.

45. *Ibid.*

46. IfZ MA 302, fol. 7224. Himmler's letter to SS-Obergruppenführer Wolff, 3/20/44.

47. IfZ MA 302, fol. 7227. Himmler's letter to Gebhardt.

48. Speer, *ITR*, p. 395.

49. Cf. Speer Office Journal, 3/16–17/44.

50. BA R 3/1607, fol. 26. Gebhardt's letter to Speer, 4/28/44.

51. BA R 3/1591, fol. 89. Speer's letter to Dr. Morell, 2/26/44.

52. BA R 3/1579, fol. 43. Speer's letter to Dr. Gebhardt, 6/6/44.

53. Speer, *ITR*, p. 370.

54. *Ibid.*, p. 653f, note 4.

55. BA R 3/1578, fol. 144. Speer's letter to Bichelonne, 10/16/44.

56. BA R 3/1578, fol. 145. Speer's letter to Bichelonne, 12/5/44. Bichelonne's death because of pulmonary embolism several weeks later may very well have been due to the surgery; but it proves nothing about Gebhardt's qualifications as a surgeon. Then as now, an embolism resulting from surgery was not entirely unavoidable.

57. BA R 3/1628. Liebel's memorandum about Dorsch's talk at Führer Headquarters, undated. In regard to the "Dorsch Affair," cf. Gregor Janssen's detailed account in *Das Ministerium Speer*, p. 157. In this description of the conflicts in Speer's ministry, the author is interested in showing chiefly Speer's reaction.

58. BA R 3/1630. Speer's letter to Dorsch, 1/27/44.

59. *Ibid.*
60. BA R 3/1515, fol. 56. Speer's letter to Hitler, 1/29/44.
61. Cf. D. Irving, *Die Tragödie der Deutschen Luftwaffe,* p. 352.
62. Cf. *ibid.,* p. 353.
63. W. A. Boelcke, *Hitlers Konferenzen mit Albert Speer.* Meeting of 4/14/44, item 1.
64. *Ibid.,* item 2.
65. *Ibid.,* item 5.
66. *Ibid.*
67. *Ibid,* item 8.
68. Speer, *ITR,* p. 396.
69. *Ibid.,* p. 397.
70. BA R 3/1516. Speer's letter to Hitler, 4/19/44.
71. *Ibid.*
72. *Ibid.*
73. IfZ, Field Marshal Milch, *Persönlichkeiten, Hitler.* (9/1/45), p. 39.
74. Cf. Walter Rohland, *Bewegte Zeiten* (Stuttgart, 1978), p. 99.
75. *Ibid.*
76. Cf. D. Irving, *Die Tragödie der Deutschen Luftwaffe,* p. 215.
77. Cf. *ibid.,* p. 209.
78. IfZ ZS 1230.
79. IfZ, Field Marshal Milch, *op. cit.,* p. 39; cf. also Irving, *Die Tragödie der Deutschen Luftwaffe,* p. 356. However, Milch's jottings do not indicate that he initiated that conversation, as Irving claims; according to Milch, it was Hitler who took the initiative.
80. IfZ. Field Marshal Milch, *op. cit.,* p. 39.
81. *Ibid.,* p. 40.
82. *Ibid.*
83. *Ibid.*
84. Quoted in Irving, *Die Tragödie der Deutschen Luftwaffe,* p. 356.
85. Cf. IfZ Ed. 100, Milch Diary, 4/21/44.
86. Speer, *ITR,* p. 404.
87. Cf. BA R 3/1637, fol. 8.
88. Cf. BA R 3/1637, fol. 10. Speer also appointed Dorsch to represent him as his commissioner for the regulation of construction and as his deputy in all matters of the Todt Organization.
89. Cf. Speer, *ITR,* p. 407.
90. Field Marshal Milch, *op. cit.,* p. 40.

91. Speer, *ITR*, p. 407.
92. *Ibid.*
93. BA R3/1549. Speer's address at the Haus am Wannsee, 5/10/44.
94. *Ibid.*
95. *Ibid.*

7. The Twentieth of July 1944

1. Cf. G. Janssen, *Das Ministerium Speer*, p. 268.
2. Cf. Speer, *ITR*, pp. 448–469.
3. In regard to the German resistance, cf. the fundamental work by Peter Hoffmann, *Widerstand, Staatsstreich, Attentat. Der Kampf der Opposition gegen Hitler* (Munich, 1969). This book includes a detailed bibliography.
4. Speer, *ITR*, p. 456.
5. Cf. Speer: *SPDI*, p. 188.
6. A statement that Speer made in 1966 contains such a belated identification. "I knew that people were bitching. *We* bitched *together* [author's emphasis]." *Der Spiegel*, No. 46, p. 58.
7. Speer Office Journal, 7/20/44, describes the flow of information about the assassination attempt to Speer somewhat differently from the way Speer does in his memoirs. However, Speer's more detailed description sounds quite credible.
8. Cf. Speer Office Journal, 7/20/44; also Speer, *ITR*, pp. 452f. G. Janssen, *op. cit.*, p. 269, claims erroneously that Speer held a press conference for a great number of journalists. Cf. Speer Office Journal, 7/20/44: "At the invitation of Reich Minister Goebbels, the Minister [i.e., Speer] will speak to the members of the Reich government at the Propaganda Ministry."
9. Cf. Speer, *ITR*, p. 453. At the time of the failed coup, several hundred members of the Todt Organization were at Führer Headquarters.
10. Cf. Speer, *ITR*, p. 454f.
11. Cf. Goebbels' report on the Twentieth of July. Radio broadcast on 7/26/44. In *Goebbels-Reden 1939–1945*, p. 343.
12. M. Domarus, *Hitler*, p. 2127.

13. Speer, *ITR,* p. 456. Cf. also the Speer Office Journal, 7/20/44: "The Minister remained in Goebbels' house until late at night; Goebbels is in charge of the measures for thwarting the military putsch."

14. Wilfred von Oven, "Der 20. Juli 1944—erlebt im Hause Goebbels," in *Verrat und Widerstand im Dritten Reich* (Coburg, 1978), p. 43.

15. *Ibid.*

16. *Ibid.,* p. 57.

17. Cf. *20. July 1944,* 4th ed. (Bonn: [West German] Bundeszentrale für Heimatdienst, 1961), p. 39.

18. A. Wagner, *Die Rüstung im "Dritten Reich" unter Albert Speer,* p. 220.

19. Cf. Goerdeler's secret memorandum for the generals about the necessity of a coup d'état, 3/26/43. In Gerhard Ritter, *Carl Goerdeler und die deutsche Widerstandsbewegung* (Stuttgart, 1956), p. 597.

20. This connection was to be established by way of Professor Ditze (teacher of economics at the University of Freiburg, Breisgau) and Professor Hettlage (on the staff of Speer's ministry). Cf. SD report of 10/2/44, in *Spiegelbild einer Verschwörung. Die Kaltenbrunner-Berichte an Bormann und Hitler über das Attentat vom 20. Juli 1944. Geheime Dokumente aus dem ehemaligen Reichssicherheitshauptamt.* (Stuttgart: Archiv Peter, 1961), p. 433.

21. Cf. Speer Office Journal, 7/21/44.

22. Speer, *ITR,* p. 462.

23. Personal information from Otto Günsche.

24. Cf. Speer, *ITR,* p. 464.

25. BA R 3/1522, fol. 43. Speer's memorandum of 7/20/44.

26. Personal information from Hans Kehrl/Dr. Wolters to the author.

27. Personal information from Speer to the author. Cf. also Speer, *SPDI,* p. 188.

28. G. Janssen, *op. cit.,* p. 269.

29. Speer, *ITR,* p. 463.

30. Cf. Speer Office Journal, 7/20/44.

31. *Ibid.*

32. Cf. Speer, *ITR,* p. 466.

33. Cf. Speer Office Journal, 7/24/44.

34. BA R 3/1552, fol. 213–217. Stenographic report of the speech given by Reich Minister Speer on 7/24/44.

35. Cf. G. M. Gilbert, *Nürnberger Tagebuch,* p. 166.

36. IfZ Ed 99/Vol. 12, Albert Speer Interrogation, 7/3/45.

37. Cf. Göring's speech to the Luftwaffe, 7/21/44, in *Ursachen und Folgen,* Vol. 21, p. 425.

38. Cf. Goebbels' speech of 7/26/44, in *Goebbels-Reden 1939–1945,* p. 342.

39. Cf. Grand Admiral Dönitz's speech to the men of the German Navy, 7/21/44, in *Ursachen und Folgen,* Vol. 21, p. 451.

40. H. Kehrl, *Krisenmanager im Dritten Reich,* p. 398. Kehrl says this meeting of the office chiefs took place on 7/21/44; the Speer Office Journal says nothing about it on that date, but it does mention such a meeting on 7/24/44.

41. H. Kehrl, *op. cit.,* p. 399.

42. Speer Office Journal, Original, 7/27/44.

43. Personal information from Hermann Giesler to the author.

44. Cf. Speer, *ITR,* p. 469.

45. Major Klamroth used this term during his interrogation by the SD. Cf. SD Report of 8/2/44, p. 125.

46. Cf. Speer, *ITR,* p. 467.

47. Goebbels' speech of 7/26/44, in *Goebbels-Reden 1939–1945,* p. 352.

48. *Ibid.*

49. Cf. SD Report of 10/12/44, p. 445.

50. Cf. H. Kehrl, *op. cit.,* p. 359.

51. SD Report of 10/12/44, p. 445.

52. BA R 55/601, fol. 175.

53. BA R 3/1555, fol. 95. Speer's speech at the "standing meeting" on Pariser Platz, 11/15/44.

54. *Ibid.*

55. Cf. Speer, *ITR,* p. 467.

56. Cf. SD Report of 7/24/44, p. 11.

57. *Ibid.,* p. 9.

58. Leonard Mosley, *The Reich Marshal.* (New York: Doubleday, 1974), p. 306.

59. Cf. SD Report of 10/12/44, p. 445.

60. Speer himself says that he read through the Kaltenbrunner Report in one night. Cf. Speer, *ITR,* p. 469.
61. *Playboy* (June 1971).
62. *Ibid.*
63. Cf. P. Hoffman, *op. cit.,* pp. 628f. In regard to the film of the execution of the conspirators, which has still not turned up despite great efforts by various people, cf. *ibid.,* p. 869, note 111.
64. Speer, *ITR,* p. 469.
65. Personal information from Otto Günsche/Frau Christian.
66. Personal information from Hermann Giesler.
67. G. Janssen, *op. cit.,* p. 270, lists the people for whom Speer interceded.
68. Cf. in this connection Speer's letter to Kaltenbrunner, 12/29/44. BA R 3/1535.
69. Cf. G. Janssen, *op. cit.,* p. 270.
70. BA R 3/1627, fol. 60.

8. Stick-It-Out Speeches and the Assassination Attempt

1. G. M. Gilbert, *Nürnberger Tagebuch,* p. 395.
2. W. A. Boelcke, ed., *Hitler's Konferenzen with Albert Speer.* Meeting of 9/7–9/9/42, item 8.
3. Milch Diary, 12/31/46. Quoted in D. Irving, *Tragödie der Deutschen Luftwaffe,* pp. 388f.
4. BA R 3/1547. Speer's speech at the Berlin Sportpalast, 6/5/43.
5. K.-H. Ludwig, *Technik und Ingenieure im Dritten Reich,* p. 439.
6. BA R 3/1548. Speer's speech at the conference of Reich orators and Gau propaganda chiefs, 9/24/43, at the Kroll Opera.
7. BA R 3/1548. Speer's speech at the conference of Gauleiters, Poznan, 10/6/43.
8. BA R 3/1549. Speer's speech at the conference of the Gau propaganda chiefs and district propaganda chiefs, 1/10/44.
9. *Ibid.*
10. W. A. Boelcke, *op. cit.* Meeting of 7/8/43, item 19.

11. Wilfred von Oven: *Finale Furioso. Mit Goebbels bis zum Ende* (Tübingen, 1974), p. 205.

12. 10,492 V-1s were fired at London between June 1944 and March 29, 1945; only 2,419, less than one fourth, actually hit the British capital. Cf. David Irving, *Die Geheimwaffen des Dritten Reiches* (Gütersloh, 1965).

13. W. von Oven, *op. cit.*, p. 393. Quoted also in Irving, *Geheimwaffen des Dritten Reiches.*

14. *Das Reich* (7/30/44).

15. In regard to the population's mood in this respect, cf. Marlis Steinert, *Hitlers Krieg und die Deutschen,* pp. 527ff.

16. BA R 3/1553. Speer at the meeting of the armaments staff, 8/1/44.

17. BA R 3/1554. Speer's speech at the conference of the armaments heads, 8/31/44.

18. Lutz Count Schwerin von Krosigk: *Es geschah in Deutschland. Menschenbilder unseres Jahrhunderts* (Tübingen and Stuttgart, 1951), p. 302.

19. BA R 3/1551. Speer at the armaments meeting in Linz, 6/24/44.

20. Cf. BA R 3/1555. Speer on 9/11/44.

21. Cf. BA R 3/1586. Speer's letter to Goebbels, 11/2/44.

22. BA R 3/1556. Speer on 1/13/45.

23. Cf. *ibid.*

24. BA R 3/1554. Speer on 8/16/44.

25. BA R 3/1555. Speer on 10/4/44.

26. BA R 3/1555. Speer at the standing conference at Pariser Platz, 11/15/45.

27. From a sworn affidavit by Hermann Giesler, 4/22/81.

28. IfZ Ed 99/Vol. 12. Interrogation of Albert Speer, 7/3/45.

29. Cf. Speer, *ITR,* pp. 486f. and *ibid.,* note 1.

30. In regard to Fritz Sauckel, cf. this book, "The Nuremberg Trial," pp. 154ff.

31. BA R 3/1697, fol. 17. Meeting of the Central Planning Committee, 10/10/42. In regard to this agency, cf. G. Janssen, *Das Ministerium Speer,* pp. 56f.

32. BA R 3/1697, fol. 17. Meeting of the Central Planning Committee, 10/10/42.

33. BA R 3/1548. Speer's speech at the conference of the Gauleiters, 10/6/43.

34. *Ibid.*
35. *Ibid.*
36. BA Slg. Schuhmacher 1271, fol. 421. Himmler's letter to all the Supreme Reich agencies and all Gauleiters, 5/27/42.
37. *Ibid.*
38. *Ibid.*
39. *Ibid.*
40. Cf. *RGB1* I, 1942, p. 165. Führer's order for the protection of the armaments industry. Cf. also Boelcke, *op. cit.* Meeting of 2/19/42, item 2; cf. also this book, "The Minister," p. 63.
41. Cf. IfZ Fa 506, 12: Reich Minister Speer on the criminal nature of false data on armaments needs or supplies, 4/18/42.
42. BA R 3/1602, fol. 52. Speer's letter to Thierack, 2/12/44.
43. BA R 3/1602, fol. 56. Speer's letter to Thierack, 3/4/44.
44. This emerges from Speer's letter to Kaltenbrunner, 6/28/44. BA R 3/1585, fol. 15 and RS.
45. *Ibid.*
46. *Ibid.*
47. Cf. Albert Speer, *Infiltration* (New York: Macmillan, 1981), pp. 107f.
48. *Ibid.*
49. *Ibid.,* p. 107f.
50. In regard to the immobilization activities and Speer's conflicts with Hitler, cf. Janssen, *op. cit.,* pp. 303ff; also the well-meaning articles by Reimer Hansen, "Albert Speers Konflikt mit Hitler," GWU, Vol. 17 (1966), pp. 596ff; and Alfred Wagner, "Die Rüstung im 'Dritten Reich' unter Albert Speer," *Technikgeschichte,* Vol. 33 (1966), pp. 221ff). These articles, as well as the cited chapters in Janssen, go along with the traditional Speer historiography.
51. Cf. IMT, Vol. XVI, p. 542.
52. Cf. *ibid.,* p. 544.
53. Cf. Speer; *ITR,* p. 508.
54. Cf. also this book, "The Nuremberg Trial," pp. 145ff.
55. Cf. IMT, Vol. XLI, pp. 416f. Statement by Dietrich Stahl.
56. *Der Spiegel,* No. 46 (1966).
57. Uwe Bahnsen and James O'Donell, *Die Katakombe* (Munich, 1977) p. 27.
58. In a 1966 interview, Speer said that he could not have made an

open attempt, because his entire family would then have been liquidated. Cf. *Der Spiegel,* no. 46 (1966). In *ITR,* p. 511, he writes, "Quite aside from all question of fear, I could never have confronted Hitler pistol in hand. Face to face, his magnetic power over me was too great up to the very last day."

59. Personal information from Otto Günsche to the author.
60. Personal information from Albert Speer to the author.
61. Cf. IMT, Vol. XVI, p. 544; also this book, "The Nuremberg Trial," pp. 145ff.
62. Dr. Wolters' diary (unpublished).
63. Dr. Rudolf Wolters in conversation with the author.
64. Dr. Theo Hupfauer had been head of the Central Office of Speer's ministry since 12/17/44. Cf. Janssen, *op. cit.,* p. 284.
65. Personal information from Dr. Theo Hupfauer to the author.
66. Personal information from Hermann Giesler to the author.
67. John K. Galbraith, *Economics, Peace and Laughter,* p. 294.
68. *Ibid.,* p. 239.
69. Schwerin von Krosigk, *op. cit.,* p. 304.
70. Quoted in Janssen, *op. cit.,* p. 311.
71. Speer, *ITR,* p. 517.
72. Erich Kempka, *Die letzten Tage mit Adolf Hitler* (Preussisch Oldendorf, 1975), p. 64.
73. Cf. Janssen, *op. cit.,* pp. 311f.
74. E. Kempka, *op. cit.,* p. 66.
75. Speer, *ITR,* p. 538.
76. Cf. Janssen, *op. cit.,* pp. 316f. No doubt, such conflicts between the dictator and his minister must have taken place; Speer told his friend Dr. Wolters about them a short time later. "Speer told me that their conversations had been duels with sharp knives, but that the Führer had remained calm on the outside. . . ." Dr. Wolters' diary (unpublished).
77. Speer, *ITR,* p. 546.
78. BA R 3/1557, fol. 27–41. G. Janssen, *op. cit.,* p. 412, note 126, describes this speech text as a draft "with corrections in Speer's handwriting." However, I feel that the corrections are Hitler's, since they have been made in Gothic script by an obviously trembling hand. Speer's corrections are in Latin letters. The author has quoted the typewritten text without corrections, since it

cannot be determined with certainty which revisions are by Hitler and which by Speer.

79. *Ibid.,* fol. 29.
80. *Ibid.,* fol. 36. The word *"zutiefst"* (profoundly) was crossed out either by Speer or by Hitler. Cf. note 78.
81. Speer, *ITR,* p. 548.
82. BA R 3/1625, fol. 2. Speer's letter to Karl Hanke, 4/14/45.
83. Cf. *Playboy* (June 1971).
84. Speer, *ITR,* p. 564.
85. On 4/22, Hermann Giesler was with his brother Paul Giesler, Gauleiter of Munich; it was here that he read Bormann's wire. Cf. Hermann Giesler's sworn affidavit, 4/22/81.
86. Personal information from Gerda Christian.
87. Speer: *ITR,* p. 568f. This also contains Speer's account of the other events that he witnessed during his visit to the Führer's bunker.
88. That was how Professor Karl Hettlage, a collaborator of Speer's, characterized him. Cf. Speer, *SPDI,* p. 134.
89. Personal information from Arno Breker to the author.

9. Speer and the Dönitz Government

1. IMT, Vol. XLI, p. 540. Statement by Baumbach.
2. Fundamental works on the Dönitz regime: Reimer Hansen, *Das Ende des Dritten Reiches. Die deutsche Kapitulation 1945* (Stuttgart, 1966); Marlis G. Steinert, *Die 23 Tage der Regierung Dönitz* (Düsseldorf and Vienna), 1967.
3. Cf. BA R 3/1661, fol. 15.
4. Cf. BA R 3/1661, fol. 15.
5. Cf. Speer, *SPDI,* p. 348.
6. Milch diary; quoted in D. Irving, *Die Tragödie der Deutschen Luftwaffe,* p. 369.
7. Speer, *ITR,* p. 585.
8. Cf. *ibid.,* note 1.
9. BA R 3/1661, fol. 15.
10. BA R 3/1661, fol. 16.

11. Walter Lüdde-Neurath, *Regierung Dönitz. Die letzten Tage des Dritten Reiches,* 3rd ed. (Berlin, Frankfurt am Main, Zurich, 1964), pp. 29f and p. 122, addendum 2. In regard to the source value of Lüdde-Neurath's memoirs, cf. Reimer Hansen, *op. cit.,* pp. 88f.

12. Cf. Marlis Steinert, *op. cit.,* p. 78.

13. Dönitz's son Peter died in action in March 1943 as watch officer on a U-boat; his son Klaus died in action in May 1944 as commander of a torpedo boat.

14. BA R 3/1576, fol. 70. Speer's letter to Dönitz, 5/21/44. He had written a similar letter to Dönitz when the latter's son Peter died in action. Cf. BA R 3/1576, fol. 69.

15. Cf. BA R 3/1576, fol. 92.

16. Cf. Speer, *SPDI,* p. 116.

17. Cf. BA R 3/1661, fol. 13.

18. Cf. Karl Dönitz, *Regierung der 20 Tage,* typescript (Nuremberg, no year). Copy in the author's possession.

19. Text of telegram in KTB OKW Vol. IV, 2, p. 1468; also in Lüdde-Neurath, *op. cit.,* p. 45.

20. Lüdde-Neurath, *op. cit.,* p. 45.

21. Speer, *ITR,* p. 567f.

22. *Ibid.,* p. 568.

23. Cf. Karl Dönitz, *Zehn Jahre und Zwanzig Tage* (Frankfurt am Main, Bonn, 1973), p. 434.

24. R. Hansen, *op. cit.,* p. 107.

25. *Ibid.*

26. BA R 3/1641, fol. 16. Under 4/30/45: "Radio Message to Dönitz —Transfer to Dönitz's Headquarters. Marginal note: "Draft [of] radio message to the Führer a[nd] appeal."

27. IMT Vol. XLI, p. 540. Statement by Baumbach.

28. The text is quoted in M. Steinert, *op. cit.,* p. 165: "Mein Führer: I have received your orders. I will justify your confidence [in me] by remaining faithful to your idea and doing everything in my power for the good of the German people."

29. BA R 62/2, fol. 20.

30. BA R 62/8, fol. 69 (draft with handwritten revisions by Dönitz). The dispatched and slightly revised text can be found in Steinert, *op. cit.,* p. 165.

31. Cf. R. Hansen, *op. cit.,* p. 113. Interpretations of the telegram *ibid;* also in Steinert, *op. cit.,* pp. 165f.
32. Cf. Lüdde-Neurath, *op. cit.,* p. 130.
33. Karl Dönitz, *Regierung der 20 Tage,* p. 15.
34. *Ibid.*
35. Speer, *ITR,* p. 568.
36. BA R 62/2, fol. 17.
37. *Ibid.,* fol. 18f.
38. Cf. Dönitz to the German People, May 1, 1945. Printed in Lüdde-Neurath, *op. cit.,* p. 132, addendum 7a.
39. *Ibid.,* p. 81.
40. Otto Dietrich, *12 Jahre mit Hitler* (Munich, 1955), p. 259.
41. Cf. J. C. Fest, *Das Gesicht des Dritten Reiches,* p. 245.
42. Lüdde-Neurath, *op. cit.,* p. 81.
43. Cf. R. Hansen, *op. cit.,* p. 119.
44. Karl Dönitz, *Zehn Jahre und Zwanzig Tage,* p. 439.
45. Cf. Lüdde-Neurath, *op. cit.,* p. 83.
46. Cf. note 27.
47. Cf. Lüdde-Neurath, *op. cit.,* p. 84.
48. BA R 3/1661, fol. 16.
49. Cf. Lüdde-Neurath, *op. cit.,* p. 84.
50. BA R 62/2, fol. 23.
51. BA R 3/1625, fol. 16. Cf. Speer's letter to Schwerin von Krosigk, 5/5/45.
52. BA R 62/11, fol. 180.
53. BA R 3/1624, Speer's letter to Schwerin von Krosigk, 5/15/45.
54. Cf. this book, "Birth of a Myth," p. 7.
55. Cf. Speer's letter to Robert H. Jackson, 11/17/45; quoted in Reif, *Kontroversen,* pp. 224f.
56. Speer, *ITR,* p. 596.
57. J. K. Galbraith, *op. cit.,* p. 295.
58. *Ibid.*
59. Written by Gauleiter Paul Wegener at Esterwegen Prison, 1/18/50. Copy in author's possession. Wegener (Gauleiter of Bremen and Weser-Ems) was part of the "inner civilian circle of the Dönitz regime" (Hansen, *op. cit.,* p. 171) and had learned this from Backe.
60. Galbraith, *op. cit.,* p. 292.

61. Lutz Count Schwerin von Krosigk, *Es geschah in Deutschland. Menschenbilder unseres Jahrhunderts,* p. 304.
62. Galbraith, *op. cit.,* p. 292f.
63. Cf. BA R 62/11, fol. 180; also R. Hansen, *op. cit.,* p. 179.
64. Cf. R. Hansen, *op. cit.,* pp. 179f.
65. BA R 3/1624. Speer's letter to Schwerin von Krosigk, 5/15/45.
66. Galbraith, *op. cit.,* p. 292.
67. Cf. also the thorough treatment in Hansen, *op. cit.,* pp. 190–199.
68. Lüdde-Neurath, *op. cit.,* p. 116.
69. *Ibid.*
70. Cf. *ibid.,* pp. 113f.
71. Cf. Speer, *ITR,* p. 592.
72. *Ibid.,* p. 592f.
73. Lüdde-Neurath, *op. cit.,* p. 117.
74. H. Kehrl, *Krisenmanager im Dritten Reich,* p. 453; cf. also Schwerin von Krosigk, *op. cit.,* p. 305. "Even during his imprisonment, Speer believed for a while that he would be called upon for the task of reconstruction."
75. Cf. Bradley F. Smith, *Reaching Judgment at Nuremberg* (New York: Basic Books, 1977) p. 218.

10. The Nuremberg Trial

1. Speer, *ITR,* p. 598; also *SPDI,* p. 33.
2. IfZ Ed 99/19. Albert Speer, *Die weitere Entwicklung des deutschen Problems in Europa.*
3. *Ibid.,* p. 3.
4. *Ibid.*
5. *Ibid.*
6. *Ibid.,* p. 9.
7. *Ibid.,* p. 17.
8. *Ibid.,* p. 18.
9. B. Smith, *op. cit.,* p. 218.
10. Galbraith, *op. cit.,* p. 293.
11. Cf. *ibid.*
12. Overall accounts of the Nuremberg Trial: W. Maser, *Nürnberg. Tribunal der Sieger* (Düsseldorf, 1977); Gerhard E. Gründler,

Arnim von Manikowsky, *Das Gericht der Sieger* (Oldenburg and Hamburg, 1967); J. Heydecker, J. Leeb, *Der Nürnberger Prozess* (Cologne, 1979).

13. Cf. IMT, Vol. I, pp. 29–73.
14. Speer, *ITR,* p. 603.
15. *Ibid.*
16. Flächsner had not found out until late October/early November 1945 that he was to be a defense attorney at the Nuremberg Trial. Personal information from Dr. Hans Flächsner.
17. Speer, *ITR,* p. 604.
18. Personal information from Dr. Hans Flächsner.
19. Cf. Speer, *ITR,* p. 601.
20. Personal information from Dr. Hans Flächsner.
21. *Ibid.*
22. Cf. W. Maser, *Nürnberg,* p. 162.
23. Quoted in Fraenkel/Manvell: *Hermann Göring* (Hanover, 1964), p. 314.
24. IMT, Vol. IX, p. 314. Göring's testimony and cross-examination, *ibid.,* pp. 268–957. While being cross-examined by Jackson, Göring stated: "I absolutely and willingly assume responsibility for even the most serious things that I have done." *Ibid.,* p. 624. And elsewhere: "I admit to the responsibility of having done everything, implementing the preparations for the [Nazi] seizure of power and solidifying the [Nazi] power in order to make Germany free and great. I did everything [I could] to avoid war. But after it arrived, I had to do anything [I could] in accordance with my duty to win it." *Ibid.,* p. 724.
25. D. Irving, *The Nuremberg Trial,* Germ. ed., p. 92.
26. Cf. W. Maser, *Nürnberg,* p. 386.
27. B. Smith, *op. cit.,* p. 221.
28. Quoted in Reif, *Kontroversen,* pp. 224–225.
29. B. Smith, *op. cit.,* p. 221.
30. Albert Speer in *Welt am Sonntag* (10/31/76). Also in Reif, *Kontroversen,* p. 225.
31. D. Irving, *op. cit.,* p. 92.
32. In regard to the theory of a "secret agreement" between Albert Speer and Chief American Prosecutor Robert H. Jackson at Nuremberg, cf. Reif, *Kontroversen,* pp. 223–230.
33. The United States provided a chief prosecutor, two prosecutors,

four associate prosecutors, and fifteen assistant prosecutors. Cf. IMT, Vol. I, p. 2.

34. In regard to the following, cf. Irving, *op. cit.,* p. 92.
35. Quoted in *ibid.*
36. Cf. *ibid.*
37. IMT, Vol. XVI, p. 476.
38. *Ibid.,* p. 531.
39. *Ibid.,* p. 616.
40. *Ibid.,* p. 594.
41. *Ibid.*
42. *Ibid.,* p. 595.
43. *Ibid.,* p. 609.
44. *Ibid.*
45. *Ibid.,* p. 614.
46. Cf. *RGBl,* I, 1942, p. 179.
47. In regard to the problem of the forced laborers, cf. H. Pfahlmann, *Fremdarbeiter und Kriegsgefangene in der deutschen Kriegswirtschaft* (Darmstadt, 1968); E. L. Homze, *Foreign Labor in Nazi Germany* (Princeton, 1967).
48. IMT, Vol. III, p. 453.
49. J. K. Galbraith: *A Life in Our Time. Memoirs* (Boston, 1981), p. 212.
50. Galbraith, *Economics, Peace and Laughter,* p. 299.
51. *Ibid.,* p. 299; and, same author, *A Life in Our Time,* p. 212.
52. IfZ Ed. 99/10 Speer interrogation, 7/4/45, p. 4.
53. *Ibid.,* p. 8.
54. Cf. Speer, *ITR,* p. 601.
55. *Ibid.*
56. *Ibid.*
57. IMT, Vol. III, p. 544.
58. IMT, Vol. XVI, p. 493.
59. *Ibid.,* pp. 483f.
60. Cf. *ibid.,* pp. 485f; *ibid.,* p. 525.
61. IMT, Vol. I, p. 376.
62. IMT, Vol. XVI, p. 478.
63. BA R 3/1547. Reich Minister Speer's address at the conference of Gauleiters and Reichsleiters, Munich, 2/24/42.
64. IMT, Vol. XVI, p. 479.
65. IMT, Vol. XIX, p. 241.

66. IMT, Vol. XLI, pp. 541f. Statement by Dietrich Stahl.
67. Personal information from Dr. Hans Flächsner.
68. Speer, *ITR*, p. 611.
69. Personal information from Dr. Hans Flächsner.
70. IMT, Vol. IV, p. 380. Naturally, Kubuschok meant the year 1945.
71. *Ibid.*
72. G. M. Gilbert, *Nürnberger Tagebuch*, p. 105.
73. *Ibid.*, pp. 105f.
74. Cf. *ibid.*, p. 107.
75. IMT, Vol. XVI, p. 543.
76. *Ibid.*
77. Gilbert, *op. cit.*, p. 393.
78. IMT, Vol. XVI, p. 543.
79. Speer, *ITR*, p. 673, note 4.
80. Cf. IMT, Vol. XVI, p. 543, and *The Trial of German Major War Criminals*, Vol. XVII, p. 32. The English text goes: "I am most unwilling to describe the details, because there is always something repellent about such matters. I do it only because it is the Tribunal's wish."
81. IMT, Vol. XVI, pp. 543f.
82. *Ibid.*, p. 583.
83. Speer, *ITR*, p. 611.
84. Cf. IMT, Vol. XLI, pp. 520–535. Testimony by Manfred von Poser. Answer to Question 21: "Herr Speer told me of his plan to turn Himmler over to the Allies in Lüneburg."
85. IMT, Vol. XIX, p. 241.
86. Cf. Gilbert, *op. cit.*, p. 396.
87. Cf. *ibid.*, p. 400.
88. Cf. IMT, Vol XVI, p. 582.
89. Gilbert, *op. cit.*, p. 396.
90. Cf. *ibid.*
91. *Ibid.*, p. 394.
92. Karl Anders, *Im Nürnberger Irrgarten* (Nuremberg, 1948), p. 125.
93. Personal information from Dr. Hans Flächsner.
94. B. Smith, *op. cit.*, p. 220.
95. Personal information from Dr. Hans Flächsner.
96. According to Albert Speer in a conversation with the author.

97. Personal information from Dr. Hans Flächsner.
98. Cf. G. E. Gründler, A. v. Manikowsky, *op. cit.,* pp. 202ff.
99. Cf. Maser, *op. cit.,* p. 48.
100. Cf. Smith, *op. cit.,* pp. 222f.
101. Cf. IMT, Vol. I, p. 413.

11. Spandau

Preliminary remark—
In *The Spandau Diaries,* Speer pursues a certain goal, and thus his picture of his years in prison is one-sided; it played a not unimportant role in the postwar development of his legend. In order to balance Speer's account, the author feels justified in establishing, or at least outlining, the things that greatly facilitated Speer's survival at Spandau. In his description, the author draws on unpublished notes by Dr. Rudolf Wolters and on writings that he has compiled for this chapter; this material, quoted as ZS SP, includes interviews as well as further unpublished documents. By no means is the author trying to trivialize the harshness of twenty years' imprisonment.

1. Speer, *SPDI,* p. 67.
2. *Ibid.,* p. 23.
3. Cf. *Der Spiegel,* No. 66 (1966).
4. This calculation is based on information supplied by Speer; cf. *SPDI,* p. 446.
5. The wealth and variety of the works that Speer claims he read could fill the library of a Renaissance man. Cf. the index of names in *The Spandau Diaries.*
6. Speer, *SPDI,* p. 71.
7. *Ibid.,* p. xi.
8. ZS SP.
9. ZS SP.
10. Personal information from Dr. Wolters.
11. Dr. Wolters' notes.
12. *Ibid.*
13. ZS SP.

14. ZS SP.
15. Cf. Trevor-Roper, *op. cit.,* p. 243.
16. ZS SP.
17. ZS SP.
18. By 1979, Speer had donated a six-figure total to Aktion Sühnezeichen. Speer indicated this approximate amount only at the author's urging. One must admit that for all his publicity-seeking, Speer did not exploit his contributions as a demonstrative gimmick in his rehabilitation.
19. Dr. Wolters' notes.
20. *Ibid.*
21. *Ibid.*
22. ZS SP.
23. ZS SP.
24. ZS SP.
25. Dr. Wolters' letter to Speer, 5/25/61.
26. Dr. Wolters' written information to the author.
27. *Ibid.*
28. Speer, *SPDI,* p. 446.
29. ZS SP.
30. Dr. Wolters' personal information to the author.
31. Cf. *Der Spiegel,* No. 16 (1975).
32. Cf. *Playboy* (June 1971); *Quick,* No. 21 (1971).
33. ZS SP.
34. Cf. *Der Spiegel,* No. 16 (1975).
35. Dr. Wolters' personal information to the author.
36. Dr. Wolters' letter to Speer, 8/27/75.
37. Dr. Wolters' personal information to the author.

12. Speer and the Final Solution—A Necessary Correction

1. Speer: *ITR,* p. xxvi.
2. According to Albert Speer in the Marcel Ophüls film *Nicht schuldig.*
3. *Der Spiegel,* No. 46 (1966).
4. Cf. Speer, Infiltrations, pp. 247–255.

5. Cf. *RGBl.*, I (1939), p. 864.
6. It was also signed by Minister of Justice Gürtner, Minister of the Interior Frick, Führer-Deputy Rudolf Hess, and, on behalf of the Reich Labor Minister, by Dr. Krohn. Cf. *ibid.*
7. Cf. Paragraph 1 of the law.
8. Cf. Paragraph 2 of the law.
9. Cf. H. G. Adler, *Der verwaltete Mensch* (Tübingen, 1974), p. 45.
10. Cf. the account by Dr. Martha Mosse, who was on the staff of the Jewish Community Office, Berlin. In H. G. Adler, *op. cit.,* p. 46.
11. This is apparent in the concluding report by the Main Resettlement Division of the Speer agency. Cf. Speer Office Journal, 1942, original, p. 108. The quoted passages from the original Speer Journal are in the copy owned by the author.
12. Cf. *ibid.*
13. Cf. K. J. Ball-Kaduri, "Berlin wird judenfrei. Die Juden in den Jahren 1942/43," in *Jahrbuch für die Geschichte Mittel- und Ostdeutschlands,* Vol. 22 (1973), p. 240.
14. Re the Gestapo supervision of the Reich Union of Jews, which the Gestapo forced to help in the resettlement throughout Germany, cf. Wolfgang Scheffler, *Judenverfolgung im Dritten Reich* (Berlin, 1974), p. 43.
15. This is apparent in a pertinent protocol; cf. below, note 22.
16. Quoted in H. G. Adler, *op. cit.,* p. 46.
17. Speer Office Journal, 1941, original, p. 21 (4/1–4/15).
18. *Ibid.*
19. *Ibid.,* p. 23 (4/16).
20. *Ibid.*
21. Speer Office Journal, 1941, original, p. 31 (5/31).
22. Minutes of a meeting in the head office of the Reich Propaganda Ministry, 3/21/41. Quoted in Adler, *op. cit.,* pp. 152f.
23. *Ibid.*
24. *Ibid.*
25. *Ibid.*
26. Speer Office Journal, 1941, original, p. 46 (6/14).
27. *Ibid.,* p. 65.
28. *Ibid.,* p. 66.
29. *Ibid.*

30. Hildegard Henschel. "Gemeindearbeit und Evakuierung von Berlin" (16. October 1941–16. June 1943), in *ZfdGJ,* IX (1972), p. 34.

31. *Ibid.,* p. 35.

32. *Ibid.,* p. 36.

33. *Ibid.*

34. Cf. Robert Kempner, "Die Ermordung von 35 000 Berliner Juden. Der Judenmordprozess in Berlin schreibt Geschichte." In *Gegenwart und Rückblick. Festgabe für die Jüdische Gemeinde zu Berlin 25 Jahre nach dem Neubeginn.* Ed. by Herbert A. Strauss and Kurt R. Grossmann (Heidelberg, 1970), p. 180.

35. Speer Office Journal, 1941, original, p. 85.

36. Cf. BA R 3/1605, fol. 121. Speer's letter to Otto Wetzel (member of the Reichstag), 4/21/42. Cf. also Adler, *op. cit.,* pp. 607f.

37. BA R 3/1605, fol. 121. Speer's letter to Otto Wetzel, 4/21/42.

38. Cf. R. Kempner, *op. cit.,* p. 185.

39. Speer Office Journal, 1941, original, p. 87.

40. Speer, *Infiltrations,* p. 255.

41. In 1980, Speer stated in a filmed interview: "I simply didn't want to know the truth—I wanted to evade the truth." Quoted in Michael Hepp, "Albert Speer: Der Sklavenstaat. Notwendige Anmerkungen," p. 9 (typescript).

42. Cf. Speer Office Journal, 1942, original, p. 97 (9/30/42).

43. Cf. *ibid.,* p. 108.

44. Speer turned the Resettlement Division over to the Berlin Gauleiter's office. Cf. Adler, *op. cit.,* p. 608.

45. IMT, Vol. XVI, p. 569.

46. *Ibid.*

47. Speer Office Journal, 1943, original, p. 44 (3/30/43). Cf. also IMT, Vol. XVI, pp. 490f.

48. BA NS 19 new/1542. Speer's letter to Himmler, 4/5/43.

49. *Ibid.*

50. Cf. *ibid.*

51. BA NS 19 new/1542. Pohl's letter to Dr. Brandt (personal staff of the SS-Reichsführer).

52. *Ibid.*

53. Cf. BA RD 77/3. *"Die Regelung der Bauwirtschaft."* Published

by the Commissioner for the Regulating of the Construction Industry (March 1943).

54. Contrary to the original intention, Speer's ministry sent two inspectors on the trip instead of one.
55. Cf. BA NS 19 new, 994. Speer's letter to Himmler, 5/30/43.
56. *Ibid.*
57. Speer, *Infiltrations,* p. 44.
58. BA NS 19 new/1542. Speer's letter to Himmler, 6/10/43.
59. G. M. Gilbert, *Nürnberger Tagebuch,* p. 30.
60. Personal information from Wolf J. Siedler to the author.
61. Speer, *ITR,* p. 133.
62. Cf. *ibid.,* p. 447.
63. *Ibid.*
64. *Ibid.*
65. *Ibid.,* p. 135.
66. Cf. Speer Office Journal, 12/10/43.
67. Cf. IfZ Ge 0108/1.
68. Sworn affidavit by Albert Speer, 6/15/77. Quoted in "Aus Politik und Zeitgeschichte," supplement to the weekly newspaper *Das Parlament* (July 29, 1978).
69. According to Albert Speer in a conversation with the author.
70. Cf. Erich Goldhagen, "Albert Speer, Himmler und das Geheimnis der Endlösung." Reprinted in Adelbert Reif, *Kontroversen,* pp. 383–394.
71. Quoted *ibid.,* pp. 387f.
72. Cf. Speer, *ITR,* pp. 373f.
73. Quoted in Reif, *Kontroversen,* pp. 388f.
74. *Ibid.,* p. 390.
75. Personal information from Albert Speer to the author.
76. Albert Speer, "Antwort an Erich Goldhagen." Reprinted in Reif, *op. cit.,* pp. 395–403.
77. *Ibid.,* pp. 396f.
78. *Ibid.,* p. 398.
79. Albert Speer, "Ein Nachtrag." Reprinted in Reif, *op. cit.,* pp. 404–407.
80. Cf. *ibid.,* p. 405.
81. *Ibid.,* p. 406.
82. Cf. above, note 79.
83. Speer, *ITR,* p. 135.

Afterword

1. Personal information from Dr. Wolters to the author.
2. Speer, *ITR,* p. xxv.
3. *Ibid.,* p. 621.
4. Dr. Wolters' letter to Speer, November 1969.

Speer and the History of this Book

1. Personal information from Speer to the author.

BIBLIOGRAPHY
AND SOURCES

PRELIMINARY REMARK

Even today, the historian investigating the history of the Third Reich encounters limits. Many witnesses of this era declared their willingness to give the author information, but they simultaneously asked him to make only partial or no use of this knowledge. The same was true in regard to the documentary material that the author was allowed to see; here, too, he was frequently asked not to use the original papers as a source. The reasons for this conduct were, as a rule, personal and often political. The author respected such requests. However, in order to guarantee the credibility of the statements made in this book, he restricted himself—not without some regret—to those sources of which he could avail himself freely. Furthermore, the author compiled his own collection of sources for this book. This material is generally indicated as ZS (*Zeugenschrifttum* = documents by witnesses) or ZS SP *(Zeugenschrifttum Spandau* = documents by witnesses, Spandau) for the chapter entitled "Spandau."

DOCUMENTS PRIVATELY OWNED AND PERSONAL INFORMATION

(ts = typescript; hw = handwritten; o = oral)

Eugene K. Bird (o)

Prof. Arno Breker (o)

Gerda Christian (o)

Karl Dönitz: *Regierung der 20 Tage.* Nuremberg, no year (probably 1946; ts)

Dr. Hans Flächsner (o, ts)

Prof. Hermann Giesler: letters and jottings from the years 1969–1981 as well as four sworn affidavits of 4/22/81 (hw, ts, o)

Otto Günsche (o)

Dr. Theo Hupfauer (o, ts)

David Irving (o)

Hans Kehrl (o)

Prof. Peter Koller (hw)

Walter Lüdde-Neurath: Albert Speer jottings of 1946. With an addendum of 1979 (ts, o).

Dr. Theo Morell: Various medical records, medical reports, prescriptions, letters, as well as notes on telephone calls (hw, ts)

Richard Schulze-Kossens (o)

Wolf Jobst Siedler (o)

Albert Speer: In regard to *Deutschlands Rüstung im Zweiten Weltkrieg* (ed. and introduced by Willi A. Boelcke), December 1969 (ts, o)

Dr. Fritz Todt: statements (ts)

Gerdy Troost (o)

Paul Wegener: Jottings in Esterwegen Penitentiary, 1959 (hw)

Dr. Rudolf Wolters (o, ts)

    Jottings and diaries (ts, hw)

    Speer Office Journal (original) 1940–1944 (ts)

    Kurzer Lebensabriss (Coesfeld, 1966; ts)

    Various letters, Wolters–Speer, 1946–1966 (hw, ts)

    Speer/Wolters correspondence 1966–1975 (ts, hw)

DOCUMENTS IN ARCHIVES

Bundesarchiv (Federal Archives), Koblenz

NS 19   Personal Staff of SS-Reichsführer
R 3   Reich Ministry of Armaments and War Production
R 43   Reich Chancellery
R 55   Reich Ministry of National Enlightenment and Propaganda
R 62   Business files of the Dönitz Reich Administration
BA Schumacher Collection

Berlin Document Center

Albert Speer files

Institut für Zeitgeschichte (Institute of Modern History)

Ed 83, Vols. I and II — Goebbels diaries

Ed 99/13 — Albert Speer, *Die weitere Entwicklung des deutschen Problems in Europa*

Ed 100 — Erhard Milch's diaries and notebooks, 1921–1945

Ge Ol. 08/1 — Trial at the Court of General Sessions at the Essen Land Court against the former SS-members Bischoff, Sander, and Busta for mass murders committed at the Dora concentration camp

Milch, Erhard — *Persönlichkeiten, Hitler.* Jottings, 9/1/45, at Kaufbeuren Camp

ZS 1230 — Helmut Heiber's interrogation of Erhard Milch

ZS 1471   Helmut Heiber's interrogation of Wolfgang
                 Thomales

PERIODICALS

pre-1945:   post-1945:

Der Angriff   *Frankfurter Allgemeine*
Das Reich   *Zeitung*
Deutsche Allgemeine Zeitung   *Das Parlament*
Völkischer Beobachter   *Playboy*
Westfälische Tageszeitung   *Quick*
                                 Der Spiegel
                                 Stern
                                 Die Welt
                                 Die Zeit, Zeitmagazin

PRINTED SOURCE COLLECTIONS, DOCUMENTATION

*Ausgewählte Reden des Führers 1938. Sonderausgabe für die Wehr-
macht.* Berlin, 1938.
Boberach, Heinz, ed., *Meldungen aus dem Reich. Auswahl aus den
geheimen Lageberichten des Sicherheitsdienstes der SS 1939–
1944. Neuwied—Berlin, 1965.*
Boelcke, Willi A., ed., *Deutschlands Rüstung im Zweiten Weltkrieg.
Hitlers Konferenzen mit Albert Speer.* Frankfurt/Main, 1969.
——, *"Wollt ihr den totalen Krieg?" Die geheimen Goebbels-Kon-
ferenzen 1939–1945.* Stuttgart, 1967.
Deutschland im Kampf, ed. by A. J. Behrendt and H. von Wedel.
Berlin, 1939–1944.
Domarus, Max, *Hitler. Reden und Proklamationen 1932–1945,* two
vols. Würzburg, 1962 and 1963.
Goebbels, Joseph, *Tagebücher 1945. Die letzten Aufzeichnungen.* In-
troduction by Rolf Hochhuth. Hamburg, 1977.

Goebbels Tagebücher. Aus den Jahren 1942–1943, mit anderen Dokumenten, ed. by Louis P. Lochner. Zurich, 1948.

Handbuch des deutschen Aberglaubens, III. Berlin—Leipzig, 1930/1931.

Heiber, Helmut, ed., *Goebbels-Reden 1932–1945,* two vols. Düsseldorf, 1971 and 1972.

———, *Hitlers Lagebesprechungen. Die Protokollfragmente seiner militärischen Konferenzen 1942–1945.* Stuttgart, 1962.

Hitler, Adolf, *Monologe im Führerhauptquartier 1941–1944. Die Aufzeichnungen Heinrich Heims,* ed. by Werner Jochmann. Hamburg, 1980.

Adolf Hitler. Bilder aus dem Leben des Führers. Altona, Cigaretten-Bilderdienst, 1936.

Hubatsch, Walther, ed., *Hitlers Weisungen für die Kriegsführung 1939–1945. Dokumente des Oberkommandos der Wehrmacht.* Frankfurt/Main, 1962.

Jacobsen, Hans-Adolf, *Ausgewählte Dokumente zur Geschichte des Nationalsozialismus 1933–1945,* Vols. I and II. Bielefeld, 1961.

———, *1939–1945. Der Zweite Weltkrieg in Chronik und Dokumenten,* 5th ed. Darmstadt, 1961.

20. Juli 1944, 4th ed. Bonn, Bundeszentrale für Heimatdienst, 1961.

Kosch, Wilhelm, *Biographisches Staatshandbuch. Lexikon der Politik, Presse und Publizistik.* Berne and Munich, 1963.

Kriegstagebuch des Oberkommandos der Wehrmacht (Wehrmachtführungsstab), ed. by P. E. Schramm in collaboration with A. Hillgruber, W. Hubatsch, and H. A. Jacobsen, Vols. I–IV. Frankfurt am Main, 1961–1965.

Kürschners Gelehrtenkalender, 1941.

Neue Deutsche Baukunst. Published by the Inspector General of Buildings for the Reich Capital, Albert Speer. Presented by Rudolf Wolters, Berlin 1941.

Die Niederlage 1945. Aus dem Kriegstagebuch des Oberkommandos der Wehrmacht, ed. by P. E. Schramm. Munich, 1962.

Official telephone book, Berlin, 1936.

Picker, Henry, ed., *Hitler's Tischgespräche im Führerhauptquartier 1941–1942.* Stuttgart, 1963.

Poliakov, Léon, and Wulf, Josef, eds., *Das Dritte Reich und die Juden. Dokumente und Aufsätze.* Berlin, 1955.

Der Prozess gegen die Hauptkriegsverbrecher vor dem Internationalen Militärgerichtshof in Nürnberg. 14. November 1945–1. Oktober 1946, 42 vols. Nuremberg 1949.

Reichsgesetzblatt. Berlin, Reich Ministry of the Interior, 1933 ff.

Reif, Adelbert, ed., *Albert Speer. Kontroversen um ein deutsches Phänomen.* Munich, 1978.

Spiegelbild einer Verschwörung. Die Kaltenbrunner-Berichte an Bormann und Hitler über das Attentat vom 20. Juli 1944. Geheime Dokumente aus dem ehemaligen Reichssicherheitshauptamt. Stuttgart, Archiv Peter, 1961.

The Trial of Major War Criminals, 22 vols. London, 1946–1950.

Ursachen und Folgen. Vom deutschen Zusammenbruch 1918 und 1945 bis zur staatlichen Neuordnung Deutschlands in der Gegenwart, ed. by Herbert Michaelis and Ernst Schraepler with the collaboration of Günter Scheel, 26 vols. 1958–1979.

BIOGRAPHIES, DIARIES, MEMOIRS, HISTORICAL STUDIES

Adam, Uwe D., *Judenpolitik im Dritten Reich.* Düsseldorf, 1972.

Adler, Hans G., *Der verwaltete Mensch.* Tübingen, 1974.

Arndt, Ino, and Scheffler, Wolfgang, "Organisierter Massenmord an Juden in nationalsozialistischen Vernichtungslagern. Ein Beitrag zur Richtigstellung apologetischer Literatur." *VHZG,* Vol. 24 (1976), pp. 105–135.

Auterhoff, H., *Lehrbuch der pharmazeutischen Chemie.* Stuttgart, 1981.

Bahnsen, Uwe, and O'Donell, James P., *Die Katakombe.* Munich, 1977.

Ball-Kaduri, Kurt Jacob, "Berlin wird judenfrei. Die Juden in den Jahren 1942/1943." *Jahrbuck für die Geschichte Mittel- und Ostdeutschlands,* Vol. XXII (1973), pp. 196–241.

Baumbach, Werner, *Zu spät? Aufstieg und Untergang der deutschen Luftwaffe.* Stuttgart, 1977.

Baur, Hans, *Ich flog Mächtige der Erde.* Kempten, 1962.

Bein, Alex, *Die Judenfrage. Biographie eines Weltproblems,* Vols. I and II. Stuttgart, 1980.

Below, Nicolaus von, *Als Hitlers Adjutant.* Mainz, 1980.

Berthold, Will, *Die 42 Attentate auf Adolf Hitler.* Munich, 1981.

Besgen, Achim, *Der stille Befehl. Medizinalrat Kersten und das Dritte Reich.* Munich, 1960.

Besymenski, Lew, *Die letzten Notizen von Martin Bormann. Ein Dokument und sein Verfasser.* Stuttgart, 1974.

Bewley, Charles, *Herman Göring and the Third Reich.* Toronto, 1962.

Binion, Rudolph, "*. . . dass ihr mich gefunden habt.*" *Hitler und die Deutschen: eine Psychohistorie.* Stuttgart, 1978.

Bird, Eugene K., *Rudolf Hess.* Munich, 1974.

Birkenfeld, Wolfgang, *Der synthetische Treibstoff 1933–1945. Ein Beitrag zur nationalsozialistischen Wirtschaftspolitik.* Göttingen—Berlin—Frankfurt/Main, 1964.

———, Review of Milward, Alan S, *The German Economy at War,* in *VSWG,* Vol. 53 (1966), pp. 570–573.

Bleuel, Hans Peter, and Klinnert, Ernst, *Deutsche Studenten auf dem Weg ins Dritte Reich. Ideologien—Programme—Aktionen 1918–1935.* Gütersloh, 1967.

Boldt, Gerhard, *Die letzten Tage der Reichskanzlei.* Vienna—Zurich—New York, 1947.

Bracher, Karl Dietrich, *Die deutsche Diktatur. Entstehung, Struktur, Folgen des Nationalsozialismus.* Cologne—Berlin, 1976.

———, *Die Auflösung der Weimarer Republik. Eine Studie zum Problem des Machtverfalls in der Demokratie,* 5th ed. Villingen, 1971.

Bramsted, Ernest K., *Goebbels und die nationalsozialistische Propaganda 1925–1945.* Frankfurt/Main, 1971.

Broszat, Martin, *Der Staat Hitlers.* Munich, 1969.

———, "Hitler und die Genesis der 'Endlösung.' Aus Anlass der Thesen von David Irving." *VHZG,* Vol. 25 (1977), pp. 739–775.

Browning, Christopher, "Eine Antwort auf Martin Broszats Thesen zur Genesis der 'Endlösung.'" *VHZG,* Vol. 29 (1981), pp. 95–109.

Buchheim, Hans, "Die SS in der Verfassung des Dritten Reiches." *VHZG,* Vol. 3 (1955), pp. 127–157.

Bullock, Alan, *Hitler. Eine Studie über Tyrannei.* Düsseldorf, 1961.

Burckhardt, Jacob, *Weltgeschichtliche Betrachtungen.* Frankfurt/Main—Berlin, 1965.

Dahms, Helmuth G., *Geschichte des Zweiten Weltkrieges.* Tübingen, 1965.

Delarue, Jacques, *Geschichte der Gestapo.* Düsseldorf, 1964.

Dietrich, Otto, *12 Jahre mit Hitler.* Cologne, no year.

Dönitz, Karl, "Ich lege Rechnung." *Quick,* Nos. 19–22 (November 1958).

——, *Mein wechselvolles Leben.* Göttingen—Zurich—Berlin—Frankfurt/Main, 1968.

——, *Zehn Jahre und zwanzig Tage.* Frankfurt/Main—Bonn, 1963.

Dornberger, Walter, *V 2—Der Schuss ins Weltall.* Esslingen, 1952.

Dülffer, Jost, Thies, Jochen, and Henke, Josef, *Hitlers Städte. Baupolitik im Dritten Reich.* Cologne—Vienna, 1978.

Engel, Gerhard, *Heeresadjutant bei Hitler 1938–1943.* Stuttgart, 1974.

Erdmann, Karl Dietrich, "Die Regierung Dönitz. Über den Umgang mit Ereignissen der jüngsten deutschen Geschichte. *GWU,* Vol. 14 (1963), pp. 359–375.

Farth, W., *et al.,* eds., *Allgemeine Pharmakologie und Toxikologie.* Mannheim—Vienna—Zurich, 1977.

Faust, Anselm, *Der nationalsozialistische deutsche Studentenbund. Studenten und Nationalsozialismus in der Weimarer Republik.* Düsseldorf, 1973.

Fest, Joachim C., *Das Gesicht des Dritten Reiches. Profile einer totalitären Herrschaft.* Munich, 1963.

——, *Hitler. Eine Biographie.* Frankfurt/Main—Berlin—Vienna, 1973.

Fraenckel, Heinrich, and Manvell, Roger, *Goebbels. Eine Biographie.* Herrsching, 1980.

——, *Hermann Göring.* Hanover, 1964.

——, *Himmler. Kleinbürger und Massenmörder.* Berlin—Frankfurt/Main—Vienna, 1965.

Fromm, Erich, *The Anatomy of Human Destructiveness.* New York: Holt, Rinehart & Winston, 1973.

Galbraith, John K., *A Life in Our Time. Memoirs.* Boston: Houghton-Mifflin, 1981.

——, *Economics, Peace and Laughter.* New York: New American Library, 1981.

Galland, Adolf, *Die Ersten und die Letzten. Die Jagdflieger im Zweiten Weltkrieg,* 13th ed. Munich, 1978.

Gatzke, Hans W., Review of Albert Speer, *Inside the Third Reich,* in *The American Historical Review,* Vol. 76, 2 (1971), p. 1562.

Georg, Enno, *Die wirtschaftlichen Unternehmungen der SS.* Stuttgart, 1969.

Giesler, Hermann, *Ein anderer Hitler. Bericht seines Architekten Hermann Giesler. Erlebnisse, Gespräche, Reflexionen.* Leoni, 1978.

Gilbert, Gustave M., *Nürnberger Tagebuch.* Frankfurt am Main, 1977.

———, *The Psychology of Dictatorship.* New York: Ronald, 1950.

Gisevius, Hans B., *Adolf Hitler. Versuch einer Deutung.* Munich, 1963.

Görlitz, Walter, *Karl Dönitz. Der Grossadmiral.* Göttingen—Zurich —Frankfurt/Main, 1972.

Gruchmann, Lothar, *Der Zweite Weltkrieg.* Munich 1975.

Gründler, Gerhard E., and Manikowsky, Arnim von, *Das Gericht der Sieger.* Oldenburg—Hamburg, 1967.

Guderian, Heinz, *Erinnerungen eines Soldaten.* Heidelberg, 1951.

Haffner, Sebastian, *Anmerkungen zu Hitler.* Munich, 1978.

Hamsher, William, *Albert Speer. Victim of Nuremberg.* London, 1970.

Hansen, Reimer, "Albert Speers Konflikt mit Hitler." *GWU,* Vol. 17 (1966), pp. 596–621.

———, *Das Ende des Dritten Reiches. Die deutsche Kapitulation 1945.* Stuttgart, 1966.

———, "Der totale deutsche Zusammenbruch 1945. Probleme und Ergebnisse der historisch-politischen Forschung." *Aus Politik und Zeitgeschichte,* supplement to the weekly newspaper *Das Parlament* (5/9/70).

———, "Der ungeklärte Fall Todt." *GWU,* Vol. 18 (1967), pp. 604–605.

Henschel, Hildegard, "Gemeindearbeit und Evakuierung von Berlin —16. Oktober 1941 bis 16. Juni 1943." *ZfdGJ,* IX (1972), pp. 23–52.

Hess, Wolf R., *Weder Recht noch Menschlichkeit. Das Urteil von Nürnberg. Die Rache in Spandau. Eine Dokumentation.* Leoni, 1974.

Heydecker, Joe, and Leeb, Johannes, *Der Nürnberger Prozess.* Cologne, 1979.

Hilberg, Raul, *The Destruction of the European Jews.* Chicago, 1961.

Hillgruber, Andreas, "Tendenzen, Ergebnisse und Perspektiven der gegenwärtigen Hitler-Forschung." *HZ* 226 (1978), pp. 600–621.

————,. Review of Werner Maser, *Adolf Hitler, Legende, Mythos, Wirklichkeit,* in *HZ* 216 (1973), pp. 456–458.

————, "Endlösung im Osten." *VHZG,* Vol. 20 (1972), pp. 133–153.

Hitler, Adolf, *Mein Kampf,* 174–175th ed. Munich, 1936.

Höhne, Heinz, *Der Orden under dem Totenkopf. Die Geschichte der SS.* Gütersloh, 1967.

Hoffmann, Peter, *Die Sicherheit des Diktators. Hitlers Leibwachen, Schutzmassnahmen, Residenzen, Hauptquartiere.* Munich, 1975.

————, *Widerstand. Staatsstreich. Attentat. Der Kampf der Opposition gegen Hitler.* Munich, 1969.

Homze, Edward L., *Foreign Labor in Nazi Germany.* Princeton, New Jersey, 1967.

Hortleder, Gerd, *Das Gesellschaftsbild des Ingenieurs. Zum politischen Verhalten der technischen Intelligenz in Deutschland.* Frankfurt/Main, 1970.

Hüttenberger, Peter, *Die Gauleiter. Studie zum Wandel des Machtgefüges in der NSDAP.* Stuttgart, 1969.

Irving, David, *Die Geheimwaffen des Dritten Reiches.* Gütersloh, 1965. (American title: *The Mare's Nest.* Boston: Little, Brown, 1965.)

————, *Die Tragödie der deutschen Luftwaffe. Aus den Akten und Erinnerungen des Feldmarschall Milch.* Frankfurt am Main—Berlin—Vienna, 1970. (American title: *The Rise and Fall of the German Air Force.* Boston: Little, Brown, 1974.)

————, *Hitler und seine Feldherren.* Frankfurt am Main—Berlin—Vienna, 1975. (American title: *Hitler's War.* New York: Viking, 1977.)

————, *Wie krank war Hitler wirklich? Der Diktator und seine Ärzte.* Munich, 1970.

————, *Der Nürnberger Prozess. Die letzte Schlacht.* Munich, 1979.

Jäckel, Eberhard, *Hitlers Weltanschauung. Entwurf einer Herrschaft.* Tübingen, 1969.

Janssen, Gregor, *Das Ministerium Speer. Deutschlands Rüstung im Krieg.* Frankfurt/Main—Berlin—Vienna, 1969.

Kannapin, Hans-Eckhardt, *Wirtschaft unter Zwang,* Cologne, 1966.

Kater, Michael H., *Studentenschaft und Rechtsradikalismus in Deutschland 1918–1933. Eine sozialgeschichtliche Bildungskrise in der Weimarer Republik.* Hamburg, 1975.

Kehrl, Hans, *Krisenmanager im Dritten Reich.* Düsseldorf, 1973.

————, *Zur Wirklichkeit des Dritten Reiches. Ergänzende Betrachtungen zum Forschungsstand der Wirtschafts- und Socialgeschichte.* No publication place, no year.

Kelley, Douglas M., *22 Cells in Nuremberg.* New York, 1947.

Kempka, Erich, *Die letzten Tage mit Adolf Hitler.* Preussisch Oldendorf, 1975.

Kempner, Robert M., "Die Ermordung von 35 000 Berliner Juden. Der Judenmordprozess in Berlin schreibt Geschichte." *Gegenwart und Rückblick. Festgabe für die Jüdische Gemeinde zu Berlin. 25 Jahre nach Neubeginn.* Ed. by Herbert A. Strauss and Kurt R. Grossmann. Heidelberg, 1970.

Kersten, Felix, *Totenkopf und Treue. Heinrich Himmler ohne Uniform.* Hamburg, 1952.

Kogon, Eugen, *Der SS-Staat. Das System der deutschen Konzentrationslager.* Munich, 1977.

Koller, Karl, *Der letzte Monat. Die Tagebuchaufzeichnungen des ehemaligen Chefs des Generalstabs der deutschen Luftwaffe vom 14. April bis 27. Mai 1945.* Mannheim, 1949.

Kuhn, Axel, *Hitlers aussenpolitisches Programm. Entstehung und Entwicklung 1919–1939.* Stuttgart, 1970.

Kuhn, Helmut, "Die deutsche Universität am Vorabend der Machtergreifung." *Die deutsche Universität im Dritten Reich. Eine Vortragsreihe der Universität München* (Munich, 1966), pp. 13–43.

Lärmer, Karl, *Autobahn in Deutschland 1933–1945. Zu den Hintergründen.* (East) Berlin, 1975.

Lang, Jochen von, *Der Sekretär. Martin Bormann: Der Mann, der Hitler beherrschte.* Stuttgart, 1977.

Lange, Karl, *Hitlers unbeachtete Maximen. "Mein Kampf" und die Öffentlichkeit.* Stuttgart—Berlin—Cologne—Mainz, 1968.

Langer, Walter C., *Das Adolf Hitler–Psychogramm.* Vienna—Munich—Zurich, 1973.

Larsson, Lars O., *Die Neugestaltung der Reichshauptstadt. Albert Speers Generalbebauungsplan für Berlin.* Stuttgart, 1978.

Ludwig, Karl-Heinz, *Technik und Ingenieure im Dritten Reich.* Düsseldorf, 1974.

Lüdde-Neurath, Walter, *Regierung Dönitz. Die letzten Tage des Dritten Reiches,* 3rd ed. Berlin—Frankfurt/Main—Zurich, 1964.

Maier, Hedwig, "Die SS und der 20. Juli 1944." *VHZG,* Vol. 14 (1966), pp. 299–316.

Maser, Werner, *Adolf Hitler. Das Ende der Führer-Legende.* Düsseldorf—Vienna, 1980.

——, *Adolf Hitler. Legende, Mythos, Wirklichkeit.* Munich—Esslingen, 1971.

——, *Die Frühgeschichte der NSDAP.* Frankfurt/Main, 1965.

——, *Nürnberg. Tribunal der Sieger.* Düsseldorf—Vienna, 1977.

Mattausch, Roswitha, *Siedlungsbau und Stadtneugründungen im deutschen Faschismus.* Frankfurt/Main, 1981.

Miale, Florence R., and Selzer, Michael, *The Nuremberg Mind. The Psychology of the Nazi Leaders.* New York, 1977.

Milward, Alan S., *Die deutsche Kriegswirtschaft 1939–1945.* Stuttgart, 1966.

——, "Fritz Todt als Minister für Bewaffnung und Munition." *VHZG,* Vol. 14 (1966), pp. 40–58.

Miller Lane, Barbara, *Architecture and Politics in Germany 1918–1945.* Cambridge, Mass., 1968.

Mommsen, Hans, *Beamtentum im Dritten Reich.* Stuttgart, 1966.

Mosley, Leonard, *The Reich Marshall.* New York: Doubleday, 1974.

Müller, Max, "Der plötzliche und mysteriöse Tod Dr. Fritz Todts." *GWU,* Vol. 18 (1967), pp. 602–604.

Norden, Eric, "Albert Speer. Interview." *Playboy* (June 1971).

Owen, Wilfred von, *Finale Furioso. Mit Goebbels bis zum Ende.* Tübingen, 1974.

Petsch, Joachim, *Baukunst und Stadtplanung im Dritten Reich. Herleitung/Bestandsaufnahmne/Entwicklung/Nachfolge.* Munich—Vienna, 1976.

Pfahlmann, Hans, *Fremdarbeiter und Kriegsgefangene in der deutschen Kriegswirtschaft 1939–1945.* Darmstadt, 1968.

Plutarch, *Lives.*

Ramme, Alwin, *Der Sicherheitsdienst der SS. Zu seiner Funktion im faschistischen Machtapparat und im Besatzungsregime des sogenannten Generalgouvernements Polen.* (East) Berlin, 1969.

Rasp, Hans-Peter, *Eine Stadt für tausend Jahre. München—Bauten und Projekte für die Hauptstadt der Bewegung.* Munich, 1981.

Rauschning, Hermann, *Gespräche mit Hitler.* Zurich—Vienna—New York, 1940.

Recktenwald, Johann, *Woran hat Adolf Hitler gelitten? Eine neuro-psychiatrische Deutung.* Munich—Basel, 1963.

Reitlinger, Gerald, *Die Endlösung. Hitlers Versuch der Ausrottung der Juden Europas 1939–1945.* Berlin, 1956.

Riess, Curt, *Joseph Goebbels.* Zurich, 1949.

Ritter, Gerhard, *Carl Goerdeler und die deutsche Widerstands-bewegung.* Stuttgart, 1956.

Röhrs, Hans-Dietrich, *Hitlers Krankheit. Tatsachen und Legende.* Neckargemünd, 1966.

Rohland, Walter, *Bewegte Zeiten. Erinnerungen eines Eisenhütten-mannes.* Stuttgart, 1978.

Schacht, Hjalmar, *Abrechnung mit Hitler.* Hamburg—Stuttgart, 1948.

———, *76 Jahre meines Lebens.* Bad Wörishofen, 1953.

Schieder, Theodor, "Strukturen und Persönlichkeiten in der Ge-schichte." *HZ* 195 (1962), pp. 265–296.

Schirach, Henriette von, *Der Preis der Herrlichkeit. Erinnerungen.* Berlin—Munich—Vienna, 1978.

Schöllgen, Gregor, "Das Problem einer Hitler-Biographie. Über-legungen anhand neuerer Darstellungen des Falles Hitler." *NPL,* XXIII (1978), pp. 421–434.

Schönleben, Eduard, *Fritz Todt. Der Mensch, der Ingenieur, der Na-tionalsozialist.* Oldenburg, 1943.

Schulze, Hagen, "Die Biographie in der 'Krise der Geschichtswissen-schaft.' " *GWU,* Vol. 29 (1978), pp. 508–518.

Schwarzwäller, Wulf, *Rudolf Hess. Der Letzte von Spandau.* Vienna et al., 1974.

Schwerin von Krosigk, Lutz Count, *Memoiren.* Stuttgart, 1977.

———, *Es geschah in Deutschland. Menschenbilder unseres Jahrhun-derts.* Tübingen—Stuttgart, 1951.

Shirer, William L., *Rise and Fall of the Third Reich.*

Smith, Bradley F., *Reaching Judgment at Nuremberg.* New York: Basic Books, 1977.

Sontheimer, Kurt, "Der Tatkreis." *VHZG,* Vol. 7 (1959), pp. 228–260.

Speer, Albert, *Architektur. Arbeiten 1933–1942.* No loc., 1978.

———, *Die Neue Reichskanzlei.* Munich, no year.

———, *Inside the Third Reich.* New York: Macmillan, 1970.

———, *Spandau: The Secret Diaries.* New York: Macmillan, 1976.

———, *Infiltration. How Heinrich Himmler Schemed to Build an SS Industrial Empire.* New York: Macmillan, 1981.

———, *Technik und Macht,* ed. by Adelbert Reif: Esslingen, 1979.

Steinert, Marlis G., *Die 23 Tage der Regierung Dönitz.* Düsseldorf—Vienna, 1967.

———, *Hitlers Krieg und die Deutschen. Stimmung und Haltung der deutschen Bevölkerung im Zweiten Weltkrieg.* Düsseldorf—Vienna, 1970.

Steinhoff, Johannes, *In letzter Stunde, Verschwörung der Jagdflieger.* Munich, 1974.

Suzman, Arthur, and Diamond, Dennis, "Der Mord an sechs Millionen Juden. Die Wahrheit ist unteilbar." *Aus Politik und Zeitgeschichte,* supplement to the weekly newspaper *Das Parlament* (7/29/78).

Taylor, Telford, *Die Nürnberger Prozesse. Kriegsverbrechen und Völkerrecht.* Zurich, 1950.

Teut, Anna, *Architektur im Dritten Reich 1933–1945.* Berlin—Frankfurt/Main—Vienna, 1967.

Thies, Jochen, *Architekt der Weltherrschaft. Die "Endziele" Hitlers.* Düsseldorf, 1976.

Thomas, Georg, *Geschichte der deutschen Wehr- und Rüstungswirtschaft (1918–1943/45),* ed. by Wolfgang Birkenfeld. Boppard am Rhein, 1966.

Todt, Fritz, ed., *Die Strassen Adolf Hitlers.* Berlin, 1938.

Toland, John, *Adolf Hitler.* Bergisch-Gladbach, 1977.

———, *Das Finale.* Munich—Zurich, 1968.

Trevor-Roper, Hugh R., *The Last Days of Hitler.* New York: Macmillan, 1947.

Vondung, Klaus, *Magie und Manipulation. Ideologischer Kult und politische Religion des Nationalsozialismus.* Göttingen, 1971.

Wagenführ, Rolf, *Die deutsche Industrie im Kriege. 1939–1945,* 2nd ed. Berlin, 1963.

Wagner, Alfred, "Die Rüstung im 'Dritten Reich' unter Albert Speer." *Technikgeschichte,* Vol. 33 (1966), pp. 205–227.

Wangerin, Gerda, and Weiss, Gerhard, *Heinrich Tessenow. Ein Baumeister 1876–1950. Leben, Lehre, Werk.* Essen, 1976.

Warlimont, Walter, *Im Hauptquartier der deutschen Wehrmacht 1939–1945.* Frankfurt/Main, 1962.

Wellers, Georges, "Die Zahl der Opfer der 'Endlösung' und der Korrherr-Bericht." *Aus Politik und Zeitgeschichte,* supplement to the weekly newspaper *Das Parlament* (7/29/78).

Wheeler-Bennet, John, *Die Nemesis der Macht.* Düsseldorf, 1954.

Winkler, Dörte, *Frauenarbeit im "Dritten Reich."* Hamburg, 1977.

Wolters, Rudolf, *Albert Speer.* Oldenburg, 1943.

———, *Stadtmitte Berlin. Stadtbauliche Entwicklungsphrasen von den Anfängen bis zur Gegenwart.* Tübingen, 1978.

Zoller, Albert, *Hitler privat. Erlebnisbericht seiner Geheimsekretärin.* Düsseldorf, 1949.

ILLUSTRATION SOURCES

The facsimiles on pages 59, 119, and 192–193 were reproduced with the kind permission of the Federal Archives in Koblenz. The originals of all other facsimiles are in the author's possession.

ACKNOWLEDGMENTS

This book could never have been completed without the support of countless people.

The author's parents enabled their son to study for a long time. He thanks them with all his heart.

The men and women of the Bundesarchiv Koblenz, the Institute für Zeitgeschichte, and the Berlin Document Center helped the author in every way. Dr. Eberhard Bohm, head of the library of the Friedrich Meinecke Institute, Berlin, always did his best to obtain books and periodicals as quickly as possible. Frau Friderieke Millack, Düsseldorf, gave the author permission to read the diaries of her deceased uncle, Erhard Milch. Herr Otmar Katz, Munich, allowed the author to consult the vast collection of Dr. Theo Morell's posthumous papers. Herr Michael Hepp, Munich, made the manuscript of an unpublished article available to me. Professor Dr. Reimer Hansen, Berlin, allowed the author to see a great deal of material. Professor Dr. Michael Erbe, Berlin, and Herr Felix Escher, Berlin, were always ready to make suggestions. Stephan Schmidt, the author's brother, read the manuscript with critical eyes. Herr Werner Duchstein, Berlin, in a series of conversations, gave the author a chance to discuss a topic that is inadequately referred to as the "human psyche." Herr Peter Gems, Berlin, enabled the author to continue working on this book when he assisted him swiftly and generously in autumn 1980. Fräulein Gabriele Jeka typed the manuscript with a great deal of patience and commitment. I would also like to recall the prematurely deceased Professor Dr. Friedrich Zipfel, Berlin, whose seminar offered a great deal of inspiration for this investigation.

I can only express my gratitude to Professor Dr. Hans-Dietrich Loock. He knows what I mean.

MATTHIAS SCHMIDT
Berlin, March 1982

INDEX